The History of the Provincial Press in England

The History of the Provincial Press in England

Rachel Matthews

Bloomsbury Academic
An imprint of Bloomsbury Publishing Inc

B L O O M S B U R Y
NEW YORK · LONDON · OXFORD · NEW DELHI · SYDNEY

Bloomsbury Academic

An imprint of Bloomsbury Publishing Inc

1385 Broadway	50 Bedford Square
New York	London
NY 10018	WC1B 3DP
USA	UK

www.bloomsbury.com

**BLOOMSBURY and the Diana logo are trademarks of
Bloomsbury Publishing Plc**

First published 2017

Library of Congress Cataloging-in-Publication Data
Names: Matthews, Rachel, 1936- author.
Title: The history of the provincial press in England / Rachel Matthews.
Description: New York: Bloomsbury Academic, 2017. | Includes bibliographical
references and index. Identifiers: LCCN 2016047932 (print) | LCCN 2017007218 (ebook) | ISBN
9781441156037 (hardback) | ISBN 9781441162304 (paperback) | ISBN 9781441100160 (ePub)
| ISBN 9781441156464 (ePDF) Subjects: LCSH: Journalism, Regional–Great Britain–History. |
British newspapers–History. | Newspaper publishing–Great Britain–History. | BISAC: SOCIAL SCI-
ENCE / Media Studies. | HISTORY / Europe / Great Britain.
Classification: LCC PN5124.R44 M38 2017 (print) | LCC PN5124.R44 (ebook) |
DDC 072–dc23 LC record available at https://lccn.loc.gov/2016047932

ISBN: HB: 978-1-4411-5603-7
PB: 978-1-4411-6230-4
ePDF: 978-1-4411-5646-4
ePub: 978-1-4411-0016-0

Cover design: Clare Turner
Cover image © ncjMedia Ltd

Typeset by Deanta Global Publishing Services, Chennai, India
Printed and bound in the United States of America

A newspaper is a living thing. It cannot stand still and live. It is no longer what it was because by remaining static it must die.

W. Vaughan Reynolds, editor of the Birmingham Post, 1957.

Contents

List of Tables and Illustrations ix

Preface x

1 Introduction 1
The provincial press: The contemporary conundrum 1
Editorial workers in the provincial press 16
The 'national' versus 'provincial' dichotomy examined 20
Reappraising the provincial press 27

2 Printers' Papers: Profiting from the Commerce of Information 31
Reimagining the early provincial newspaper 31
The newspaper's place in the commercial landscape 33
Early ventures in the newspaper industry 36
Establishing a market: 'Freshest advices' and circulation wars 41
The reader, cure-alls and books 46
Advertising and profit 49
The emergence of local journalism 54

3 The Provincial Press and Political Patronage 59
The political bent 59
Politics and the battle for a free press 61
Communities of interest and profit 69
Industrialization: Demarcation and news work 74
The good of the community and representation 79

4 The Impact of 'New Journalism' 85
The emergence of 'news' 85
The development of news presentation as a sales technique 89
The influence of New Journalism on content and production 92
New Journalism and the *Midland Daily Telegraph* 98
Commercial success as an organizing factor 105

5 The Corporatization of the Provincial Press 111
The growth of chain control 111

The consolidation of ownership: Pattern and process   115
Lord Rothermere: Ambition and resistance   122
Newspaper costs as a driver for consolidation   128
Consolidation of ownership: Royal Commissions   130
Commercial practice and the good of the community   135

6   The Provincial Press in Wartime   139
    Conflict is good news for newspapers   139
    The provincial press and the community in the First World War 141
    Publishing in the face of the adversity of the Second World War 145
    The business of newspaper publishing in wartime   149
    The provincial press and morale   155

7   The Deunionization of the Provincial Press   163
    New technology   163
    The changing motivations for newspaper ownership   167
    Rising costs and competition   173
    Computerization. The end of an era?   178
    The legacy of new technology: Working practices and content   183

8   The Digital Turn   189
    Interpreting the crisis in local news?   189
    Digital beginnings   190
    Redefining the provincial press in a digital age   199
    Where now the future for local news?   206

Bibliography   219
Index   232

List of Tables and Illustrations

Figure 2.1   *The Northampton Mercury*, vol. IV, no. 293, 6 January
             1723–4, p. 1. Newspaper Image © The Warden and Fellows
             of All Souls College, Oxford   42

Figure 4.1   *Midland Daily Telegraph*, 1 February 1895, p. 1. Newspaper
             Image © The British Library Board. All rights reserved.
             With thanks to The British Newspaper Archive
             (www.BritishNewspaperArchive.co.uk)   100

Figure 5.1   *Derby Daily Telegraph*, 12 August 1929, p. 1.
             Newspaper Image © Mirrorpix. All rights reserved.
             With thanks to The British Newspaper Archive
             (www.BritishNewspaperArchive.co.uk)   125

Figure 6.1   *Midland Daily Telegraph*, 6 May 1940, p. 1.
             Newspaper Image © Mirrorpix. All rights reserved.
             With thanks to The British Newspaper Archive
             (www.BritishNewspaperArchive.co.uk)   151

Table 5.1   Chain ownership of newspapers 1921–48   116

Table 5.2   The National Chain Publishers' shares of provincial
             morning, evening and weekly newspaper circulations in
             Great Britain in 1937, 1947, 1961 and 1974   117

Table 5.3   The largest ten publishers of provincial evening newspapers
             in 1974 and their share of the total circulation of provincial
             evening newspapers in the UK in 1961 and 1974   121

Table 5.4   The largest ten publishers of provincial weekly newspapers
             in 1974 and their share of the total circulation of provincial
             weekly newspapers in the UK in 1961 and 1974   122

Table 5.5   Distribution of costs of newspaper production 1938
             compared with 1974–7   129

Table 6.1   Number of newspapers published in the UK
             in 1948 and 1961   154

Table 8.1   Circulations of selected daily titles   194

Table 8.2   Local newspapers: declining number of titles in 1985–2014   201

Preface

This work is the culmination of my somewhat tumultuous relationship with the provincial newspaper. For many years this was the environment within which I worked as a journalist, and it was here that I grew to love the all-encompassing view of life which it afforded. At the same time though my colleagues and I were subject to the strictures of a working environment which was being squeezed by the quest for everlasting shareholder payouts. We worked longer and longer hours, with fewer and fewer staff, but such was our professional pride that we were driven to produce the best papers we could. Despite this it was personal circumstance, rather than disillusion, which prompted my move to academe and afforded me the opportunity to reflect on my experience as a working journalist. This work began there, as a kind of a quest; the search for the halcyon days of the provincial newspaper – a time when its operation was dedicated to the public interest 'watchdog' role, which had been inculcated into me via training and my newsroom acculturation. But instead of finding a high point against which decline could be measured, I discovered an industry which had always been just that – an industry, focused on turning a profit, for which the 'public interest' was little more than a stance to add legitimacy to its economic intent.

Surprisingly I also discovered that to date there is no singular study which considers the development of the provincial paper over a sustained period of time. This says so much about the status accorded to these titles, despite their long-standing success as commercial products and their establishment as fixtures of the communal imagination. I recognize the ambition of my intent to address this gap.[1] For this reason, this study has concentrated on titles in England; this is due not only to the sheer size of the task of investigating the provincial press which makes containment a necessity, but also to differences in governance which affect the relationship between the local and London-based national press in Scotland, Wales and Northern Ireland.[2]

---

[1] Wiles covers 1700–1765, Black 1621–1861; Boyce et al. do scope newspaper history from the seventeenth century to the present day, but the chronological section is a consideration of press development as a whole rather than factions within it.

[2] That is not to say that the methodology employed here is not significant to the structure of the provincial press in these areas. Indeed, national boundaries are significant definers of newspapers

However, rather than cataloguing where and how individual papers began and ended, I have concentrated on the development of the provincial newspaper as a specialist media form, aligned with a set of norms and practices which can be distinguished and charted over time. In doing so this study also seeks to rescue the study of the provincial newspaper industry from the amnesia which besets most contemporary considerations, which are cut off from this historic context. The contemporary landscape of disruption makes this approach particularly apposite. Following in the spirit of James Curran, this approach is driven by the contention that 'history and media studies are fundamentally connected insofar as one can only really begin to understand the contemporary media landscape if one knows something about how communication technologies – and their social uses – have changed over time' (2002: 20). Where this study diverges from Curran, and his criticism of the 'medium history' approach of most media history, is in its unashamed concentration on one media form. Curran suggests that a better approach is to 'offer a general history of the account of the development of modern British society in which the history of the British media is inserted … to dissolve linear narratives – whether they progress or regress – in favour of complexity' (ibid.: 149). However, this approach works best when all media are considered, and so this study seeks to establish the provincial press as 'an essential building block' in this landscape and to engage with it as a discursive form. In doing so we can use history to challenge and analyse those constituent parts.

Of course any work of this scope owes a debt to the many people who assisted in its production. A special acknowledgement is due to Professor Bob Franklin, who has championed contemporary research into the provincial press. Similarly, Professor Martin Conboy's early support lent encouragement to the project. Not least among those who deserve recognition are the many staff at the local archives and libraries around the country who have helped me piece together the often fragmentary evidence which remains in relation to the business of regional newspapers. Particular thanks are due to the Cumbria Archive Service, which facilitated my examination of the extensive holdings relating to the CN News group in Carlisle, and the Cumberland & Westmorland Antiquarian and

and as such, the Scottish press may be considered fairly similar in its essential terms as the English or Welsh local press (see McNair (2006) and Thomas (2006) for scoping studies of the structure of the local press in Scotland and Wales). Indeed, their increasing remoteness from the London-based press suggests an increased emphasis on the provincial press in these areas, and Tunstall (1996: 62) suggests that Scotland has traditionally resisted the dominance of the London press.

Archaeological Society for their generous funding support for this stage of my study. I owe a particular debt to the document supply team at the Lanchester Library at Coventry University, for whom an obscure reference is seen as a challenge to be met with success. Similarly, I am grateful for my own institution, Coventry University, for the research sabbatical funding which enabled me to concentrate on the preparation of the final manuscript, and to my friends and colleagues whose encouragement has seen me over the finish line on more than one occasion. My family has in many ways lived and breathed the progress of this project for many years – particularly my youngest child Gabriel, who is as old as it is. Finally, as a journalist I was taught that news is people and, in many ways, so is history – even the history of a business. Behind this history lies the very real experience of all those who have worked to produce local and regional newspapers. Ultimately this work is dedicated to them.

1

Introduction

The provincial press: The contemporary conundrum

When film director Ridley Scott imagined a dystopian future in his 1982 film, *Blade Runner*, he made the cars fly, but put the hero on the street corner reading a printed broadsheet. Sommerville (1996) comments that, in the way fish did not discover water, we think of news as being an essential part of social consciousness and for many that is still inextricably linked with a product printed on paper, despite the expansion of digital technology. The newspaper is, therefore, embedded in the landscape to the extent that it is hard to envision a world without it. This is particularly true in England, which has traditionally had one of the highest consumptions of newspapers per head in the world.[1] At a local level, this translates to the notion of the daily or weekly newspaper as a faithful friend, the regular appearance of which is a ritualistic part of community life. This ubiquity though is a chimera; despite their apparent fixedness in the place in the cultural imagination, the newspaper – whether at national or local level – has never had an absolute presence, and currently its reach might be described as fragmentary at best. As I write, the circulations of printed newspapers are in such a continued and long-term state of decline that the dominant narrative surrounding their future is one of extinction. This is particularly so in the face of the impact of digital technology which has disrupted long-standing assumptions underpinning the perceived relationship between form, content and purpose.

It is this fragmentation which has prompted this retrospective look at the provincial press in England. Just as we are now more likely to search for a new house using the internet than via the pages of these papers, these titles are also available online, so that websites now outnumber printed products. Additionally

---

[1] There is further discussion of the consumption of newspapers in Chapter 5.

digital technology has challenged this once-definitional relationship with place[2] and has undermined not only our reading and buying habits but also revenue streams for these titles, which further problematizes the definitional process. Provincial is here a term particularly suited to the discussion of newspapers in England, which is overwhelmingly dominated by a London-centric view of nationhood. In England, the prevailing definitions of newspapers connect to three main characteristics: frequency of publication, geographical reach and business model. In turn, these characteristics have been linked to a hierarchical ranking of newspaper forms aligned with their perceived significance. Accorded first place within this definition are the daily, 'national' newspapers – which are themselves subdivided into 'quality', mid-market and tabloid. National titles are here defined as those headquartered in London but circulating across Britain.[3] At the bottom in terms of status are the local free sheets pushed unrequested through the letterbox. Provincial therefore signifies those titles which are based outside of the capital and is contiguous with the definition of 'local paper', used by the Newspaper Society, the body which represented such titles until recently.[4] The 'local press' as a whole relates to those newspapers which define themselves as circulating within a defined geographical area; within this classification they are usually further subdivided to the 'regional press', which circulates across larger geographical areas such as English counties, meaning the 'local press' is largely understood to focus on a town or district level.

These titles claim fealty to the locales in which they operate via their names, which also proclaim their role as information purveyors. Their circulations range from just a few thousand to those which sell more than 90,000 a day.[5] Thus they are the *Derby Telegraph*, the *Plymouth Herald*, the *Newcastle Chronicle* the *Rutland Times* or simply *The Cornishman*. Such is the nature of the business that titles coexist and overlap so that one county can host multiple titles circulating

---

[2]   Before its merger with the News Publishers Association, the Newspaper Society claimed there were 1,100 titles circulating in the UK and 1,700 'associated websites'.

[3]   Even this classification is open to question. Some London 'national' titles take on geographical nomenclatures – such as *The Mirror*, which is renamed the *Daily Record* in Scotland (MacInnes et al. 2007: 189). The London *Evening Standard* also has an ambiguous position here; its origins lie alongside 'national' titles like *The Times*, with which it competed and its circulation has historically been higher than that of many nationals (Williams 2010: 110).

[4]   The Newspaper Society was amalgamated with the News Publishers Association in 2014 to form the News Media Association. This is no part due to the fragmentation of the industry by the digital as discussed in Chapter 8.

[5]   Figures produced by the Audit Bureau of Circulations for August 2013 show the largest sale for a daily title to be that of the *Express & Star* (Wolverhampton) at 90,612 (*Press Gazette*, 28 August 2013a). The smallest sale for a weekly title was that of the *Herne Bay Gazette* at 2,245 (*Press Gazette*, 28 August 2013b).

within its boundaries, ranging from those daily organs which are seen to have status and influence, such as the *Manchester Evening News* or the *Yorkshire Post*, to the smallest titles, like the *Herne Bay Gazette*, or the *Grantham Times*. The relationship between paper and town can run deep, and the loss of titles can prompt protest and anxiety from those who feel bereft of a paper they might not even buy. For those readers who have stayed loyal to the habit of local newspaper consumption, the title will be the place where they look to for news of their area. These range from reports of those landmark events and issues which shape our physical and imagined environment to those personal details which resonate with us on an individual level, such as the deaths of those we know. And they are served up by teams of journalists who are themselves perceived as embedded in those areas, dedicating their hours to solitary attendance at countless 'parish pump' events.

It is this conception of the local newspaper which those working within the industry foreground in their memoirs of their experiences. Perhaps unsurprisingly for those who have made a living out of writing, personal accounts of time spent on newspapers abound, as do works on varying issues such as training or production. Some offer a useful insight into the industry; Morris (1963), for example, who captures his foray into the provincial news industry in *I Bought a Newspaper*, describes in detail his battle to establish an independent title in the face of opposition from group-owned newspapers in the 1950s. His account heroizes the campaigning editor, committed to his locale and dedicated to giving a voice to the voiceless. Richard Stott (2002), who progressed to edit national titles including *The Mirror*, offers an insight into the life of the local reporter when he recalls his training on the *Bucks Herald* in the 1960s. His nostalgic view positions the committed local journalist at the heart of the community, describing the chief reporter Phil Fountain as 'a local newspapermen (*sic*) to his fingertips, who could have made Fleet Street without any bother. But he loved Aylesbury and he knew it inside out. Local councils and courts were meat and drink to him. Immaculate shorthand note, all the councillors and the coppers at his beck and call, the holder of 1,000 borough secrets' (2002: 90). It is a view epitomized by Clive Joyce, editor of the *Kidderminster Shuttle*, writing to publicize the annual Local Newspaper Week. 'We must never forget that a local newspaper stands and falls on its relationship with its community' (Newspaper Society 2009). These partisan recollections, mediated by memory, contribute to the mythology of the local newspaper as a steadfast pillar of the community. As such they can themselves become stitched into the fabric of the values which underpin the provincial newspaper industry and the attitudes towards it, which this history seeks to interrogate.

Beneath this apparent simplicity, then, is a heterogeneous and numerous accumulation of titles, which would lay claim to being a local newspaper, and it is this variety of responses which makes telling the story of this particular media form challenging. Defining what it is to be a provincial newspaper, as this history will demonstrate, is not as straightforward as those memoirs would have us believe. Few answers are to be found within the canonical body of scholarship, which so often passes over the provincial newspaper in favour of the metropolitan titles, despite the fact that the latter is eclipsed by the former in terms of circulation and profitability for much of its history.[6] This book then seeks to reappraise the status of the provincial press by taking a longitudinal approach, which not only exposes the fragility of the distinction between provincial and national titles but also begins to unveil the claims to legitimacy which the provincial newspaper industry has constructed. As such, those claims which underpin the place of newspaper in the national psyche – such as its ability to serve the interests of democracy, or as an 'objective' narration of the latest events – are contextualized within a historic framework which enables us to revisit those 'absolutes' with a reinvigorated critical engagement.

The central position of this book is that the provincial newspaper is, and always has been, a commercial venture to its core. This is in itself not new; in particular the evening newspaper, which dominated the provincial press for much of the twentieth century, has long been acknowledged as the financial powerhouse for the provincial news industry as a whole and, indeed, for the national industry where those titles were co-owned. However, my argument goes further to suggest that profit is the principle around which all other elements of the newspaper – including its name, content, relationship with the reader and, significantly, social standing – are organized. Such is the power of this principle that it has governed the centrality the provincial newspaper claims for that ill-defined notion of 'community', despite the fact that the commercial structure of its business model can precisely undermine this position. This interpretation is

---

[6]   Bob Franklin has challenged this position with an extensive canon of work building on a flurry of academic studies in the 1970s. His work with David Murphy (1991) eruditely states the case for why the regional newspaper should be given full attention, and his argument remains relevant twenty-five years on. Others who have sought to redress the imbalance in scholarly attention to the local/regional press include Wiles, whose 1964 work on the origins of the provincial press is unrivalled in its scope and detail, Ian Jackson (1971), Cox and Morgan (1973) and more recently Andrew Walker (2006a).

at odds with the established construction of the role of the provincial newspaper at points in its history; in particular it conflicts with the dominant narrative of the twentieth-century newspaper to serve the 'good of the community'. Such is the sway of this value that it is embodied in professional norms and values – and perpetuated in training and standards of practice – and continues as an ideological justification for much local journalism today. This historicization, therefore, critiques the absoluteness of this value and instead suggests that it has been used to shore up the social legitimacy of what is in fact a highly commercial product. In doing so, it challenges the apparent immutability of these concepts by revealing that they are in fact highly contingent and even wrought with contradictions. This is particularly apposite in the current landscape where the contradictions are increasingly apparent.

A key example of the fracturing of the ideological justification for the provincial newspaper industry is the way in which news workers increasingly feel unable to meet the value of serving the good of the community, which they see as core to their raison d'etre. This position is perpetuated not only via training but also via the justification for routines which underpin local news practice, such as the understanding of the newspaper as a watchdog, which means local titles scrutinize local institutions such as courts and councils. This position is itself wrought with the contradiction inherent in the conceptualization of commercial circulation areas as some sort of homogenous community with an apparent unified set of interests, which can be served by journalists. These tensions are explored at length in the closing sections of this work in relation to the twenty-first-century provincial news workers. But such is its significance to the industry for nearly 200 years that, in addition, this claimed relationship between journalist and community has become the motif of this study, which seeks to establish the path by which it has become embodied as an ideological value, defined by a discourse of public service.

The thesis set out here is that the relationship between the provincial press and the community has been overstated and oversimplified by the industry, which has drawn upon it for its justification since its emergence in the nineteenth century. During that era, the marriage of the newspaper, which was positioned as an institution, with other civic institutions was largely one of convenience; this coincidence increased the status of newspaper owners, and their products, and the coverage of those institutions ensured a regular diet of content for the purpose of newspaper production. But there was nothing in the nature of the provincial newspaper which made that relationship absolute, and so, any claims to serving the public interest of a community were always tempered by the primary purpose of the newspaper as a business. Additionally, the notion of 'community' itself has been presented as a non-problematic ideal by the local newspaper, whereas, in practice, the notion is largely aligned to a constructed advertising market which developed in confluence with people living in a geographical area. This commercial nature of community at once stripped it of any claim to absoluteness, and this history demonstrates at key points how the newspaper addressed different publics at different times in order to expand advertising revenue. Again, this makes any claim to serving the 'public interest' questionable because of the ill-defined nature of the newspaper's public itself.

Therefore, this work also charts the emergence of the critique of the extent to which the provincial press performs this social function. Significantly, this position holds most sway at times of overt commercialism for the newspaper business. The first Royal Commission into the Press in 1947 was specifically related to fears about the impact of consolidation on the ability of titles to work in favour of their communities. Similarly, Jackson's seminal work (1971) focused on a provincial press which had been through an extensive period of consolidation and was largely owned by a few, huge corporations. As a result, he understood that, for these titles, the good of the community was a conscious strategy whereby papers – and in particular the highly successful evening papers – located themselves geographically with a content and commercial strategy of reaching as many people as possible in an area, thereby creating a targeted readership to 'sell' to advertisers. These papers specialized in a varied 'diet' of local content, which enabled them to attract large volumes of advertising and so run at a healthy profit. As such they presented themselves as a local 'watchdog' even though their centralized and remote ownership was weakening their 'licence' to make this claim (Bromley and Hayes 2002: 199).

However, while these criticisms address the way in which newspapers might be able to enact their service to the community, what they do not question is that status of this purpose in relation to the provincial press. This assumption of its centrality suggests that, such was the power of the ideological value that it became entrenched and established as absolute as these critiques emerged. Therefore, in calling for the 1947 enquiry, journalists and MPs did so to preserve the ability of the newspapers to serve their communities. Similarly, when Jackson wanted to demonstrate what a community loses when its newspaper 'dies' (1971: preface). This perspective continues to be articulated in contemporary debates about the state of the local news industry in the wake of digitization. Complaining that 'clickbait' had replaced reporter-generated copy for the *Croydon Advertiser*, editorial worker Gareth Davies articulated this position when he said, 'Local press should be a vital part of democratic accountability and a force for change, not an exercise in generating clicks by any means' (Ponsford, 31 July 2016).

The issue here is the 'should' in Davies' statement. As this work demonstrates, there is nothing implicit in the provincial newspaper business which makes serving the public interest a necessity. Indeed, the significance of advertising revenue to the finances of this sector means that for much of its history, the reader – in whose interest it would claim to function – is significant only as a target for that advertising market. That is why the free newspaper works. The irony is that the relationship between newspaper and community, which might best be described as adventitious, has developed to have such significance for those within and without the industry. In particular, the extent to which news workers see serving the good of the community as part of their professional ideology must be recognized. There is no doubt that for the thousands of often poorly paid and overworked journalists working in local and regional news rooms, the idea that they are serving some sort of public good has motivated them to continue in what can be a thankless role. Davies described himself as 'heartbroken' by what he saw as detrimental changes to his title, and I see no reason to doubt the sincerity of his statement. The problem here is the very demand for social purpose from a commercial entity whose primary goal is to generate profit; at times an avowed social role might have helped that primary purpose, such as during the era of the Second World War. At other times, though, this has not been the case, and in particular, the contemporary picture for the industry is one in which the form of journalism which supports the social purpose is simply too demanding of editorial resources for the current business model to support.

Jackson's work is particularly useful for the way it facilitates a deeper analysis of the way in which that ideology of news workers is held in balance by the emphasis on the bottom line of the newspaper business; it enables us to map through time the extent to which that ideology is supported by, or conflicted with, the dominant modus operandi for particular companies. Jackson accepts that the local newspaper's first role is to act as a local watchdog or 'moral guardian', safeguarding the reader against the actions of local institutions, but it can also bolster the community by suggesting improvements and celebrating success. In addition, it reflects what happens in those communities by recording a myriad of events. Together these roles enable a title to 'project itself as a community conscience, idealist, standard bearer of local pride and recorder'. He then maps the extent to which these roles are aligned with a set of professional journalistic practices which govern the content of these titles. Chief among these is an overwhelming emphasis on local content (just three of forty-five stories of 10 column inches surveyed by Jackson were non-local) within the paper and on the front page. Thus a title is able to give prominence to, and campaign for causes and issues within the geographical area with which it is aligned. For Jackson the commercial monopoly held by a title over its circulation area can add to the degree to which a community identifies with a title; because there is only one title, it can be seen as 'our paper' by a readership. Therefore, a second feature identified by Jackson is the 'local mass circulation' enjoyed by titles, which brings with it a need for accuracy – because expert local readers would notice mistakes – and an assumed mandate for the watchdog role.

These roles also account for the importance attached by local papers to local institutions – particularly councils – and their relationships with them. For Jackson, local papers feel 'responsible towards these institutions' and want to maintain the 'esteem' of them. In a similar process, local papers set out to propagate family values and formulate 'a network of ideal values for their readers', thus assuming the role of 'socialising medium'. The result is a number of recurring themes in terms of the content of a local newspaper including crime and subsequent court hearings, exposure of error, neglect or faulty procedure (as an adjunct to the watchdog status), acts of heroism and public service indicating good 'citizenship', local celebrity – to include personal landmarks like wedding anniversaries, coverage of local institutions and organizations – including sport. Jackson's analysis suggests that those within the local newspaper industry saw the reporting of local government as their 'prime function', and research carried out nearly twenty years later demonstrated that 23 per cent of the stories analysed in eighteen weekly papers came from councils or regional authorities (Franklin and Murphy 1991: 64). The newspaper's approach to this content is couched within the context of enhancing the status of a given community and the image of that community acts as a 'reference point' in coverage. Drawing on the example of the ritual of installing the mayor into a council, Jackson sees the interests of title and authority aligned because both ascribe to the notion of serving the good of the community, and such reports present a picture of 'ordered, constructive activity – a series of positive contributions to local community life' (Jackson, 1971: 110). Even the reporting of what Jackson terms 'disorder' news, including crime and violence, can ultimately have a positive effect on the community, he argues, by promoting the work of the police and legal system, which ultimately 'reassures' readers (ibid.: 93).

> The version of local life that is variously reflected can be seen as a confrontation of the agencies of community order and disorder. On the side of order are the community leaders, local heroes and achievers, and those who attain a transient celebrity status in context of home or work; centenarians, non-retirers, lucky winners etc. … Community disorder manifests itself in reports about the agents and victims of disasters, accidents, crimes and institutional discord or neglect. The presence of such reports in the local Press should not be allowed to mask the fact that it presents institutional leaders in their normal, positive roles. (Jackson 1971: 273)

The idealized standards of the paper mapped here are those articulated by the *Darlington Evening Despatch* in 1968, that 'a newspaper should reflect the community it serves – warts and all. When a mirror it holds to society reveals neglect, injustice, inhumanity, ignorance, or complacency, the mirror should not be clouded but polished, so that these things can be eradicated rather than ignored' (ibid.: 286). These themes are aligned with those embodied within the training syllabus of the National Council for the Training of Journalists. Since its inception, a knowledge of court reporting and local government have been identified as essential components of the qualification for those wishing to work in the regional newspaper (NCTJ.com 2014); this in turn aligns with the required ability of a local newspaper reporter to report on the courts and councils. In this way the ideology of the journalist as local guardian is disseminated to would-be entrants into the industry and is subsumed into a pattern of work routines. It is an ideological position which can be found both in the trainee and the editor alike, as former editor Sara Hadwin expressed, 'The role of an editor is to produce a newspaper which serves the community in which it circulates and is bought willingly because it has the long-term interests of its readers at heart, satisfies their curiosity, enriches their lives, expands their horizons and helps and informed enlightened public opinion to emerge' (2006: 146).

That the relationship between newspaper and community can be so naturalized demonstrates its appeal for a range of stakeholders both inside and outside the industry itself. Such is its normative power that it is the basis for continued criticism for these titles, which are said to cover less local government, or fewer local court hearings, or which rely too much on public relations generated material. It is this naturalization which this history sets out to challenge. By charting the development of the business model in tandem with the ideological value, this normative concept can be interrogated so that we can problematize the very notion that the role of the provincial newspaper is to serve the community. Additionally, we have the challenge that, because the relationship between newspapers and communities are largely adventitious, the possibility exists that their operation may not support communities at all. Providing an answer to this question is largely beyond the scope of this study, but critiquing the relationship does reveal its constructedness, and this position has been expressed at times in the ongoing debate about the function of the provincial press. Cox and Morgan (1973) argue that local newspapers idealize, rather than benefit, communities; to this end their organizational structure is geared around the business of the newspaper itself, rather than a social role. This shifts our understanding of those who work in the organization; for instance, the editor is reframed from the campaigning hero, to someone who deals in the business of news so that the community is only of secondary interest in a news room which relies on tried and tested sources to fill newspaper pages. 'They [editors] will give more detailed news, and news of neighbourhood concern, only if it fits into their perceptions of what the readership in aggregate will take. They are entrepreneurs dealing in news. ... There are comparatively few payoffs, from their point of view, in the effort of going outside well-worn routines' (Cox and Morgan 1973: 142). This perspective is echoed by Simpson (1981) who analyses editorial practice in terms of its functionality to the newspaper business and understands it as a cost to be controlled, rather than a public service. Additionally, Franklin and Murphy (1991) offer an analysis of the degradation of the watchdog function of the newspaper in tandem with an analysis of its corporate structure. These perspectives are all given due consideration in the course of this work, and the variance in emphasis between the provincial newspaper as public servant and moneymaking venture in turn informs the typology developed here. As such this work charts the development of the industry in these key terms in order to facilitate a deeper understanding of the discursive construction of the good of the community and so reframe the debate about its significance. In particular this approach demonstrates the primacy of advertising income to the nature of the provincial newspaper; in turn, this acknowledgement enables a reassessment of the discursive claims to legitimacy, which the industry continues to draw upon. This work is then an attempt to employ history as a tool to map the shifts in the balance of weight given to the role of the provincial newspaper as a financial instrument and as a community player. Significantly this process enables us to reframe the debate about the purpose of local journalism, which has been largely polarized for the past seventy years between those who argue it should serve the public and those who argue it should make money. A more useful starting point is to understand why these positions are so entrenched so that we can instead ask that **if** we believe the local press should be a vital part of democratic accountability, then **what** sort of business model can support a local press able to take on that mantle.

This approach has much in common with the work of Martin Conboy, who has been at the forefront in the revival of historical approaches to media history. In his 2004 work, *Journalism; A Critical History*, Conboy draws on Foucault to question the value system which operates through, and is acted upon by, the practices of journalism. Significantly this posits journalism within the network of relationships sought by Curran. As Conboy explains,

> 'Journalism is therefore made up of the claims and counter-claims of a variety of speakers on its behalf. What journalists say about their work, what critics and political commentators say about journalism, the perceived effects of a language of journalism on society, the patterns of popularity among readers and viewers of journalism, all take their place in defining the discourse of journalism'. (ibid.: 4)

Conboy's approach leads him to interrogate and re-evaluate what have traditionally been seen as core values of journalism, such as its ability to function as a 'fourth estate', its claims to 'objectivity' or the way in which its 'economic imperative' is often 'obscured' (ibid.). This study takes a similar approach, not to a set of practices which may be considered as journalism or news as Conboy has done, but to a set of products which may be defined as provincial newspapers, with its own associated set of practices and values.

My contention is that an historical understanding of these shifts in emphasis between the components of the provincial press – and in particular within the context of this study, its claims to serve a community – enables us to understand the medium in relation to the development of society on a macro level; it also enables us to challenge those components which are often presented as absolute and to critically engage with the ideological construction and function of those to the media. In this context, the provincial newspaper-centric approach of this position contextualizes its hegemonic claims to perform certain functions – particularly serving the good of the community – and, in doing so, challenges them. History enables us to do this because, as Foucault writes, 'the search for descent is not the erecting of foundations; on the contrary, it disturbs what was previously considered immobile, it fragments what was thought unified, it shows the heterogeneity of what was imagined consistent in itself' (1984: 82). This history differs in so much as it does not seek to create a grand narrative of the provincial press, as is so often the case at times of uncertainty. Neither does it identify a 'golden age' for provincial press, by arguing for a time when local papers functioned in a way which deserved the normative reverence they sought to command. Instead it reveals the discursive construction of the provincial press 'in its specificity; to show in what way the set of rules … put into operation is irreducible to any other' (Foucault 1972: 139).

This approach is made possible by a particular conception of what it is to practice journalism and, to be a journalist. We understand journalism as a practice primarily concerned with news so that the main concern of journalism is constantly changing as the specifics of the subject matter in hand shift. So one day a provincial journalist might be covering a political conflict, but the shifting news agenda means the next day attention turns to perceived tragedy or the to-ings and fro-ings of local luminaries. In the words of Vaughan Reynolds, the editor of the *Birmingham Post* newspaper, 'There is nothing so dead as an issue which has lived its days … a newspaper must be forward looking. If it is a live paper, that is because it is perpetually self-renewing, changing with current demands while preserving standards of abiding value' (Whates 1957: 243). This association with the new, though, belies the ritualization of the news-gathering process which governs the day-to-day workings of journalists, and the restrictions of the wider contexts of regulatory, legal and practical constraints. Therefore a more useful definition of journalism practice is as a range of communicative actions; implicit in this understanding is the dynamism of the process of journalism which becomes a matter of constant negotiation between journalist and public framed by constraints such as public expectation or, significantly for the conception of journalism put forward here, that which is 'commercially viable' (Conboy 2004: 3).

Rather than considering journalism and its forms as fixed and immutable, or at least without legacy as if catapulted into our presence fully formed, this conception necessitates a consideration of these competing facets in their own right. The provincial press then becomes elevated to an object of study; by understanding it as a discursive form, it can be recognized as a social object, the presence of which can be considered as manifestations of the power relationships in society, which in turn has implicit and explicit ramifications for the understanding of and practice of provincial journalism. Particularly significant for this study is the way in which this approach reveals the contingency of what is often considered absolute within this media form. For instance, instead of accepting that it is the role of the local press to cover the local council, we can instead ask why this is considered an absolute practice. Why is it that such news values have become naturalized within the practice of local journalism to the extent that they have achieved the status of lore? By doing so, we are able to take a fresh look at those claims which the provincial press would have us take as constant principles. We can examine how these very claims serve the interests of the various vested interests, whether they be those of newspaper workers, newspapers owners or external; those claims can be repositioned within the changing shape of the provincial press and in relation to how it has positioned itself at different moments. In turn this can help us to assess in whose interests those positions function.

The provincial newspaper may therefore be considered as a cultural form, which frees it from a set format – such as being printed on paper – and foregrounds it as a process of communication with its own set of aims and practices. This is a useful approach for the historian of the newspaper because it enables an approach which recognizes it as an evolving form. One signifier of this constant evolution is the fact that those things which we currently call newspapers have taken the names 'corantos, newsbooks, diurnals, gazettes, news-sheets, mercuries, intelligencers, periodicals, tabloids, newspapers and journals' (Williams 2010: 4) at different points in its history; in the digital age they might equally be named, news websites, apps and tablet editions or, even news brands, in recognition of emerging forms of publication for what have been household names, albeit on a localized scale. This is significant to the historicized newspaper which has at its heart the tension between claims to continuity and the process of evolution, and our ability to navigate those twin drivers may well hold the key to re-envisioning the newspaper for the future. At least an inability to let go of what are seen as non-negotiable characteristics may be harmful so that it is an obsession with paper as a medium, which is signalling the end of the 'newspaper', according to Jeff Jarvis (2007) rather than anything in the nature of the newspaper itself. Contradictory as this may sound, for Jarvis, what is important is not the form but the purpose. It is the newspaper as an 'organising principle' – which delivers a certain form of information to a certain audience.[7] As well as offering a way to look forward,

---

[7] This position is discussed in the concluding chapter.

this view of the newspaper also offers us a way to look back – to negotiate those many-named publications to identify a particular form of communication which we might take into our history. This perspective acknowledges that of Jeremy Black (2001) who predicates change itself as a defining characteristic of the newspaper. While paper is always part of Black's product, he cites a shift in emphasis between other key components, such as the content of that product, the way in which it makes money and its perceived influence, as all shifting over time.

This then gives us the framework within which we can chart the emergence and presence of the provincial newspaper as a specialist institution, refined in relation to particular circumstances, in particular locales, at particular points in history, and formed by the special interaction of those key aspects associated with news practice. As Black has argued, 'Each period of English newspaper history can be presented as one of transformation, shifts in content, production, distribution, and the nature of competition, and the social context' (2001: 1). As such it considers a range of issues associated with it including ownership, contents, its relations with audience and readership and technology and even its relationship with the mode of delivery – that is whether on paper or online. This change, though, is set against the relief of what is constant for the newspaper; for instance, that it is centred around communication but that it is an institution which mutates and shifts in response to external and internal factors. As such, identifying those continuous aspects not only gives us the different forms of a newspaper, as we differentiate divergence between communication institutions through time, but also enables us to identify what is continuous for each of those institutions. It enables us to identify those first principles from which others can be seen to emanate and around which they circulate and settle. So, for the provincial newspaper, we have the idea of its relationship with geography and, its subsequent relationship with the community within that area. What is particularly evident when reviewing the history of the provincial newspaper is the allied centrality of profit to its operation. From its earliest appearance as an opportunistic business venture in the hands of printers, the provincial newspaper has overwhelmingly been a vehicle for making money, and that money has largely come from advertising. What may be surprising is the way in which this motive takes precedence over both the geographical area, the relationship with local communities and even the urge to disclose the latest news – none of which can be identified as unwavering principles. Instead it is the commercial logic of the advertising-rich provincial newspaper which has sustained it for much of its existence as a highly profitable business model, and which has dominated and governed its cultural position.

The centrality of this perspective of political economy therefore contextualizes competing historiographical perspectives – including social, technological and political, although these others are emphasized to varying degrees throughout the period discussed. So, while the position of the provincial press in relation to politics dominates its narration for much of the nineteenth century, this perspective wanes with the ascendency of the mass-market press. Equally, technology takes centre stage as computerized production impacts on the industry in the 1970s and 1980s, but is insufficient to explain the full context of deunionization in the industry. What dominates these varying perspectives is the impact that operating for profit has had, not only on the evolution and day-to-day structure of the provincial newspaper but also on its ideological values, as experienced by those working in the sector via their associated routines, and by the wider social context. This is particularly marked during the Second World War, for instance, where the provincial newspaper industry might be understood to foreground its role in the community during this era of national crisis as a way of preserving a highly successful business model.

This approach to the provincial newspaper, therefore, interrogates those normative concepts themselves by comparing their evolution and operation at different points in time and, in so doing, this longitudinal approach extends the existing theorization of this process. For example, the dichotomy between the accounts which position a 'free' provincial press against market forces has been well rehearsed, particularly in the late-twentieth-century era of the highly commercialized local newspaper (see for instance Franklin and Murphy 1991; Curran 2003). This history extends that perspective backwards in particular, in an attempt to identify when and why those normative concepts emerge so that they can be revealed and interrogated. Simply, if we believe that the market is the driver for the provincial press, to what extent does this influence the key concepts employed by it, such as serving the interest of the community, or acting as a watchdog or even being aligned to a specific geographical area? It enables us to ask why the industry has come to make such claims and in whose interests they are made – to treat those claims as a specific discourse, in the Foucauldian sense, which 'give expressions to meanings and values

of institutions or practices and, in doing so, claim authority for themselves'
(Conboy 2011: 5).

Editorial workers in the provincial press

A parallel theme arising from the consideration of what it is to be a provincial
newspaper is that of what it is to be a journalist working within these titles,
and the routines and practices which can be described as journalism. This is a
particular apposite question within the long view of the provincial newspaper
because the journalist is not always part of that story; this is particularly so at the
beginning, when titles are in the hands of printers who are skilled in production
rather than content, and in the landscape of the second decade of the twenty-
first century when the 'citizen' journalist is harnessing technology to publish
outside of formal business structures. This recognition in itself interrogates the
centrality of key ideological values associated with the work of the provincial
journalist to that practice.

The coming-and-going of the journalist within this history counters the
mythology of the industry, which naturalizes their presence. The job, though
tough, is presented as unproblematic; journalists are either born with a 'nose
for news' or the practice of journalism is a trade to be learnt on the job with
no more reflection than that which applies to skilled labour. Delano recalls
L. Mencken's glib description of journalism at the beginning of the nineteenth
century as 'a craft to be mastered in four days and abandoned at the first sign
of a better job' (2000: 262). Marr suggests that 'journalists have a blurred social
status, a foggy range of a skills, an ill-defined purpose and a ludicrously romantic
haze where a professional code would normally be' (2004: 5). These approaches
suggest the complexity which presents a 'conceptual dilemma' for the practice of
journalism (Elliott 1978: 172); a journalist can be a force for good – as typified
by Woodward and Bernstein – or a muckraking scoundrel who is to be despised.
As such, the journalist is 'constructed in history somewhere between hack and
hero' (Conboy 2011: 167), and his or her 'multiple identity' as an 'individual
professional, the citizen with social responsibilities, and the worker as part of a
collective' (Harcup 2002: 103) is wrought with tension.

This is no less true for the journalist in the provincial press than for that
of the mythologized figures exemplified by our Watergate heroes. Countless
national journalists started their career in local papers and recall their early

days with fondness and respect for the grounding it gave them. The provincial press has traditionally been seen as the training ground for all journalism, and until recently a common form of entry into journalism was via a formal apprenticeship with a local paper. This structure is reflected in differential pay rates, which reflect the apparent differential status between national and local titles. Encouraging more women into journalism, Emilie Peacocke, then editor of the *Daily Telegraph*'s Woman's Department, proclaimed the provincial press as an 'incomparable' training ground (Cranfield 1930).[8] This is the training extolled by Richard Stott, whose first big story concerned the Great Train Robbery, which took place on his Buckinghamshire 'patch' in 1963. Similarly, Harold Evans, the legendary editor of the *Sunday Times* newspaper, began his career on a weekly paper in Lancashire; John Humphrys, who hosts *Today*, the flagship current affairs programme on BBC Radio 4, left school at the age of fifteen to join the *Penarth Times*. This history is populated with the names of those figures through time who have used the provincial press as a springboard to journalistic greatness.

The competing classifications of journalism as a trade or profession are also epitomized in the tension between the trades union, the National Union of Journalists and the Institute of Journalists. The latter envisioned journalism as 'an autonomous profession able to organise and rank its members, regulate their ethical conduct and determine certain conditions of their employment' (Delano 2000: 271). Yet those who have measured journalism against traditional definitions of a profession have found it wanting. As Gopsill and Neale explain,

> Journalism does not work in the manner of a profession as most people understand the term when they think of say, medicine, accountancy or law. These are closed shops, with high barriers to entry; they are regulated by professional associations, and, most importantly, the practitioners often control the fees they are paid. … In economic terms journalists are simply hired hands, or pens. This is why they need, and 100 years ago, formed a union. (2007: 4)

In tandem with this, then, is the fact that neither does journalism have a set code which practitioners are obliged to sustain – despite the development of various optional standards by competing organizations including the Press

---

[8] The history of the female journalist is even more complex. When Emilie Peacocke was writing, the presence of women on the staff of newspapers was in its infancy, and most women were present as correspondents or as editors of specialist content aimed at women. The expansion of women into the profession was driven by a wish to attract different advertisers in a process explored in the section on New Journalism in Chapter 4.

Council, Press Complaints Commission and latterly the Independent Press Standards Organisation (IPSO). A journalist who breaks the code may face repercussions but cannot be 'struck off' and barred from practising, in the same way as a medical or legal professional might be. Consideration of the practice of journalism over time also suggests that its status has shifted and developed in sometimes non-linear ways, for instance, facing reversal due to the impact of technological innovation in the 1980s and 1990s, and, more recently, with the impact of digital innovation. This is despite an increased emphasis on education and the increased visibility of journalism as an undergraduate programme. There are also the attempts from within journalism to resist professionalization either by emphasizing the individual over efforts to collectivize (Elliott 1978) or by undermining shifts in their own occupation (Conboy 2011). The result is that the questions which confront those working as journalists – for instance with reference to organization, regulation and independence – are little changed in a century (Delano 2000: 261).

Alternative views on the question of professionalism have begun to extricate journalism from this impasse and complement a historical analysis of what it means to practice journalism. Elliott has reframed the debate to consider it an 'occupation', from which a living can be made, and links it to a set of practices and an accompanying ideology which develops in line with the evolution of the context in which it is practised (1978: 172–3). The development of this occupation is both complex and perhaps contradictory; for instance, the role of the 'professional' editor is associated with the need to be independent of political interference; but this only came at the turn of the twentieth century when journalism became organized according to an industrial process which enabled it to be commercially successful. Rather than being 'free', the irony is that this journalism was in fact made up of strategic rituals dominated by the technology of the telegraph and the skill of shorthand which enabled verbatim 'objective' reports and fast news. To give value to this increasingly commodified work, these journalists increasingly ascribed to the value of serving the public interest. Journalism and the journalist are not, therefore, fixed in time but instead might be thought of as a spectrum,[9] which can be defined by a set of 'professional imperatives' which inform what journalists do, for instance, fact checking and scrutinizing information.

---

[9]   Conboy posits five types of journalist – the radical pamphleteer, the man of letters, populist scribe, hack and the enlightened editor (2011: 166).

These values are not abstract ideological constructs, but actualized, organizing principles which inform the way in which journalists work. As such, neither are those practices fixed, and the development of key techniques which might be considered unchallenged are traced through the course of this work. This includes the emergence of the inverted pyramid as a storytelling technique in the provincial press at the turn of the twentieth century and the related values of objectivity (see Chapter 4). The way in which those practices are experienced can similarly be employed by journalists to challenge the systems in which they work, for instance by being aware of the limitations placed by industrial structures on their ability to work in a way they would see as being 'professional', such as being able to exercise individual discretions or serving the public interest. These palpable tensions between those values and the realities of working life are discussed in the closing section of this book in relation to news workers in the provincial press of the twenty-first century.

The notion of professionalism employed in this thesis is therefore aligned with that expounded by Delano and developed by Deuze, who defines his approach as 'understanding journalism in terms of how journalists give meaning to their news work'. Journalism is understood in terms of the dominant occupational ideology which informs how journalists see themselves and their praxis, although there may be variations in its application over time and between media (2005: 443–5). To chart the development of journalism is to chart the development of 'values, strategies and formal codes characterizing professional journalism and shared most widely by its members' and which 'validate and give meaning to their work' (ibid.: 445–6). To do so necessitates a full consideration of the context in which those people are working, so the media form to which they relate. Key to this are those values which legitimize the occupation of journalism in society, and Deuze suggests that these values are not fixed but are renegotiated and repositioned in relation to other factors, including, critically, the perception of the media form to which journalists are aligned. It is this understanding which shifts us away from a 'naïve' definition of journalism as a profession; instead 'it is by studying how journalists for all walks of their professional life negotiate the core values that one can see the occupational ideology of journalism at work' (ibid.: 458). Therefore, the ideologically informed practices of journalism carried out by those who might be considered to be professionals are contextualized by their historicization. This enables an approach to the notion of journalism and professionalism which recognizes not only its shifts but also its constants and the way in which its significance is understood by the wider society. Significantly for this work it also enables key concepts – such as that of journalists working to serve the good of the community – to be understood historically and in terms of their relationship to the lived experience of news workers as well as their significance for news organizations and their cultural context.

The 'national' versus 'provincial' dichotomy examined

On 18 December 2013 the multimedia editorial team of the *Liverpool Post* documented the final edition of the long-established and respected, regional newspaper via a live blog. The event marked the end of 158 years of continuous publication, and yet the demise of a once-significant daily title went largely unnoticed by the wider population; media commentator and former regional daily editor Steve Dyson claimed the decision was 'common sense' (*Theguardian. com*, 12 October 2013), citing a sale of 6,000 copies in a city with a population of 500,000. Just a handful of readers even bothered to comment on the *Post's* own blog of the landmark day (*Liverpooldailypost.co.uk*, 18 December 2013). Announcing the closure of the title in its own columns, Trinity Mirror North West managing director Steve Anderson Dixon said: 'Sadly, the Liverpool city region no longer generates the demand in terms of advertising or circulation, to sustain both the *Post* and the *Liverpool Echo*. The *Post* is a wonderful and much-loved old lady who has simply come to the end of her natural life' (*www. liverpooldailypost.co.uk*, 10 December 2013). The closure was an especially poignant reminder of direction of travel for the industry. Just eight years earlier Granada TV (which holds the commercial television franchise for the Liverpool region) had featured a two-part documentary about the newspaper to mark its 150th anniversary. It is also one of the few regional papers to be subjected to academic scrutiny, which resulted in the seminal work by Harvey Cox and David Morgan *City Politics and the Press* (1973). The significance of the paper, then called the *Liverpool Daily Post*, and its sister title *The Liverpool Echo*, seemed significant with a combined circulation of nearly 500,000 copies per day at the end of the 1960s.

The *Liverpool Post* is among a swathe of once-loved local newspapers papers to have been closed in recent years; the early section of this book catalogues the development of the *Northampton Mercury* as among one of the first provincial titles in England. In October 2015 the title folded just five years shy of its 300th anniversary, one of eleven free distribution newspapers deemed uneconomical by owners Johnston Press. The demise of these papers reveals the duality of the perspective from which such local papers are viewed. On the one hand they are 'rags' which can be dispensed with when no longer needed; on the other they are an integral part of the local landscape. What both sides would appear to agree on is that these newspapers have had their day – a view formed against a backdrop of falling advertising revenues and declining sales. Typical of this is the attitude of media analysts FTI Consulting, whose 2013 report tells of an industry in terminal decline in the face of a digital media revolution. Yet in terms of other indicators, the provincial press remains successful. In the same year the now-defunct Newspaper Society identified 1,100 regional and local newspapers in the UK – with 1,600 associated websites. The print products alone reached 31 million readers a week. Since then, some titles have closed (forty-six according to research carried out by the trade paper the *Press Gazette*), but nearly as many have launched. And as I write, the business continues to yield substantial profits, albeit at a level which has been drastically reduced by the dual impact of the digital revolution and the economic recession.

Local newspapers are more popular, in terms of aggregate circulations, and command more trust than national newspapers in England. They return higher profits and for much of their history they have outsold and been read by more people than the national press; it is even debatable if the 'national' newspaper has had national reach for much more than fifty or sixty years. In the 1950s the *Manchester Guardian* changed its name and moved its base to London; before then, the London daily papers could hardly claim national circulation. Tom O'Malley (2014) has carried out new research, which suggests that although the London 'nationals' were pushing for sales in the 1950s, they were only partially successful. In the main, the London 'class' newspapers were read in the south of England. This is borne out by the evidence of the Hulton Readership Survey, aimed at guiding advertisers. Most titles had northern editions which were produced outside of London and had considerable differences in content from their metropolitan editions. The *Daily Express* and the *Daily Mail* also printed Scottish editions. Even so, areas of the United Kingdom remained immune to the charms of these London-based titles, particularly Northern Ireland and Scotland but also the major northern conurbations around Newcastle (Seymour-Ure 1996). The Royal Commission on the Press of 1947 concluded that these titles did not serve the nation, but instead represented the interests of the south of England and 'to this extent performed a function similar to that of the larger provincial morning papers' (Royal Commission 1947: 8). In 1947 the major 'quality' provincial titles also outsold the London papers. *The Times* sold 195,000 a day, while the Manchester *Daily Despatch* sold 475,000, the *Yorkshire Evening Post* 204,000, *the Birmingham Mail* 200,000 and the *Newcastle Journal* 146,000. The highest selling provincial title was the Manchester-based Sunday, the *Empire News*, which sold some 2 million copies, putting it in the top four bestselling Sundays at the end of the war (Seymour-Ure 1996: 20).

MacInnes et al. (2007) go further and suggest that the 'national' definition preferred by titles assumes that circulations, national identities and institutions map seamlessly against each other; in fact though, titles do not circulate equivalently across the UK and the competing claims of titles to serve the national interests of Wales, Scotland and Northern Ireland further undermine the notion of 'national'. This complexity is such that it renders the 'ultimate utility of the construct "the British national press" rather doubtful' (2007: 201). The idea of a 'national press' then privileges a 'metro-centric version of British nationalism' (Rosie et al. 2006: 330). As such it is better understood as a discursive position taken by 'political actors' who 'may seem to reproduce a popular banal national consciousness to legitimise the state' (MacInnes 2007: 189). The relative contiguity between Parliament and 'Fleet Street' means the voice of the metropolitan press has also historically been heard clearly by politicians, despite what have at times been relatively small circulations (Koss 1981: 21). In tandem with this is the academic privilege given to the notion of journalism as a fourth estate, which again focuses attention on the relationship between newspaper and politician.

In fact the development of the newspaper in England is such that it is hard to disentangle the national from the regional for much of the period under consideration here. Predicating the national newspaper as the dominant form fails to recognize that the origin of the press in England is regional in shape with a distinction between London and the provinces more accurate. Walker (2006a) argues that during the nineteenth century the regional press was significant enough in its own right to be seen as forming a national network. There is also evidence that the largest provincial titles were also held for national influence (Cranfield 1978). When the London press did extend its reach beyond the capital, there remained an often-symbiotic relationship between the two forms of paper, exemplified, for instance, by the traffic in content and staff between the two in formalized and structured ways typified by career progression codified in the National Union of Journalists. The dominant businesses also failed to distinguish between the two – holding regional and national titles alongside each other for profit at least, if not for prestige. This cross-ownership of national and local titles continues to be an attractive proposition, exemplified by Johnston Press plc, which in early 2016 bought the national *i* (denoted by a single lowercase letter) newspaper. The irony is that the provincial press is at least, in part, to blame for this lesser status. The centralized and overwhelmingly conglomerate ownership of newspapers charted by this history has meant that provincial titles have at times provided subsidies for those London-based titles, owned largely for influence and vanity. This left the provincial titles vulnerable to asset-stripping, which has in turn affected their prestige (Tunstall 1996).

This overwhelming emphasis on the 'national' press goes a long way to explain the extent to which scholars have become preoccupied with the study of the relationship between newspapers and the process of democracy. Early examples of writing about newspapers suggest this as a preoccupation (see Raymond 1999). In this account the study of the history of the newspaper becomes the study of the development of a 'free press' – that is free from government control – which Curran and Seaton in the classic *Power Without Responsibility* term the 'orthodox' interpretation of the British press (2003: 3). This interpretation bestows the newspaper with the power of democratization by information; an informed population, empowered by the burgeoning newspaper industry once the taxes on knowledge had been abolished in the mid-nineteenth century, became politically literate because of the free circulation of newspapers. It is the Habermasian idea of the public sphere made concrete – refined into 'politics by public discussion' by Mark Hampton (2004: 8) – and it is a notion which has such leverage to have become mythologized and which has been given a renewed vigour by Michael Schudson (2008) who sets out 'why democracies need an unlovable press'. This conception is invoked in contemporary arguments about the newspaper press in the UK, including the discussion of state regulation of the newspaper industry by Lord Justice Leveson, who said, 'The press, operating properly and in the public interest is one of the true safeguards of our democracy' (House of Commons 2012: 4).

Yet even this notion of 'fourth estate' – and the allied conception of a free press – is an area of contestation for historians. Koss refines the notion of a free press into a press which is free to be partisan in the wake of the abolition of the 'taxes on knowledge' in the mid-1800s. In a process which is related to the development of the provincial press, these allegiances were not fixed but shifted and changed with the fortunes of those they chose to support. And it was easy for the press to shift away from them altogether to favour a form of a conservatism which appealed to the mass readership of a highly industrialized process of newspaper production in the early years of the twentieth century. No metric exists by which to ascertain the exact extent to which the press held influence over the political process. However, what is significant is the extent to which both readers, writers and politicians subscribed to – and exploited – the notion that this influence existed so that the 'power of the press' became a 'conceit' to which all parties ascribed at the same time as the newspaper refined its commercial operation (Koss 1984: 7). Mark Hampton moves the process of commercialization to the centre of this process and argues that notion of the press as fourth estate emanates from within the industry itself and, as such, serves as an organizing factor, and as a discursive position, for that industry. This is true of national and provincial newspapers which 'create an arena for public discussion on the "questions of the day."' (2004: 9). Newspapers also 'represent' their readership by reflecting their views and by 'crystallizing them into a powerful form that could bring pressure to bear on Parliament' (ibid.).

For the regional press, this notion has become refined into the idea of the local paper as a 'watchdog', existing to serve 'the good of the community'. Both Walker (2006a) and Black (2001) have discussed how the provincial press of the mid-nineteenth century was aligned more to national rather than regional interests, although Jackson (1971) traces the origins of local news to the eighteenth century. Gliddon (2003) provides a model for a shift to a more localized version as the motivation for ownership of newspapers moves away from political influence to making money. Work by Taylor (2006) on the *Cambridge Evening News* evidences the process by which a title constructs a community and uses the interests of that community as an organizing factor for news values. As such newspapers begin to construct this concept as they develop into sophisticated mass-market products, with improvements in elements including content and production. These improvements, such as organizing local content together and highlighting it through better labelling (see Chapter 4), have been brought together under the auspices of New Journalism.[10] Bromley and Hayes (2002) suggest that in the interwar period, titles contributed to the formation of a civic identity and this notion is evidenced by those working with the newspaper industry; as such, by the time of the Second World War, it is firmly established as an ideological value which gives meaning to the work of journalists and is,

[10] These developments have been thoroughly theorized by Horst Pottker (2005) and Martin Conboy (2004) and are discussed in the context of the English provincial newspaper by Donald Matheson (2000).

therefore, articulated by those within the industry (Fletcher 1946; Hansard 1946; see Chapter 6). Jackson (1971) suggests the relationship with the community drives aspects of provincial journalism practice, such as the coverage of local government, which seeks to represent local life in a positive, organized fashion. However, this position has been criticized by those who challenge the ability of the local newspaper to perform this watchdog role, either through lack of distance between journalist and politician (Cox and Morgan 1973) or because of the structure of local government press relations itself (Burke 1970). This means the concept of serving the good of the community is based more on rhetoric than reality (Murphy 1976).

There is no doubt that the provincial newspaper industry is part-way through a transformation wrought by the pushes and pulls of the digital revolution of the past twenty years or so. These changes, which have undermined the traditional business model for local news, are characterized as having 'radically altered virtually every aspect of news gathering, writing and reporting' by Bob Franklin (2013: 1). Change is evident everywhere, but the inability of the industry to make money from the web versions of their titles, and the subsequent precariousness of the news they provide, has created a complex pattern of reactions. The discussion around the closure of the *Liverpool Post* typifies the different viewpoints on the issue. Writing his last column for the paper, Editor Mark Thomas said, 'Some politicians, and some people in public life in our own city region, who will today be celebrating the end of the road for the *Liverpool Post*. Without our scrutiny, they may be tempted to breathe just a little more easily' (*www.liverpooldailypost. co.uk*, 18 December 2013).

These contemporary arguments continue to be rehearsed at the highest level and were called upon in support of calls to the British government to grant business rate relief for those papers which continue to operate networks of local offices in 2015. The roots of this debate though are to be found in post-war Britain in the context of the concentration of ownership of the provincial newspaper industry and the comparisons between those detailed discussions in the 1947 Royal Commission on the Press, and these debates now demonstrate the inertia that has surrounded these issues for more than fifty years. This is in no part due to the fact that, despite its complexity, the industry presents its commitment to the community as a truism which renders changes such as moving from broadsheet to tabloid, daily to weekly or even from paper to online incidental to the industry's core purpose.

Of course, a significant reason for looking back is to enable us to better understand where we are now, and to give us 'a clearer context in which to explore claims concerning the inevitability of change or conservatism within journalism today' (Conboy 2011: 6). This history pays particular attention to this process in regard to the concept of existing for the good of the community because of its centrality as an established value for those working in the provincial newspaper industry. To do so it has drawn on not only pre-existing press histories, but also a wealth of primary material, drawn from archival holdings. Empirical evidence has also been found in statistics and reports from professional organizations focusing on particular issues, such as that produced by the think tank Political and Economic Planning in 1938, or the three Royal Commissions into the press in the twentieth century, each of which gathered contemporary evidence. These form an invaluable snapshot of the industry in a moment of time but again are related to a particular line of enquiry and so will present a picture of only relevant aspects of an issue. The consolidated nature of the industry means there are few extant archives relating to the economic structure of particular titles over a sustained period of time; therefore, when it comes to applying that to individual newspaper titles, the trail of evidence is often hard to follow.

This approach, therefore, sets out to contribute to the scholarship of the provincial newspaper in three key ways. First, by promoting the consideration of the provincial press as an essential building block of the media system as a whole, it demands a reassessment of key concepts related to this system. For instance, if, as O'Malley suggests, (2014) the readership of the 'national' press was largely concentrated in the south-east region of England during the Second World War, the corollary is the need to reassess the extent to which regional newspapers were key players in issues surrounding censorship or morale during the conflict. Second, by reappraising the significance of the provincial press we are able to contextualize a significant area of journalism practice. Mark Hampton (Hampton and Conboy 2014) argues that only by integrating the historical consideration of journalism with broader historiographies can its distinctive qualities be appreciated. 'Simply put', Hampton argues, 'journalism, whether as a genre or as professional ritual, needs a location – a delivery mechanism … the type of journalism that can be practiced is intimately intertwined with the nature of the media organization, and it's status in the wider society' (ibid.: 158–9). Third, it is hoped that a deeper understanding of the development of the provincial press will contribute to the way in which future historians approach the products of the industry. Bingham and Conboy argue that historians have a tendency to consider the products of the news media 'without properly considering their distinctive stylistic and institutional traits' (2013: 1). Bingham also suggests that, as a result of the increasing availability of newspapers to researchers due to digitization, 'in the future historians will examine press content far more extensively and with greater sophistication' (Bingham 2012: 320). But, for the reasons discussed above, this consideration will only be effective when the context for that content is given appropriate weight.

Reappraising the provincial press

By putting the business model at the heart of this approach, this history contextualizes and explains the changes which have defined key moments for the provincial newspaper throughout its existence. Some of these have had a slow-felt influence, such as move towards monopolistic ownership patterns throughout the twentieth century, while others may have caused a seismic shift in practice, such as the repeal of Stamp Duty in 1856 which paved the way for a cheap, accessible regional press. In doing so, I suggest that the history of the local press may be divided into six distinct stages, each characterized by a shift in emphasis between the key elements of state control, political economy and significantly ownership, social influence and production techniques – typically driven by new technology. This is not the first typology of the press to be charted, and similarities may be drawn between the classification offered here and that of Nerone and Barnhurst (2003), who have documented the development of the US press in relation to its form and its relationship to the wider social context. Nerone and Barnhurst also categorize the development of newspapers into six phases; they are dealing with the US press, but the American geography is such that the newspaper industry has stuck more closely to a provincial model than the distinct regional/national dichotomy experienced in the UK, making theirs a useful comparison for the typography I offer here.

In brief their six stages are: first, the Printer's Paper where newspapers are produced by printers and filled with information culled from elsewhere. Second, as papers become established and competition increases, newspapers are harnessed by political parties and embrace partisanship as a way of attracting a wider readership; as such, the Editor's Paper is born because one person is given the role of making sure the product speaks with a single voice and advocates a point of view. The third stage, the Publisher's Paper, sees newspapers which diversify in the face of increased commercial opportunity. The Publisher's Paper in turn paves the way for mass circulation as newspapers become industrialized; thus during its fourth stage newspaper content is compartmentalized along advertising lines. In the fifth stage of development Nerone and Barnhurst describe how newspapers are increasingly owned by chains and, in turn, monopoly positions develop. As a reaction to the power of such owners, the Professional Paper develops, staffed by reporters who include objectivity and independence among their values so that they can faithfully map the society they serve. And it is this model which the authors posit is under threat in the sixth and final stage of newspaper development which we find ourselves now – that of a Corporate Paper where the reporter's ability to uphold those values is threatened.

In outline my analysis posits the six phases of regional news development, which are analysed in depth in the following chapters, marked by the shift in dominance of certain characteristics. These are: first, the local newspaper as opportunistic, entrepreneurial creation; second, the characterization of the local newspaper as fourth estate; third, the impact of New Journalism; fourth, the growth of chain control; fifth, the marketization of newspapers and, finally, the impact of digital technology. It is important to recognize that these phases are not distinct and neither are they to be seen across the whole industry at any one time; as Nerone and Barnhurst say, 'Historically, the different types have nestled within each other in complicated ways' (2003: 439). However, by charting this typology this history sets out to distinguish the contingent from the permanent in the history of provincial newspapers, characterized as it is by continuity and change, and to analyse what role is ascribed to the industry both by itself and by society and to ask what purpose this process may serve.

The first stage sees the creation of newspapers by non-specialists – usually, although not exclusively, printers – who make the most of the advent of news as a commodity in the eighteenth century by setting up newspapers. At this stage newspaper revenue comes from advertising and the promotion of complementary business interests aligned with production and distribution networks. Women are among those actively involved in the newspaper trade as proprietors, either holding interests until sons come of age, or in their own right. In the second stage, with the loosening of state control and the repeal of Stamp Duty and Advertisement Duty, the economic conditions become such that these papers become bigger in terms of circulation, pagination and status.

Industrialization means newspapers can only be accessed by those with sufficient wealth, making ownership a way of raising status and public profile. It is in this period, approximately from 1855 to 1880, that we see the origins of the rhetoric of the liberal notion of the free press and of the press as 'fourth estate' despite a reliance on commercial income. It is also during this period that women are largely excluded from the front line of provincial newspaper production.

The third stage sees the provincial press develop a more overtly commercial demeanour with the impact of 'New Journalism' and the development of the notion of reader as mass audience. This is manifest in the design of newspapers and an increased professionalization of the journalist, including the emphasis on the professional value of serving the good of the community as a localized version of the fourth estate. Women once more enter the provincial newspaper workforce, as providers of diverse content designed to widen the advertising appeal of the product. The fourth stage is examined as the rise of a new economic structure comes to the fore in the second quarter of the twentieth century; rising circulations result in the elimination of competition by acquisition. While some contemporary narratives posit this as the heyday of the local press, two separate Royal Commissions express anxiety about the process, which is broken only by the interregnum of the austerity of the Second World War. The trading conditions surrounding the operation of newspapers in the Second World War are so exceptional as to warrant their own exploration, although it is not considered a stage of development in terms of the schema above. Significantly the industry sets aside commercial rivalry to emphasize their public service to communities as a form of war service.

Since the 1970s, this consolidation of ownership has continued virtually unchecked. The result is the fifth stage of development, the dominance of a highly profitable, market-driven business. The profit is nearly wholly dependent on advertising revenues and the impact of this – epitomized by the advent of free sheets which trade a cover price for mass circulations – have a dramatic effect on the internal dominance of newspaper departments. The financial bottom line takes prominence over the editorial department, and the newspaper companies rationalize costs and concentrate on eliminating competition and establishing monopolistic positions within areas so that they can capitalize on advertising revenues.

Thus the stage is set for the final phase of the schema outlined above; the dramatic effect of the advent of the internet on the business model of the provincial press. That, together with the post-2008 banking crisis recession, is explored in the closing section of this book. Companies have found it harder to establish a secure revenue stream in terms of either advertising or selling access to content. The industry has now become a story of plummeting circulations, in which cost-cutting strategies have resulted in fewer people, producing more, but lesser-quality, content, and accusations that the regional press is becoming so homogenized that it no longer deserves the moniker 'local'. As such it has disrupted the very basis of what it means to be a journalist working in the provincial press and has destabilized professional concepts which give value to news work. Significantly, this discussion concludes with the suggestion that the future for the industry may lie, not in the quest to rescue the dominant business model from its current digital disruption, but in a re-evaluation where public service offers more hope than profit.

2

Printers' Papers: Profiting from the Commerce of Information

Reimagining the early provincial newspaper

AT THE

Printing Office

Against the *Swan-Inn* in GLOUCESTER.

WILL be shortly published, Weekly, a *News Paper* intitled, *The GLOUCESTER JOURNAL*, which will contain not Only the most authentick Foreign and Domestick News, but also the Price of Corn, Goods, etc, at Bear Key in London, and all other Trading Cities and Market Towns 50 Miles round. The Paper will be suitable to all Degrees and Capacities, and will be collected with all the Care that money or Industry is capable of procuring.

N.B At the aforesaid Printing-Office, any Shop-keepers or others may Have all Sorts of Bills and Advertisements Printed after the best Fashion; as also their Signs or any other Ornaments very curiously in-Graved on Wood, at reasonable Rates.

When Robert Raikes wrote this advertisement for his new paper, *The Gloucester Journal* in March 1721, he outlined a vision for a complex business proposition. His '*News Paper*' would disseminate trusted, 'authentick' news, together with commercially useful information from London and beyond. Significantly this information was to be circulated across a wide area and was to be produced to the highest standard for an audience, of 'all Degrees and Capacities'. Robert Raikes was not, though, a journalist as we would understand it; instead, he may be best understood as an entrepreneur who staked a position at the forefront of the emerging newspaper market. His was one of the earliest provincial newspapers;

largely opportunistic, these publications were borne of the expansion of printing made possible by the relaxation of state licensing in 1695. This enabled printers to expand from their centralized locale in London to regional centres which had hitherto been closed to them and to try out new ventures taking in a wider geographical area. The first regional title in England is accepted as being the *Norwich Post*, which was founded in 1701, although other newspapers vie for the honour of being the oldest. These include *Berrows Worcester Journal*, which for a time claimed to have been founded in 1690, although stronger evidence survives for its being available from 1709 (Williams 1916). Other towns with early publications include Bristol, Exeter, Newcastle and Nottingham. The search for the origin of the provincial press by establishing which was the founding of the form is a misplaced ambition because it assumes that the provincial newspaper was born ready-made. Instead, its early history is marked by ephemerality so that identifying factors such as name and sequence of publication were not an established part of these newspapers,[1] which came and went with the fortunes of their publishers and their other business interests.

The reasons for this ephemerality go to the heart of the nature of these publications; these titles were not originally founded as newspaper publishing businesses in themselves, but as adjuncts to other allied interests. Therefore it is perhaps best to think of these newspapers as nodes in wide-ranging networks of entrepreneurial activities involving not only printing, but also bookselling, the production and sale of patent medicines and the distribution of these and other goods. These entrepreneurial pioneers were taking advantage of a burgeoning market for regular, printed information – which might be termed 'news' – which had become established in London in the seventeenth century. As such, the successful purveyors of these early publications had business acumen as well as skills and interests aligned to the evolving practice of making newspapers. It was these entrepreneurs who were able to make the most of this emerging market to found titles which yielded profits and so enjoyed longevity. By the end of the century such was the strength of these enterprises that newspapers were recognized as stand-alone ventures which yielded considerable profits and status.

This conception of the early provincial press, then, is more complex than the accepted scholarly assessment. Cranfield (1962) and Aspinall (1973) largely explain these titles as printers' by-products, filled with 'cut and paste'

---

[1] Wiles' research (1965) resulted in a compilation of titles which existed between 1700 and 1765. This clearly demonstrates those which came first and also the longevity of each.

content and printed between the usual jobbing fare of these artisans. However, while it is true that these titles relied heavily on content from the London newspapers, evidence suggests that these papers were much more than a part-time occupation to the extent that Barker has defined them as 'highly profitable commercial ventures in their own right' (1998: 97). Neither was the transmission of information purely one way; as the provincial press established so titles went back into London where original content would be scrutinized, particularly as political content grew. Neither were those involved in this industry solely printers. Those involved in the burgeoning newspaper industry were drawn from a wide range of backgrounds, and, while some were sole printers, others were businessmen with diverse interests, which happened to chime with the opportunities afforded by the characteristics of newspapers. The *Norwich Gazette*, for instance, was founded in 1706 as a rival to the *Norwich Post* by Samuel Hasbert, who was a distiller by profession and who brought in printer Henry Cross-grove from London to produce the paper the (*Norwich Post*, 1951). Similarly, Francis Howgrave, printer of *Howgrave's Stamford Mercury*, was first an apothecary, and John Berry, who founded the *Lancashire Journal*, was a watchmaker (Cranfield 1962: 50).

This examination therefore attempts to elucidate those networks which made the first newspapers an attractive business proposition for a watchmaker, or beer seller. What was it that facilitated that early profitability and what was the interplay between these papers and allied financial interests? In turn this enables a reassessment of the practice of producing those newspapers by emphasizing the intentionality of this process and so understanding it as an emerging form of what we understand as journalism, rather than a haphazard process carried out by production technicians. In doing so we can begin to explain the process by which these titles were able to rise in status to the extent that they were to become thought of as key to the democratic process during the nineteenth century.

The newspaper's place in the commercial landscape

The origins of the newspaper in the seventeenth century are largely outside of the scope of this study,[2] but it is worth outlining its development in order

---

[2]   See for instance, Black (2001) and Raymond (1996).

to illuminate the commercial relationships under consideration. During the preceding hundred years, the commodification of information had been achieved by a combination of factors which linked the emergence of news with trade networks and social prestige and so which formed the environment for the emergence of the newspaper as we would understand it. Key to this was the provision of a certain type of information – that which was useful to commerce; its regularized dissemination created a demand for updates and so created a market for information itself. Significantly this conceptualization of disposable information enabled it to be commodified and packaged into an industrial product, the newspaper, which could be numbered and sold (Sommerville 1996).

Sommerville dates the emergence of 'a constant flow of publications' from one publisher to Germany around 1600, edging across Europe – and closer to England – during the next twenty years or so. These titles built on the tradition of personal letters, which communicated commercial information on matters such as shipping or prices; indeed, the first printed products used fonts which mimicked handwriting in an homage to these origins. Instilled in the reader of these products was the idea that they were 'current with developments' by juxtaposing a variety of reports within a regular publication. Discarding yesterday's newspaper symbolized for the reader that they were factual and forward-facing. Jeremy Black (2001) charts how the first news pamphlets in English appeared in Holland to serve the mercantile classes' interest in news of the Thirty Days War; in 1620 'corantos' appeared in London, and these began to appear regularly and were numbered to create sequenced information. These early corantos – referring to the 'current' of information – were presented in pamphlet form, with around twenty-four pages including a title page in England, although their European predecessors were news-sheets – a folio half sheet printed front and back in double columns. They were not necessarily regular and linear but were repetitive and began to benefit from the authority accorded to print over handwritten media. Additionally, they appeared alongside other time-based printed products, including newsbooks and astrological publications in a newly founded market for ephemera. Black draws on research to suggest that these were popular and were disseminated across the country, and as such, suggests that their popularity is indicative of a wider cultural shift in the significance of news. While trade demanded knowledge of 'forriegn transactions', low-cost printed ballads containing 'strange newes' and providential tales proved more popular with the home market.

In 1644 the popularity of the news market – fuelled by the Civil War – was demonstrated by the presence of around a dozen weekly newsbooks in London. Cromwell drew on legislation to effectively create a state censor of news and at the Restoration the press was formally controlled via the Printing Act of 1662. However, this did not halt the development of the newspaper in terms of form and content, ranging from the arrival of imported titles to the appearance of purely commercial advertisement sheets. The newspaper, as a purveyor of printed news or commentary, was established in its own right as a form which 'offered a predictable sequence of communication for which the only real counterpart was the weekly sermon' (Black 2001: 9). It was thus poised to 'mushroom' with the lapse of state control in 1695 – described as a 'watershed' by Michael Harris (1978: 83) – and by 1713 total annual sales of newspapers in England were 2.5 million, rising to 7.3 million in 1750 and 10.7 million in 1756 (Black 2001). Exact circulations of individual titles are hard to evidence, but Ferdinand (1997: 125) concludes that in the early 1700s, a sale of 200 copies was considered enough to keep a paper going; by the 1760s, the most successful papers were expecting a sale of 3,000–4,000 (Black 2001).

While neither reduce newspapers to purely commercial institutions and recognize the way in which newspapers became highly politicized during the English Civil War, both Black (2001) and Sommerville (1996) emphasize the press as business and its contents as a commercial product. In this conception not only did this content supposedly appeal to the capitalist classes, its presentation did too – because they bought the newspapers containing it. Presenting information as a quotidian product gave it a 'shelf-life', that is, formed it into a commercial product which was ongoing to produce a steady revenue stream. This information also claimed to be 'true' and covered a wide geographical area. In 1624 an early editor, Thomas Gainford, noted the growing demand for 'weekely Newes' (Sommerville 1996: 25).

Significantly, Black argues, the early titles were run on a commercial footing, the currency of which was the value of news as a particular form of information linked to fact, and the importance of this commercial role is evident in the Stamp Act in 1712, which introduced taxation on newspapers, and the later advertising duty, which levied a fee on adverts.

> A new world of printed news had been born. Newspapers were different to other forms of printed news or commentary, such as pamphlets and prints, because they were regular and frequent. They therefore offered a predictable sequence

of communication for which the only real counterpart was the weekly sermon. (Black 2001: 9)

Black suggests that the biggest challenge to the business model of these official 'stamped' eighteenth-century titles was taxation, which kept prices high and the titles the preserve of upper and middle-class readers (ibid.: 20).

Early ventures in the newspaper industry

The first provincial newspapers to be produced in England were, therefore, produced by those who saw an opportunity to profit from this emerging need for news to facilitate trade, which underpinned early capitalism – the 'commerce of information' as termed by Samuel Johnson (Ferdinand 1997: 211). As such, the commercial logic of these products was integral to their foundations, determining the way in which content was presented to the needs of a certain audience. 'News was a commodity. This meant that a commercial dominant was always the driving force behind innovation and change in the production of news and it was this which attracted printers and publishers to invest in it in order to make a profit' (Conboy 2004: 23). This logic went beyond the news content of these titles to include other characteristics including advertising and the way in which these titles were distributed to their audience. As such they offered a range of commercial opportunities in addition to the sale of the paper itself.

One of the early publications which might be termed a provincial newspaper was the *Bristol Post Boy*, which was probably founded in 1702 (Penny 2001). Just two pages long, it survived until December 1715 – possibly killed off by competition from the *Bristol Post Man*, which had been launched in August of that year by Sam Farley, the son of an Exeter printer whose family was to become a publishing dynasty and who published a variety of titles in Bristol and Salisbury as well as Exeter itself. The number of competing titles in Bristol and their varied longevity indicate that the local newspaper business was not a stable one. Rival titles included the short-lived *Bristol Weekly Mercury*, founded in 1716, the *Oracle*, founded in 1742 and two further rival titles launched by Sam Farley and his brother Felix in 1748. Wiles concludes that of the 150 papers founded in 60 cities in England from 1701 to 1760, half lasted fewer than five years (1965: 25).

William Parks typified the entrepreneurial spirit which underpinned the creators of England's early provincial papers. Writing in the columns of the first paper in Berkshire, the *Reading Mercury* in 1723, he clearly sets out his aspirations. 'When a Scarcity of News Happens, we shall divert You with something Merry. In a few Words, we shall spare no Charge or Pains to make this Paper generally Useful and Entertaining, since we find ourselves settled in a Place, which gives all the encouraging Prospects of Success' (Wiles 1965: 32). Reading was not Parks' first venture into print; he had already attempted to create the *Ludlow Post-Man*, which seems to have survived for just two years from 1719 to 1721 (Wiles 1965: appendix B). Rather than deter him, this failure seems to have spurred him to success. The business was successfully run by Anna Maria Smart from 1762 until 1809 when she left it to her daughters (Onslow 2000).

The New-castle Gazette was short-lived, but the remaining copy demonstrates the mercantile origins. At this time the busy port cities of England not only served as export markets, but also functioned as national transport hubs at a time when it was easier to sail round Britain than drive across it. Thus *The New-castle Gazette*, subtitled *The Northern Courant*, from 1710, concentrated on shipping news, which would have served the mercantile classes of the city. Just one edition of the two-page publication, billed as 'an Impartial Account of Remarkable Transactions Forreign (*sic*) or Domestic, from 23 to 25 December 1710, survives, although it is thought to have been published for two years. Its front page demonstrates the news networks, which both supplied its columns and provided its selling point. Content was drawn from as far afield as St Petersburg and Genoa, but also significantly from shipping ports around Britain, including Harwich, Deal, Yarmouth and nearby Shields. Thus, the arrival of a ship from Genoa was news in its own right, but it also brought news of the British Navy and its part in the Battle of Sargossa, fought as part of the War of Spanish Succession in August 1710. The item also included details of shipping movements so that readers learnt that 'Two Men of War ... are put into Leghorn. All the French Men of War that were fitting out at Thoulon, are put to Sea, and five of them are cruising in the Heighth (*sic*) of Corsica' (*The New-castle Gazette*, 23 December 1710: 1).

This edition of the *Gazette* typifies the form of these early newspapers, although most went on to use bigger pages and increased the column counts to three (Black 2001). These printer's papers, which were very similar to those cited by Nerone and Barnhurst (2003) as operating across the Atlantic in America, were not yet staffed by professional journalists; instead their content was largely 'cut and paste' – that is taken from other circulating publications, sometimes acknowledged and sometimes not. Checking facts was practically impossible because of the nature of communications and the original copy which was included was mostly provided by readers.

However, while the production process may not have been demarcated and departmentalized, for instance along editorial and printing, it did have its own complexities and commercial drivers. The production process itself dictated the organization of content; the oldest news was found on page one and the latest on page three. This was because pages one and four were printed first, and sometimes days earlier than the last pages to be printed; this is evident in the correction of stories between the front and inside due to the arrival of later information (Ferdinand 1997). Without headlines, these papers used varying, specially designed typefaces if possible to add variety to products, although Raven (2014) notes that most innovation in printing emanated from London and provincial printers were less likely to be able to afford new fonts. The last news to be included was sometimes printed in smaller type and even in the margins if the shortage of space necessitated (Wiles 1965: 57). Illustrations were also rare, and those which were printed used carved wooden blocks; as a consequence they were largely reserved for titles on the front page because using them slowed down production (Penny 2001: 10).

These papers may have been produced in the provinces, but they carried content from across the world. And most readers looked to their provincial paper to provide news of the wider world, rather than a replication of the local news they would still get verbally. In terms of circulation these titles were not local in the sense that we now understand, covering perhaps a local authority area or a county, but were regional, covering wide areas in an effort to create a sustainable circulation. Precise circulations are hard to evidence; Cranfield suggests a sale of between 1,000 and 2,000 by the mid-century, and Barker suggests that a profitable weekly newspaper would require a sale of at least 1,000 by the third quarter of the eighteenth century. At the upper end the *York Chronicle* claimed to sell 2,500 copies and the *Salisbury Journal*, a sale of 4,000 by 1780. Producing this number of newspapers with a hand press – which could process 250 sheets an hour – would not have been easy. For this reason some printers invested in multiple presses, and John Feather (1985) has demonstrated that the *York Courant* used three presses in the 1720s and that by the 1770s the *Birmingham Chronicle* had four, and Aris's *Birmingham Gazette* had five. An estimated five people read each copy, and Barker suggests that just eight per cent of the provincial population read a newspaper – with most of these being the urban areas. This means the readership was overwhelmingly middle class, as evidenced by the subscribers to the *Salopian Journal*, most of whom were 'amongst the middling sorts'. There is no evidence of who bought copies for cash.

Those who were best placed to take advantage of the opportunity to produce newspapers were the printers themselves – who had both the means of production and also the newly found freedom provided by the lapse of licensing; this had 'emasculated' the Stationer's Company, which had hitherto regulated their practice (Harris 1981). In 1700 there were around seventy master printers in London and just twelve in the provinces; by 1740 this last figure had grown to forty with printing presses operating in some forty-five towns (Raven 2014: 37). These printers though did not function alone, neither did they only publish newspapers. Instead, the periodical productions were one among a series of complimentary ventures, the balance of which varied according to specialism, opportunity, investment and partnership. A necessary ingredient, though, was good business sense. Barker draws on documentary evidence to compare the fortunes of the profitable *Chelmsford Chronicle*, which made more than £313 a year in the 1790s, compared with the *Hampshire Chronicle*, which recorded a loss of £191, despite only slight disparity in the income from sales and advertising and despite the Hampshire title being slightly smaller, and therefore, cheaper to run. For this reason, Barker suggests that many ventures failed simply because of poor management.

John White, who founded *The Newcastle Courant* in opposition to the *Gazette*, typifies this development. Involved in no fewer than three newspapers, he has been termed 'the most influential Northern newspaper printer-entrepreneur of his generation' (Gardner 2008: 72). He was the son of a printer, also called John, who was originally from London but who had married into a York family and had operated a printing press in York from 1680. John White senior was honoured for his work in November 1688 when King William II appointed him the official printer for York and the 'five northern counties' (Davies 1868). His son left to start his own business in Newcastle in 1708, possibly drawn by the growing prosperity the city enjoyed courtesy of the coal industry; both his father and grandfather also had existing links in Newcastle.

The success of *The New-castle Courant*, which was to achieve the record of being the longest running eighteenth-century provincial newspaper, has been attributed to two factors: first, the quality of the product itself, courtesy of

White's enhanced abilities as a printer, and second, his ability to create and defend a wide circulation area to sustain not only his newspaper business, but also his allied interests in general printing, books and medicine-selling. Gardner suggests that his 'less-than-honest skills in the removal of competitors' papers' also helped his cause (2008: 72). White not only appropriated the subtitle from the *Gazette*, but also mimicked the mix of content and tri-weekly publication pattern.[3] His production skills were put to use, making *The New-castle Courant* a more attractive and readable paper. Gardner describes the *Gazette* as 'printed on one folio sheet, both sides of which were crammed with news that was printed with small, worn (and therefore difficult to read) type' (2008: 77); in contrast, White was able to use a larger typeface of better quality, augmented with decorative woodcuts. White amassed quite a collection of these blocks, some of which he may well have inherited from his father and which were used to illustrate the other products he printed like the popular chapbooks[4] as well as the newspaper (Bigmore and Wyman 2014: 182). This developed technical ability is indicative of his prosperous background; the Whites enjoyed enough wealth to both live comfortably and invest in more expensive type than that available to most printers. This shows in the pages of the paper itself. *The New-castle Courant* of Saturday 4 August to Monday 6 August 1711 is a four-page publication which evidences White's prowess as a printer. Although there is no cover price printed on it, Cranfield suggests that it sold for one penny, roughly equivalent to £7 in current values (1962: 41). Carrying the number three, it is illustrated with two woodblock illustrations in the title – one of a ship and one of a 'post-man'. A woodblock illustrates the first letter of the edition, something which carried on until after his death. Such was the pull of the illustration that Saywell, the publisher of the *Gazette*, followed suit in his own title. White also sought to beat the competition in terms of content, by paying for local correspondents to supply news from the port (Gardner 2008: 77) and even printed a second edition of his title on 11 August to carry news of a Russian victory over the Turks, which must have arrived after printing of the edition had begun – the earliest noted example of such an innovation (ibid.: 77–8).

[3] London newspapers had established the tri-weekly pattern of publication to align with the postal days in the capital.
[4] The chapbook was the paperback of its day. Popular pamphlets, they carried illustrations and although production was predominantly in London, provincial printers also made them.

Establishing a market: 'Freshest advices' and circulation wars

What is clear from the legacy formed by the remaining papers from the eighteenth century is that publishers were keen to emphasize the freshness of their 'advices'. It is likely that the same agents who distributed the paper may also have contributed to the paper's columns. The account books of the *Hampshire Chronicle* show that agent Thomas Baker was regularly paid for sending reports to both the Winchester-based paper and its sister publication, the *Salisbury Journal* (Ferdinand 1997: 73). However, the length of time from news source to publication very much depended on the distance to be travelled – for instance Wiles estimates that it took four months for news from India to reach newspaper columns. This did not stop publishers boasting of their efforts to supply readers with the latest news, even going to the lengths to employ their own riders to bring in news from London, and newspaper columns attest that this system was not failsafe, perhaps because of the dependability of the horseman or because an accident – or worse – had befallen them. The very publication date of the paper would also be organized around the availability of news, with the arrival of the post a key factor in determining not only on what day but also at what time editions came out, with printers working through the night to meet morning sales (Wiles 1965).

The ability to both gather and disseminate news was, therefore, a factor to be considered in the foundation of newspapers. It is probable that this was a reason for partners Robert Raikes and William Dicey to move to Northampton to found the second of three joint ventures (they were associated with the *St Ives Mercury*, in Cambridgeshire, the *Northampton Mercury* and the *Gloucester Journal*). Though they were key figures in this period of the provincial newspaper industry, again only fragmentary evidence remains of their businesses.[5] However, what does remain – when coupled with the documentation of their titles themselves – gives us a picture of a sophisticated operation which elucidates the elements of a successful provincial newspaper in the eighteenth century.

A history of the *Northampton Mercury*, published by the paper itself in 1901, describes the relationship between Dicey and Raikes as that of printer

---

[5] The life of Robert Raikes Jr is well documented. He took over the *Gloucester Journal* on his father's death and founded the Sunday School movement. Gloucestershire librarian Robert Austin researched and catalogued the origins of the newspaper. Many of Austin's findings are now held by Gloucestershire Archives.

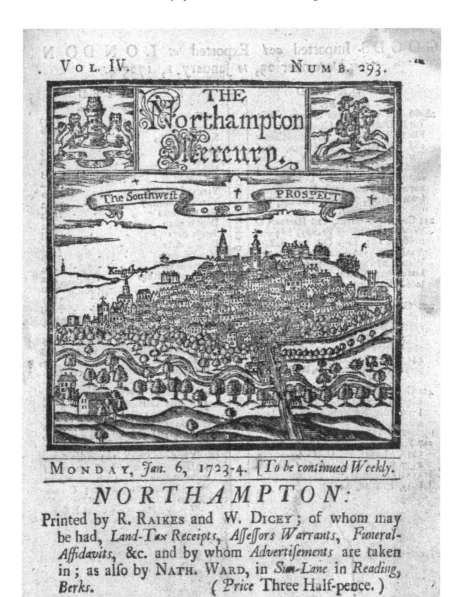

Figure 2.1 *The Northampton Mercury*, vol. IV, no. 293, 6 January 1723–4, p. 1.
Newspaper Image © The Warden and Fellows of All Souls College, Oxford.

to business manager. Raikes himself was from a family of merchants in Hull; as such, he would have likely been used to the earliest mercantile publications. In terms of production, Dicey's name appears on the *St Ives Mercury* (1719), which promised to be an 'Impartial Intelligencer, being A Collection of the Most Material Occurrences, Foreign and Domestick. Together with An Account of Trade', and the imprints tell us that William Dicey was 'near the Bridge'; significantly for the future development of Dicey's business, we also learn that 'all sorts of Books are printed' too, and indeed Dicey was to become one of the leading publishers of chapbooks in the country. Raikes is named as the publisher of the *St Ives Post-Boy* (1718–19), which was possibly a continuation of an earlier *St Ives Post*. This imprint situates Raikes in 'Water Lane', also 'near the Bridge'. Whether or not they shared premises is not known; neither is there firm evidence as to why the newspapers ceased, although it is possible that Raikes may have offended the local gentry with his publication (Norris 1910: 481). Norris does suggest that the sole remaining copy of the *St Ives Mercury* he possessed may be considered a model for the *Northampton Mercury* because of similarities in the format. Described as a 12-page paper, numbered pages 61 to 72 (so the editions could be bound into continuous volumes), the first page carries the title and the last adverts. Significantly the woodcut of Fame, with an open scroll, is the same as that on the first copy of the *Mercury* (Norris, ibid.).

The first edition of the *Northampton Mercury* appeared in the town on 2 May 1720. It seems likely that Northampton was perceived as a profitable site for a newspaper business; with good transport links, it was on the main route from London to Manchester, Liverpool and Sheffield with intersecting country roads. This meant good access to the London papers which provided much of the 'cut and paste' content for these early newspapers and equally good access to the means of distribution for the newspaper itself. The historical account written in 1901 of the early *Mercury* offers an intricate account of Dicey's efforts to be first with the news and the advantage offered by the town's location. Dicey had become a freeman of Northampton in order to gain the right to print there, and in addition to the newspaper, he printed other material, including chapbooks which were advertised in some of the earliest editions of the *Northampton Mercury*. A selling point of the three-halfpenny newspaper, which carried a Monday date, was that it offered a digest of the London newspapers. These could be received in the provinces via a variety of ways, including by being sent by clerks to the post office, who would charge £6 annually for a selection (Harris 1975). In addition, Dicey apparently devised a schedule which enabled him to include the latest London news from the Saturday morning papers in the *Mercury* by taking advantage of the rest time they spent in Northampton so that his digest could be carried for sale on the same coaches which carried those London papers as they completed their journey. To do so, Dicey employed a man on horseback who could do the London–Northampton journey in eight or nine hours and so could outrun the coaches. Two pages of the *Mercury* were printed on Thursdays; this enabled two compositors to finish printing the remaining two pages on Saturday evening in time to put the *Mercury* on the same coaches which carried those London papers a couple of hours later. Those coaches then

> carried with them huge packages of the *Northampton Mercury* for Derby and Sheffield, for York and Durham and Newcastle; for West Chester (Chester) and Liverpool; for all the great towns. Over half England, as soon as on Monday morning … a Saturday's London Paper could be procured, there could be purchased for the same money *The Northampton Mercury*, dated Monday and containing all the London news. (*Northampton Mercury*, 1901: 67)

The evidence suggests a prodigious circulation area for the title; in addition to the coaches, newsmen distributed papers regionally, taking them to Leicester, Lutterworth; Coventry and Birmingham; Leamington Spa and Warwick; Banbury, Woodstock and Witney; Dunstable, Luton and Hitchin; Hinckley, Tamworth and Lichfield, Peterborough, Stamford, Bedford and Cambridge. Coaches also took the papers east to west to Norwich and Gloucester. Similarly, Robert Raikes boasted of a substantial circulation area in the South West and Wales for his *Gloucester Journal* and used it to advertise his paper in 1728. This was accomplished via a system of named agents, each serving one of twenty-one 'divisions'; in addition the paper was sold at the printing office in Gloucester and in the offices of booksellers in Bristol, Salisbury, Worcester, Hereford and Taunton.

In creating his Gloucester title, Raikes had preserved a circulation area co-terminus with that of the *Northampton Mercury*, so ensuring that he could continue to work cooperatively with William Dicey. It seems likely that such cooperative arrangements were not unique, with neighbouring titles publishing at different times of the week in order to sell to the same people. So, the *Bath Journal* published on Monday, while the *Bath Chronicle* published on Thursday. As such, they contributed to establishing a market for newspaper buying which benefited both (Barker 1998). Personal contacts may also have influenced the extent of Benjamin Collins' network for his *Salisbury Journal*, which extended to his home town of Faringdon near Oxford, and so beyond the accepted boundary of his paper's intended circulation area. Similarly, he saw his area as sizeable and understood his title as a rival to the *Gloucester Journal* – nearly 60 miles away. John White sold his Newcastle paper via a network of booksellers and grocers in fifteen towns, in addition to several itinerant chapmen who between them covered Northumberland, Westmorland and Cumberland, the Borders of Scotland and parts of Lancashire and Yorkshire. In order to strengthen his position in Yorkshire he worked with his stepmother Grace White, who had inherited the use of his father's printing materials, and his nephew Charles with whom she worked, to establish the *York Mercury* in 1719. The *York Mercury* and the *Newcastle Courant* both served just two towns – Stockton and Darlington, again suggestive of a cooperative working arrangement. When this was threatened by the accession of Thomas Gent to control of the *York Mercury*, who sought to expand into *Newcastle Courant* territory, White's response was to set up a *York Courant* in direct opposition and to employ a series of tactics to drive Gent out of business (Gardner 2008).

> His business was to go to the houses of my customers and, substituting his papers in the room of what I sent, and the prices of good were lowered by one third, supposing their riches in Newcastle would support them through all expenses whilst they endeavoured to ruin me at York. (Gent 1821: 163–4)

Gent goes so far as to accuse White of procuring a fake *York Mercury* on unstamped paper in an effort to provoke a prosecution (ibid.: 166). His paper stopped in the early 1730s, while White was also to see off two Newcastle competitors during the same period. As such these battles could be bitter and could continue to the death, either of titles or proprietors. Jeremy Black suggests that papers would undermine their rivals in an attempt to establish a monopoly hold over their market, for instance by publishing derogatory comments in their columns. One particularly colourful attack is documented by Wiles when the *Northampton Mercury* condemned the first issue of the *Northampton Journal* as 'Bum-Fodder' and attacked the 'doating Brain' of its creator, James Pasham (1965: 29). The attacks may have worked; the *Journal* subsequently folded.

In Norfolk a vitriolic war of words was also fought via the columns of competing titles. Printer Francis Burges had moved to Norwich from London in 1700 and began publishing the *Norwich Post* a year later, using paper from nearby mills in Taverham. Described as a 'gentle soul', it was after Burges' death that the war of words broke out between the *Post*, run by his widow, Elizabeth, and two new titles, Hasbart's *Gazette* and the *Post-man*. A history of the *Post*, produced by the Norfolk News Company, suggests Mrs Burges had rejected an offer of business partnership from Hasbart, made via a letter published in his paper in December 1707. Hasbart responded to this rejection by calling her title 'obsolete' and filled with the 'Effluvia of a Dunghil', which always stinks when stirred' in his paper of 10 January 1708. These insults escalated to aggressive business tactics; he undercut the *Post*, selling his title at one halfpenny (the *Post* was a penny) and offered free advertising (Norfolk News Company 1951: 10). The *Norwich Gazette* was equally critical of the editor of the *Norwich Post-man*. Mrs Hasbert responded by publishing the *Yarmouth Gazette* from May 1708 – probably with the intention of securing advertising in that area. The war ended when Elizabeth Burges died in 1708, even though the paper persisted for another four years or so, probably produced by her administrator. The *Post-man* stopped publishing at around the same time.

The reader, cure-alls and books

The extensive circulation areas described here were necessary to sustain a sale at a time of varying levels of literacy. The networks of newsmen who took the papers about – some of whom wore uniforms to make themselves instantly recognizable – were therefore significant to attempts to build sales. Beyond the sale of newspapers, these extensive networks sustained those allied business interests. Aris of Birmingham used his newsmen to sell diverse goods, including mathematical equipment, and books (Beaven 1993). It was the relationship between these distribution networks and the sale of books and medicines which was significant to the business model of the provincial newspaper and which meant substantial gains were to be had by those who could master these systems.

James Raven (2014) describes bookselling and newspapers as distinctive but mutually supportive industries. Key to this was distribution, as both books and newspapers could share the networks on which their sale relied. For the regional bookseller and printer, the newspaper offered another revenue stream and also offered an advertising platform for their products. Michael Harris' analysis of the London newspaper also demonstrates clearly the interlocking relationships between booksellers and newspaper publishers, the complexity of which demonstrates why unravelling these commercial ventures – particularly when archival evidence is fragmented and scant – is so problematic. Harris

(1981) suggests that newspapers presented an advantageous opportunity to those who sold and produced books precisely because publishing literary works was a risk-laden business which encouraged cooperation in the form of joint ownership, described as 'congers'. In return the printers gained respectability by their association with the booksellers. As such, most London booksellers were involved in the distribution of newspapers and, as London newspapers depended on a provincial sale for their profitability, it is natural that this practice would diffuse outwards. This involvement extended to group ownership in London to give booksellers more control over titles, which as I have charted, could have a precarious existence. As an exemplar, Robert Walker, who produced six London newspapers including the *London and Country Journal* designed for distribution in the provinces, took this as far as producing provincial titles, including the *Cambridge Journal and Weekly Flying Post* (1744–66), the *Warwick and Staffordshire Journal* (1737–43), the *Shropshire Journal* (1737–9), the *Lancashire Journal* (1738), the *Derbyshire Journal* (1738) and the *Oxford Flying Weekly Journal* (1746–8). Cranfield (1962: 54) suggests that Walker was largely a sleeping partner in these titles, which he used to advertise the books he also produced, for instance giving away a copy of the *Derbyshire Journal* with each instalment of his *History of the Old and New Testaments*. Another successful bookseller, Benjamin Collins, cross-subsidized the *Salisbury Journal* from his other business interests, which also included banking and property. It is also worth noting that when Collins bought the rival *Hampshire Chronicle* in 1778 he did so as part of a consortium. Although sole ownership remained the dominant structure of provincial titles in the early part of the century, (Harris, 1978) such joint ownership served to spread the risk of running a newspaper, and Ferdinand goes as far to suggest that by the mid-eighteenth century group ownership was the norm rather than the exception for provincial papers (1997: 62).

This diversification is demonstrated by Raikes and Dicey, who outlined their business interests on the front of their newspaper for Monday, 20 November 1721:

> Of whom may be had Land Tax Receipts, Assessors Warrants, Funeral Affidavits. … Likewise all manner Stationary Wares, as Shop-books, Pocket-books, Papers, Pens, Ink, Wax, etc. Likewise Dr. Bateman's Pectoral Drops, and Radcliffe's Purging Elixir: the first fam'd for the Colic, Pains in the Limbs and Joints, Agues, and all Ailments of the Breast and Bowels. The second is the very best of purging Medicines; witness the many Certificates we daily receive from our Readers and their Friend. These Medicines are sold at 12d the Bottle

with printed Directions how to take them, and Certificates of their Cures. (*Northampton Mercury*, 20 November 1721)

Here they list the various documents produced by a jobbing printer as well as sundry associated items. Prominent though are the medicinal cures which formed a substantial trade for the Georgian printer to the extent that the relationship between the newspaper and these cures has been described as 'intimate' (Porter 1986: 22). Bristol printing dynasty, the Farleys had their own Farley's Bristol Toothwater and Durham mustard (Penny 2001), and Black notes that the biggest advert in the *Leeds Mercury* of 11 July 1738 was for Daffy's Elixir – a cure-all sold by the newspaper's printer (2001: 60–1). This cross-ownership was in no doubt due to the access both newspapers and medicines needed to a sustainable distribution network in order to achieve a sustainable sale. Equally important for the patent medicine business was advertising. This was largely because of the position of the patent medicines in the Georgian field of health care. Not quite of the same standing as 'official' doctors, the purveyors of these 'quack' cures nevertheless posed a significant alternative to what were then unreliable medical practices – with the added advantage of obviating the need to pay a doctor's fee. Like the early founders of newspapers, the creators of quack cures were entrepreneurs, who sought to market their products to as wide an audience as possible using a variety of strategies, including distinctive packaging. Most important was advertising which Roy Porter (1986) describes as having reached 'saturation' point courtesy of the newspaper, establishing these cures as household names, and equally ensuring the profitability of newspapers because of the volume of advertising involved.

The strength of this interdependency is hinted at by fragmentary evidence of these business relationships. The *Gloucester Journal* advertised the patent for Dr Bateman's Pectoral Drops as 'to prevent Counterfeits, and to secure the Property of this Medicine to Benhamin Okell, the sole Inventor thereof, and to J Cluer, of Bow Churchyard, London; R Raikes at Gloucester, and W Dicey at Northampton' (*Gloucester Journal*, 8 August 1730). 'Chymist' Benjamin Okell was said to have invented the cure and was connected to the Northamptonshire Bateman family via marriage (Burnby 1988). J. Cluer in this instance refers to John Cluer – who was William Dicey's brother in law; Dicey himself took over the printing business at Bow Churchyard in 1736 and passed it to his eldest son, Cluer Dicey, in 1740. However, William's will left to Cluer his 'third part and share of in and unto Doctor Bateman's Pectoral Drops and all other medicines

and shares in medicines drops waters and other preparations made or vended …
at [his] wholesale warehouse in Bow Church Yard, London' (Stoker 2014: 115).
This bequest was subject to legal action by Cluer's sisters, the documentation of
which demonstrates that by the 1750s the patent medicine business had been
completely separate from the substantial printing business accrued by Dicey
(which included chapbooks and broadsides as well as newspapers) to the extent
that Cluer had asked his father to 'ease him from the burden of managing the
printing business' (ibid.). In the same vein, Porter continues to suggest that
John Newbury, who co-founded the *Reading Mercury*, did so to support his
wholesale medicine business; a leading figure in the development of children's
literature, Newbury even managed to get a mention of his product – Dr James's
Powder – into one such publication. As previously noted, Francis Howgrave was
an apothecary before he was printer of the newspaper in Stamford.

Advertising and profit

A key component of these newspapers from their earliest beginnings was,
therefore, advertising, and its commercial significance is demonstrated by the
imposition of duty under the Stamp Act of 1712, which charged one shilling
on every advert. The act also demanded that newspapers themselves be printed
on taxed paper, which was supplied in the form of pre-cut 'stamped' sheets
to demonstrate that it had been paid. The act was to be levied on 'all Books
and Papers commonly called Pamphlets, and for and upon all News Papers, or
Papers containing publick News, Intelligence or Occurrences' at the rate of one
halfpenny for a half sheet and one penny for a full sheet (Oats and Sadler 2002).
This meant printers had to use sheets which had been pre-stamped to show that
the duty had been paid. Initially this was done in London, but over the course of
the century official Stamp Offices were opened in Edinburgh, Manchester and
Dublin to meet the needs of regional publishers.

The Stamp Act of 1712 prompted titles to publish in pamphlet form of more
than one sheet, which incurred the smaller duty of two shillings per sheet paid
on just one copy of each sheet. The Stamp Act of 1725 extended the tax to
newspapers of more than one sheet. However, Wiles concludes that the effect
on circulations was both 'slight and temporary' (1965: 22); the price increase
may even have helped provincial titles to compete with the metropolitan
press because they could offer a digested read in one product. Rather than

subscribing to one or more London papers, Benjamin Collins urged his readers to buy his *Salisbury Journal*, 'which not only contains the Marrow of them all, but the Gazette News, and other Intelligence three days before any of "em"' (Ferdinand: 110). The tax rose incrementally until its peak in 1815 – the stimulus for a concerted campaign to overturn this 'tax on knowledge'. Gibb and Beckwith (1954), in their comprehensive history of the *Yorkshire Post*, record how its forerunner, the *Leeds Intelligencer*, was subject to one-and-a-halfpenny Stamp Duty in 1777, half its cover price, rising to two pennies duty in 1789 and four by 1815, the effect of which was to increase the cover price to seven pence. At the same time, advertisement duty was payable at one shilling, which doubled in 1780 and rose to three shillings sixpence in 1815, regardless of how large the advert was. It is not surprising that the abolition of both taxes by 1855 was hailed as the 'emancipation of the press' by the *Intelligencer*.

While Stamp Duty may not have affected the rise in the number of newspapers produced, it did affect how those papers were produced and the cost of doing so.

Walker notes that the cost of machinery needed to produce a paper was relatively low (2006: 376); however, printers did need to keep a stock of pre-stamped paper, which necessitated a considerable initial investment – especially in the provinces where stamped paper had to come from London until the regional centres were established. However, because the 1712 Act had imposed duty on papers printed on half sheets or whole sheets of paper, printers were able to circumvent its punitive impact by simply using one-and-a-half sheets and classifying the paper as a pamphlet – at least until that specific loophole was closed. Wiles's extensive research into the surviving newspapers from this period leads him to conclude that in the thirty years after the loophole was closed the size of the half sheet gradually doubled to a page measuring around 16 inches by 22 inches (Wiles 1965: 51), enabling printers to increase the available copy in their papers though not the cost-incurring number of pages.

Despite taxation, advertising revenue remained key to a newspaper's profitability. Publishers would be flexible in how adverts could be sent into them, announcing wide-ranging drop-off points and out-of-town agents in addition to the ability of people to visit the printer's office. When Elizabeth Burges opened her *Yarmouth Gazette*, she told readers that 'advertisements are taken in at Yarmouth every Saturday at the Three Wrestlers, where any Person may speak with the Printer about any other business whatsoever' (Norfolk News Company 1951: 9). Adverts were also gathered via the network of newspaper agents, who would be found in coffee houses and other meeting points; newsmen who delivered the titles were also paid to collect adverts. The volume of advertising was, therefore, also aligned with the distribution networks titles could command. As such, improved transport links[6] signalled by the investment in turnpikes enabled newspapers to double circulations from around 1,000 in the 1720s to more than 2,000 in the 1760s. Equally though these improvements made it easier for the London newspapers to penetrate the regions; this, together with the activities of the Post Office Clerks of the Road, who distributed London newspapers, meant that by the mid-1760s more than twenty thousand metropolitan titles were sent out three times a week to the regions.

As advertising became an established practice, newspapers would experiment with special offers and variable pricing; some extended to using 'advertiser' in their title and even attempted to produce papers free-at-the-point-of-sale, although Raven suggests that an inability to maintain a large circulation made these attempts 'financial disasters', yielding as little as a third of a penny per printed copy (2014: 120–1). Wiles notes that in 1718 the *Plymouth Weekly Journal* charged three shillings for an advert, whereas a year later the *York Mercury* charged just two. Some publishers specified how long adverts could be and some charged according to length. Publishers also used claims of wide circulation to justify their advertising rates, and many sent copies to London coffee houses to add to their attractiveness as an advertising medium (Wiles 1965). Cranfield (1962) draws on evidence from newspapers themselves to suggest that until the revised Stamp Act of 1725, which tightened up the definition of a newspaper, most charged two shillings for a small advert. After this, the price rose to two shillings sixpence but even so the volume of advertising continued to grow to account for around one third of total content by 1730. The flow of adverts, however, was not constant. Beaven suggests that *Aris's Gazette* in Birmingham has most adverts in spring when house and land sales would be at their peak. Other adverts in the paper were for luxury products, including hats, chocolate and coffee, and Aris's other interests – including a stagecoach service, which would have accorded with the transport needs of the newspaper itself. Adverts also tended to be targeted at publications – so cheaper papers advertised soap while the most expensive advertised property and the exclusive services of

[6] Hobsbawm (1967) reports that the cost of transporting goods overland in early-eighteenth-century Britain was so high as to be 'prohibitive', for instance, in the middle of the century the price of a tonne of goods could be doubled by a twenty-mile long journey. This made investment into such things as turnpike trusts, and canals, worthwhile.

visiting doctors. Generally the quality and quantity of adverts increased with the quality and quantity of papers sold.

Justifying a rise in the cover price in July 1743, Aris described his costs:

> Out of every paper one halfpenny goes to the stamp office, and another to the person who sells it … the paper it is printed on costs a farthing and … consequently no more than a farthing remains to defray the charges of composing, printing, London newspapers and meeting, as far as Daventry, the Post, which last article is very expensive. (quoted in Briggs 1949: 13)

The advertising duty was doubled to two shillings in 1757, which had the effect of halving the number of advertisements placed in newspapers; but advertising duty revenues rose nonetheless from £912 in 1713, to £3,158 in 1734, £33,662 in 1774, £46,284 in 1784, £69,943 in 1794 and £98,241 in 1798. By the end of the eighteenth century, half of all duty collected was raised by adverts in the provincial press; this meant that an average of £2 a week was raised in post-tax profit by these titles – half of their total revenue (Raven 2014: 129). By the end of the eighteenth century, adverts were given prominence on a front page devoted to such announcements (Penny 2001: 10). From his study of the development of the *Salisbury Journal* and *Hampshire Chronicle*, Ferdinand proffers that the cover price covered the costs of printing and distribution, but advertising was where the profit lay (1997: 74).

As the number of adverts increased, so the pressure of space grew for publishers who wanted to keep some space for editorial content. This meant setting adverts in smaller type, although typographical features were used to highlight key words as layout developed during the course of the eighteenth century, and sometimes holding adverts back so as to preserve the balance between news and commercial notices, as pointed out by William Craighton in his *Ipswich Journal* number 914 (7 August 1756), who said, 'A considerable Part of a News Paper ought to be allowed for News, and also for many things which are equally agreeable to the Readers of it' (Wiles 1965: 172). It is likely that readers were also entertained and informed by the scope of the diverse range of adverts, which ranged from simple 'to let' announcements to complex marketing strategies. Often they furnished the most 'local' content in these titles. The adverts in the *Northampton Mercury* of 6 January 1723 are typical. On page eleven of the twelve-page pamphlet style newspaper are two adverts – one for a farm to let in Ely, Cambridgeshire, and one for information concerning a horse stolen in Kingsthorpe, Northamptonshire. The whole final page is given over to adverts, although just three paragraphs are not for products concerned with the paper. The remaining space is given to extolling the virtues of mustard on sale at the printing office, the obligatory advert for Dr Bateman's Pectoral Drops and a personal testament describing how this cure had relieved one reader of rheumatism. This content is little changed by the edition of the *Gloucester Journal* on 9 June 1730 (the first available via the Gloucestershire Archives), although the volume of adverts has increased. This paper – with a four-page publication priced twopence – has adverts on pages two, three and four. Such is the quantity that one third of page three and half of page four are filled with adverts including property and businesses to let around the county and region. A notice tells us that adverts are taken in not only in Gloucester but also in Bristol and Taunton. A noticeable feature is the inclusion of adverts for books 'sold by the distributors of the paper', including *A General History of Executions*, which, we are told, will be sold in volumes through the year.

This ability to command substantial revenues from advertising is testament to the commercial sophistication which these titles enjoyed. Such was the success of these titles that they were seen as valuable commodities, yielding returns for shareholders and being prized as family inheritances. The will of Robert Raikes, granted probate in 1755, demonstrates that he had amassed significant holdings of property in three locations in addition to the Gloucester print shop. Although the property was left to his wife and son, he was wealthy enough to dedicate the income from the rents from these to his business associates. As this chapter has demonstrated, women were often in charge of the business of running newspapers, either in their own right or, as in the case of Raikes' wife Mary, as holders of the interest until their sons came of age. The *Gloucester Journal* passed to Robert Raikes Jr when he was twenty-five. He sold it in 1802 for £1,500 and an annual income of between £300 and £500. The corollary of this is that those who were disappointed to be not left something often resorted to legal action – such as that taken after Dicey's will. Similarly, when Andrew Brice failed to leave his *Brice's Weekly Journal* to two of his employees, they were so piqued as to set up a rival title. As the century progressed, this profitability made newspaper ownership an attractive proposition for men of standing – or may indeed have brought standing for those who owned them. Thus, George Burbage, who owned the *Nottinghamshire Journal*, was made a sheriff in 1773 and elected Senior Council of the Corporation in 1790. James Simmons, who founded the Kentish Gazette, enjoyed similar positions of rank, serving as sheriff, the government's Distributor of Stamps for Kent and MP (Barker 1998). Whether the provincial newspaper promoted men to positions of rank or whether men of rank were attracted to newspaper ownership is impossible to establish; however, what is clear is the gains from the business were enough to warrant such an association.

The emergence of local journalism

The introduction of Stamp Duty tells us something about how these newspapers were seen in their contemporary cultural context. The implicit recognition of the duty on adverts was that newspapers were a commercial product – just like soap, which was also taxed under the same statute – and economically significant enough to be a source of revenue for a government which needed to fund the War of Spanish Succession. Oats and Sadler (2002) contend that at this stage newspapers were viewed as a luxury item, and while commentators such as Adam Smith would condemn the tax on soap, newspapers were omitted from such debates. The significance of advertising to these titles also suggests that their function in relation to the burgeoning consumer market, which was being created as the nation industrialized, was equally significant. Raven (2014) argues that these titles played a key role in establishing 'commerce' by supporting a range of businesses via advertising; provincial newspapers were a key element of creating a 'consumer mentality' at a time when rising disposable incomes enabled more spending on consumer items. This role is embodied in the print shop itself, which was often at the heart of local business life, selling a range of products and items useful to daily life, like tickets and timetables and maps. This positioning facilitated expansion into other areas of commercial life so that some print shops operated as employment agencies or even local banks. Similarly, their access to distribution networks enabled them to deliver and sell goods on behalf of others. It is not surprising then that Robert Raikes advertised his paper as being 'useful' to the business user first and to the reader second, so that its being 'profitable' was put before its being 'pleasant' (see *Gloucester Archives NV261: Advertisement*). This role was amplified by the presence of papers in coffee houses where business people, many of whom lacked formal commercial premises, would meet to discuss and do business (Black 2001).

However, the emphasis on the freshness of the news – and the detailed attention paid to getting and disseminating that content as described above – signifies that editorial content of these titles was neither incidental or accidental; as noted, early experiments with free newspapers funded by adverts alone were a failure (Raven 2014). These producers were not only establishing the newspaper as a business, but were innovating in the collation of content in a process which had not yet been termed journalism. Conboy has argued that journalism 'crystallises in practice under very specific economic and political constraints' (2014: 66); therefore the content of the early provincial newspaper must be contextualized by both its economic purpose and the regulatory framework in which it operated. A diverse content was clearly a key selling point and seen as one weapon among many to increase circulation. Favourite subjects included deaths and executions, leisure activities, such as bull baiting and cockfighting, alongside cricket and bell ringing. In addition, these papers ventured into more feature content such as songs, poems and stories and even novel serializations including Defoe's *Moll Flanders*. Readers' letters were also regularly included in the columns of these early newspapers and later developments saw sport make it into the editorial columns having originally been included as lists of results and other information in advertisements. Crime was especially popular to the extent that some papers gained a reputation for the quality of their crime reporting. The same topic also gave newspapers one of their first claims to acting for the public good by alerting would-be criminals to the penalties they would face if caught (Black 2001: 54). While there is evidence of some local news – Wiles (1965: 255) charts local content in the *Norwich Post* in 1708 as including news of the city, such as market prices, baptisms and burials and even the story of a soldier who had escaped from the city's Castle prison – it was not a staple element of content until the mid-1700s. Andrew Walker (2006: 376) suggests that local news only gained prominence in the latter decades of the eighteenth century when there were enough competing newspapers to focus circulation areas on more defined areas.

Such a diverse range of content had to be selected, organized and presented. While the practice of using headlines had not yet been established, the printers would insert small headings and swop typefaces for emphasis, which would signal that they thought an item of particular note. This tactic is used in the *Gloucester Journal* of 9 June 1730 to draw the reader's attention to a particularly dramatic story which still makes for good reading.

> John Doyle and John Yound, two Highway-men, were carried on Monday the 1st Instant, from Newgate, and executed at Tyburn, the former on a mourning coach, the latter in a Cart; they both seem'd to behave themselves in a becoming Manner, and Care was taken of their Bodies by their friends, in order to be decently interred. (*Gloucester Journal*, 9 June 1730: 2)

The same edition carries other reports of robberies alongside adverts for stagecoach services, indicating that safety on the roads was a cause for concern and hence worth the typographical innovation. As such, the role of an editor, who selected content with a view to keeping a reader by drawing information from a diverse range of sources, developed as an established practice in the provinces, as it was in the London press. Barker (1998) documents that William Clachar was paid a salary to run the *Chelmsford Chronicle*. Charles Pugh founded the *Hereford Journal*, but lived in London and paid Rathbone to act as editor. Anne Ward owned the *York Courant*, but employed an agent to run it. The unprofitable *Hampshire Chronicle* was managed by a paid man, John Wilkes. Wiles suggests that the established practice in 'most' provincial newspapers was 'a commendable attempt to gather news and to prepare it for a special community of readers' (1965: 208). Therefore, while the subject matter of these papers may not have appeared to be particularly local, the suggestion is that the content was selected with a particular audience in mind.

At the same time, Conboy (2004) reminds us that the press was not 'free'; licensing had lapsed but had not ended, and similarly the legacy of the seventeenth-century legislation restricted not only who could print but also what they could print. These restrictions continued into the eighteenth century with the laws of libel and the prohibition of reporting of parliamentary proceedings, which was not relaxed until 1771. The penalties for these were severe and sometimes violent. Philip Bishop, for instance, the printer of a paper in Exeter, was prosecuted for printing a ballad which compared George I to Nero. He was sentenced to life imprisonment, having his ears cut off and nailed to the pillory and 'to be whipped at the cart's tail three several market days' (Cranfield 1978: 182). Fortunately perhaps, he died before the sentence could be carried out. The publishers of the papers who printed reports of Parliament were also called to the House to account for their actions. This happened to Robert Raikes more than once – in 1727 and 1728 – for which he was held in custody by the Serjeant-at-Arms. The second offence, the reports of proceedings recount, was the fault of his staff, Raikes said, who had been ordered 'not to insert in his Journal any of the Votes or Resolutions of this House'.

This meant that producing these newspapers was a balancing act as publishers sought to keep on the right side of the law and maintain profits. The latter included brokering political interests, a concern which became more significant after the rising costs of newspaper production following the imposition of the Stamp Act. This made political subsidy – for instance via the payment for the inclusion of politically motivated content – more significant as a revenue stream particularly when the capital costs of setting up a newspaper rose with the Stamp Act of 1712, which has itself been interpreted as an attempt to limit the potentially seditious nature of the newspaper. Thus even in the eighteenth century, we can see the provincial press beginning to broker its position in relation to the political process. While not yet espousing the position of a 'fourth estate', the discourse of a free press was employed by these early editors and was often quoted in editorials. They were not above venturing opinions, either as appendages to stories or as stand-alone pieces and were starting to align themselves with the interests of their readers. Robert Raikes Junior, who succeeded to the editorship in 1757, is most famous as the founder of the Sunday School movement. His philanthropic tendencies were first exercised via the pages of the newspaper in what we would now call campaigns. The first of these was to improve conditions for the inmates of Gloucester prison in 1768.

As their role matured and their circulation areas focused in the face of competition, some editors used politics and the public interest as a way of carving out a position for their product. Barker (1998) suggests that local reform organizations in particular used their local titles to garner support for their causes. Drawing on evidence for the *Hampshire Chronicle*, she demonstrates that politicians could pay to have content inserted – but that was not true of all political coverage. In Cambridge for instance, Benjamin Flower launched his radical *Cambridge Intelligencer* to compete with the pro-Tory *Cambridge Chronicle*. Walker (2006) notes that many of these provincial radical titles were short-lived, perhaps because of the risk they ran in alienating what was already a fairly precarious readership. A campaigning title, which aligned itself with a potential readership, particularly drawn from the newly emerging middles classes, was more likely to enjoy success. The *Leeds Intelligencer*, which was to become the *Yorkshire Post* in 1866, was one such paper which owed its fortunes to the industrial revolution, which saw Leeds grow from a market town to an industrial city. By the early 1800s the paper had nailed its pro-Tory colours to its editorial mast during a particularly hard-fought election battle, possibly in a bid to secure the most affluent advertising market against more radical rivals, including the *Northern Star*. But the paper was equally known for its campaigning stance and it often stood the corner of social causes which might be understood as being in the interest of the public. These included the need to improve Leeds' sewage system in the face of recurrent cholera epidemics (Gibb and Beckwith 1954). Significantly these titles were also sent to a London readership – and incorporated into the London papers – in a process which saw provincial politics used to influence the national stage (Barker 1998: 141).

In fewer than 100 years the provincial newspaper had come far, developing into a mature commercial business which was carving out a role for itself in the creation of civic identity in relation to the creation of specific reading publics. The newspaper was establishing for itself a prominent discursive function as the purveyor of 'news', and Conboy attributes this again to the diverse mix of content and polemic which engaged the reader as an active participant in making sense of the rich variety of information presented by these papers. Eighteenth-century newspapers were established as a 'generic hybrid between public information source, community identity and profit which constitutes journalism' (2004: 42), which helped to cement the social identity of the emerging bourgeois classes who negotiated the plethora of 'advices' put forward in their columns. Some analysts have equated early newspapers with a coffee house culture – and a burgeoning public sphere; for Black, the eighteenth-century newspaper performed the role of a 'secular sermon' (2002: 176), disseminating the values of 'moral politeness' to the emerging bourgeois classes. What both of these processes depended on was the creation by the paper of a readership, in a civic and market sense. As such the titles created an 'imaginary community' (Anderson 1991) and positioned themselves as serving the interests of that community by adopting causes in their benefit. However, the price and circulation of these titles suggests they were mostly read by the middle classes. At the same time, those involved in newspapers amassed sufficient standing to enact that process and take an active role in the civic life of the middling sorts. It is this which legitimized the commercial imperative of the provincial newspaper and which was to enable it to take up the position of the guardian of democracy, which was to dominate the next phase of its development.

3

The Provincial Press and Political Patronage

The political bent

The nineteenth century is the period within which the English provincial newspaper is characterized by the link between ownership and political influence in a process which has contributed to the continued emphasis on the relationship between journalism and democracy. In this period, regional newspapers developed into titles overtly aligned to political parties to the extent that by 1860 they could be categorized according to their politics (Milne n.d.). At the same time, though, these titles were also turning into large-scale propositions, reliant on production on an industrial scale, and it is no surprise that Lee sees this epoch as one in which two varying constructions of the provincial press – 'one of fourth estate, with proprietorship a form of public service … the other as a press as an industry' (1978: 118) – vie for supremacy. The relationship between politics and paper was not, however, one of exploitation in which political persuaders hijacked the newspaper for its communicative power. Instead it was a matter of mutual dependency with political purpose a pillar of the newspaper's business model, underwritten by an ideological belief in the educative power of the newspaper. In this way it is used by newspaper owners to maintain the elite business model for the provincial press in opposition to the burgeoning radical press in the first half of the nineteenth century. Once Stamp Duty was abolished in 1855, such was the synergy between party political allegiance and profit that politics became increasingly codified in the articles of incorporation for titles; it also provided the basis for chain ownership and, as the century progressed, more owners could be found in Parliament as MPs. The relationship waned only as titles responded to the new business model necessitated by the fierce competition of mass circulations with an increased emphasis on popular content which would maintain profits and satisfy shareholders.

In light of this, the marriage between the regional press and the politicized notion of the fourth estate might then be best considered one of convenience.

For the newspaper proprietors this ideological position could be articulated into a social purpose and could be employed in varying ways at varying times. One captivating narration of this position is the campaign to end Stamp Duty – the so-called 'taxes on knowledge'. Such was its success that Boyce (1978: 21) suggests that the press created the 'political myth' that the press was able to act as part of the system of checks and balances in a democratic society. In this understanding, the press bridged the communicative space between public opinion and political institutions and, therefore, enabled that opinion to act as a sanction against political 'misrule' (ibid.). Such was the success of the myth that utilitarian philosopher John Stuart Mill 'thought that the case for an independent press was so self-evident that it need no longer be put' (Boyce 1978: 22).

For the provincial newspaper, this position was refined in relation to the audience a title sought. The dominant characterization was one which foregrounded its function as an educative political persuader. This conception was underwritten by a belief that newspapers could influence public opinion, and, specifically, that provincial newspapers could be used to influence the opinion of people in a set locality. Both extant and new newspapers became polarized by labels which defined them as liberal or conservative in a usage of terms which predates their application to political parties. This is perhaps not surprising given the national background of reform which dominated the period in question, and many scholars have concentrated on this definition of the press at this time in their analysis of its operation.[1] However, this oppositional positioning, which Barker (1998: 139) suggests is due largely to the preferred London newspapers used as content sources by provincial papers, masks a nuanced variety of practices by both those working within the industry and by those looking to exercise influence – either via content or by their connection with a business which yields status both socially and financially. As such, any political posturing was tempered by a need to make money, which meant that the most successful newspapers were often those who refined their politics so that they had as broad appeal as possible in a given area. A 'one size fits all' approach to achieving this had not yet been established within the industry. Therefore a variety of responses are to be found within the landscape of the provincial newspapers as proprietors and producers experimented within a still-evolving landscape, in the face of rapid industrialization and advances in production technologies.

---

[1]   See, for instance, Aspinall 1973; Asquith 1978 and Briggs 1949.

The material and political circumstances under which the regional and provincial newspaper operated were to alter radically during the nineteenth century. State control loosened with the abolition of Stamp Duty in 1855, which paved the way for mass-produced newspapers. The printing process improved because paper was no longer stamped, it no longer had to be cut and fed into the newly developed steam presses in sheets and instead could go in on a roll. This was soon followed by the mechanization of composition with the introduction of the Linotype, first used in Britain by the *Newcastle Daily Chronicle* in 1889 (Milne n.d.). The Linotype could set five to six thousand ens (the smallest printer's measure) per hour, compared with one thousand by hand. By 1902 there were more than 1,100 Linotype machines in use – mostly in the provincial newspaper industry. At the same time, the process of newsgathering and dissemination benefited from the communications revolution in the form of the railway and telegraph. This led to less reliance on cut and paste and correspondence, and the use of professional reporters as industrialization itself necessitated an increasingly demarcated and professionalized workforce.

In the year before the repeal of Stamp Duty there were 289 provincial papers. By 1871 this number had not only grown to 851 and a daily provincial press had become established; ten years later evening papers would be added to the industry's make-up. These improved papers were increasingly owned and produced to exert influence so that titles became institutions alongside those they sought to hold to account; the status of the editor rose and owners enjoyed a social prestige associated with their commercial activity and may even have bought into the industry as a way of securing their social positions. Significantly, the industry legitimized its social role within the rhetoric of the fourth estate, which had to be reconciled with the business of newspapers itself (Lee 1978). This epoch of the provincial press is then best understood by the interrogation of a number of contextualizing themes: first, the role of the government control and politics; second, the increased significance of localized communities of interest to the provincial newspaper business model and third, the industrialization, and demarcation, of provincial newspaper practices.

Politics and the battle for a free press

The development of the provincial press in eighteenth-century England had demonstrated that these titles could yield significant profits and, therefore, could become status symbols for those entrepreneurs who established successful businesses. By 1801 provincial newspapers outsold metropolitan newspapers; however, theirs was still a liminal social status which made them ambivalent targets for politicians who may have recognized their potential, but who were as yet unwilling to cavort with the press. Additionally, Aspinall (1973) suggests that the practice of provincial newspapers was not yet developed enough to extend to such features as editorial writing which would provide a vehicle for political expression. However, evidence suggests that these titles could intervene in debate, and Money (1971) demonstrates how titles in the Midlands took oppositional positions on both national and regional political issues in the late eighteenth century. Stamp Duty was also seen as an implicit recognition of the potential of the provincial press to be politically influential; this levy was understood by many to be a punitive one, the effect of which was to limit those who could afford to buy a newspaper. In this way it was seen as a 'measure of the fear of the ruling classes at what might happen if the masses gained access to a cheap and financially independent press wherein dangerous doctrines could be daily disseminated' (Milne n.d.: 15–16). Indeed, the spirit of the law was to enable government control of newspaper content by, in effect, limiting their availability.

The very attitudes of politicians towards newspapers were split. The conservatives deplored what they saw as a dissimulating industry which had the power to challenge the establishment. They argued that Stamp Duty meant they were in the hands of respectable men because of the amount of capital needed to own one. The liberals, on the other hand, professed an abhorrence of taxation, the effect of which was to curtail the freedom of the press. The Tory *Carlisle Patriot* was among those provincial titles to rehearse these positions.

> The liberty of the press will find an advocate where ever there is a Freeman; but where can an apologist be found for its licentiousness? What can be said in favour of those petulant animadversions on public measures, and of that unceasing abuse of public men which constitutes the greatest part of the reading in some of our newspapers? Do the writers of these articles suppose that the nation will be regulated in her opinions by the standard of their own narrow party politics, and that she can ever mistake the intemperate ardour of their comments for the genuine spirit of patriotism? ... They tend to raise popular discontent, and make the people dissatisfied with the establishment. (*Carlisle Patriot*, 1 February 1866: 3)

The status of ownership of a provincial newspaper was, to some extent, contradictory. Those who would criticize, dismissed provincial titles in particular as the products of a lowly trade; Stamp Duty limited ownership to those of means who could afford to stock up on stamped paper and to pay the necessary sureties to government against libel. It also limited the business model of official titles to one of high-price, low turnover. At 7d. these newspapers were expensive, and individual copies were priced out of the reach of the working man – who additionally may not have been able to read.[2] This meant that newspapers were accessed via communal practices, such as via the coffee house which would take multiple titles, with one in Manchester said to take 96 papers a week. Subscribers would also join forces to fund reading rooms, paying one guinea a week for the provision of wide variety of reading material. In rural areas, landlords would buy newspapers for their pubs, and they would be read aloud so that content was made available to those who were illiterate. It was this link between alcohol and news which prompted the Temperance Society to join the campaign for the repeal of Stamp Duty. Informally, groups would also club together to buy papers, and Aspinall (1946) reports how weavers in York would buy one copy between them – which was then read out to them. This means that titles had readerships many times their circulation with the most popular newspapers thought to have around thirty readers per copy.

Andrew Hobbs has gone as far as to argue that the provincial press formed such a developed network of publications by 1836 that it performed a role similar to that which we ascribe contemporaneously to the national press. Not only did provincial papers outsell the London press, Hobbs argues, but with the advent of the daily mornings especially, their status grew so that the 'provincial press was the majority newspaper press for more than a century'. In this period the numbers and types of provincial papers grew from the usual weekly newspaper, typically serving a market town or borough, to include city morning papers, such as the *Manchester Guardian*, the 'weekend regional miscellany paper', which often focused on sensational content, and the urban-based evening paper (Hobbs 2009: 16–17). Added to this was the organization of the provincial newspaper industry – including shared aspects such as telegraphed news and advertisements – which added to its cohesiveness. This may well account for the potential of the provincial press not only to exert, but also to be seen to

---

[2] Literacy levels prior to the abolition of Stamp Duty have generally been portrayed as low, largely on the premise that the 1870 Education Act somehow revolutionized levels of literacy. However, evidence suggests that the act instead built on previous provision and that literacy was well established prior to its inception. In 1835, for instance, research suggests that only one in twenty people in Bristol could not read. Lee (1976) cites the founder of the *Driffield Times*, who wrote in 1860 that 'almost universal' literacy was a good reason for setting up his newspaper.

exert, political influence which was to become such a characteristic of its existence in the second half of the nineteenth century. In the same way that politicians saw the country as a network of connecting constituencies, so they saw the provincial newspaper industry as a network of publications which could be used to reach the electorate. The notion of the newspaper as influential was to become entrenched in the public psyche. Contemporary commentators JM Ludlow and L Jones (in their *Progress of the Working Class, 1832-1867*) wrote of the illegal penny press which became established as a rival to taxed titles, and which is discussed in more detail later in this chapter: 'The cheap newspaper and periodical cannot perhaps be defined strictly as educators. Yet, for good or evil, and probably on the whole for good, they are very powerful ones' (Lee 1976: 27).

Milne goes so far as to say that politics was the 'lifeblood' of these papers, at a time when the nation was gripped by the debate surrounding the expansion of the franchise, exploited by politicians because they were 'cheap, immediate and regular' (n.d.: 13). However, direct political intervention in newspapers – which extended to subsidy – was largely reserved for London newspapers, although there is some evidence of this practice in the provincial press. Palmerston, for instance, donated £1,000 to help found the *Hampshire Independent* in support of the Liberal cause (Grant 1871). More usual though was an indirect government influence, largely executed via favouritism in the form of payments or the release of information to certain journalists. Financially, payments, pensions and government adverts were used to support certain titles. Life could also be made difficult for those titles who did not toe the government line, for instance via local officials who would flag up titles which were potentially seditious, or via disruption to those circulations which depended on the system of delivery via the post office (Asquith 1976).

When the Whig party attempted to further their cause via newspapers, they did so via indirect influence rather than out-and-out ownership. Asquith suggests the party controlled a large number of provincial newspapers in the early 1800s by getting supportive editors to include sympathetic content. This enabled the opinions expressed in the newspaper to be perceived as independent. Even this though was problematic, and both the *Bristol Mercury* and *Bath Journal* are reported to have demanded payment for political material so that in effect the copy was treated as an advert. In Liverpool in 1807, just one of four editors would compromise their position by including Whig copy because they did not want to alienate their readers who might disagree with the position. On the opposite side of the political coin, in Westmorland in the north of England, the

Lowther family operated via a complex network of associates to exploit the press in 'as if it were their own'. This was done without ever taking direct ownership of a newspaper, or contributing to the foundation of a new pro-Tory title, the *Westmorland Gazette*, instead leaving it to the 'gentlemen' of Kendal to fund the venture. Lowther exercised influence over editorials provided for the *Carlisle Patriot* by providing material to those who wrote them (Aspinall 1973: 354–6). In this way the operation of political influence via these titles was refined within a localized context as columns of local newspapers were exploited by local elites who sought to shore up their own positions as well as those of the government.

Equally, the development of titles in Manchester demonstrates how newspapers could be used to challenge those elites. This was particularly so as the century progressed and legislation sought to reform entrenched systems of power at a local level by the modernization of local government systems.[3] In this way the institutionalized provincial newspaper – and those involved in it – could take their place as a key part of that process. In Manchester, a 'band' of radical businessmen, who had made their fortunes in the textile industry, saw newspapers as their way of promoting politics, perhaps, but also as a way of challenging the hold on municipal power enjoyed by a 'select circle' of Tory Anglicans, for whom positions of authority were 'self-perpetuating; not only was the selection of officers in the hands of the same individuals for long periods of time, but outgoing officers could themselves nominate their successors – as was the case with churchwardens and overseers' (Turner 1991: 138). In this instance, the reform of local government was as much a goal of their efforts as political power.

In 1836 there were a total of 221 stamped papers in England, Wales and Scotland, including 79 in London, 83 in the English provinces, six in Wales and 53 in Scotland, according to official Stamp Office figures. Of those provincial papers, the biggest seller was the *Leeds Mercury* with an annual sale of 270,000, closely followed by the *Lincoln, Rutland and Stamford Mercury*, with a circulation of 260,000 (Whorlow 1886). However, there was also a growing and successful unstamped, and therefore illegal, press, comprised of a variety of titles.

Because the unstamped press was unofficial, it is hard to gauge its extent; by 1830, Whorlow suggests that, another unnamed, unstamped paper had a

---

[3] The Municipal Corporations Act of 1835 reformed a largely closed system of local councils where members preserved their ruling interest by promoting friends and family to positions of authority. The majority had been Tory. Under the terms of the new act, all male ratepayers could vote in elections and councils could levy taxes to fund municipal improvements.

circulation of two million copies – a circulation equivalent to one eighteenth of all stamped papers. This figure was based on a seizure of 40,000 contraband copies of the publication.

The unstamped press professed to represent the interests of the working man, building on a tradition of radical newspapers established at the turn of the century. Among those who founded titles was William Cobbett', whose *Political Register* achieved a circulation of 50,000 a week, distributed via a network of independent sellers who could order bundles and take the profits. The political content of the *Register* was issued as a 2d pamphlet to evade Stamp Duty. However, these and other radical titles were subject to government repression via the Six Acts, introduced in the wake of Peterloo in 1819.[4] The penny unstamped papers of the 1830s were illegal within the terms of the Six Acts; they were based in London and sold via a system of street sellers – who often bore the brunt of prosecution. Originally quarto publications, the titles developed into broadsheet publications which competed with the official stamped newspapers in content as well as form and were sold via the shops of working class radicals. Despite efforts to seize copies, these papers were 'too profitable, too well organized and had too much public support to be suppressed' (Hollis 1970: 106).

Significantly, the existence of a burgeoning unstamped press demonstrated that political principle and profitability could be mutually supportive. Additionally, the business model, which was to find its apotheosis in a mass readership, can be traced back to these newspapers because they relied on a low cover price and large circulation. Many of these titles, which were initially set up to further the aims of committed political radicals, were short-lived, but the most successful were 'creditable' one-sheet newspapers produced in line with professional norms and which launched the careers of journalists. Hollis (1970) suggests that these titles were as attractive to middle-class radicals as their working class audience, and it was this apparent respectability which was a threat to the stamped press. Weiner (1969) suggests that a circulation of 3,000–4,000 was needed to make an unstamped paper commercially viable, but some, including the *Poor Man's Guardian*, sold close to 10,000. Hollis suggests many achieved 'readerships' of many more – up to 50,000 – via the oral process described above in pubs and in

[4]   On 16 August 1819, eighteen people were killed when the cavalry charged at a peaceful crowd of 60,000 gathered to hear pro-reform speakers at St Peter's Field, Manchester.

workshops, and the most successful touched a sale of 40,000, at a time when *The Times* had a sale of 10,000.

These papers sold well in the provinces with at least half, and up to two-thirds, of all titles sold outside of London, where the owners might have been based. Most of these went to the large industrial conurbations and sophisticated, clandestine methods of distribution developed to meet demand. Ingenious methods were used to circulate illegal titles - with one resorting to transporting them in coffins. The proprietors took the trouble to tour the provinces and took steps to include local content to make their products more attractive; Hetherington, for instance, favoured the publication of letters from the provinces in his *Poor Man's Guardian*. Publishers, journalists and vendors of unstamped papers faced imprisonment or confiscation of equipment should they be caught, and the popularity of these papers is evidenced by the number of prosecutions. In 1835 alone, 800 people were imprisoned following cases brought by the Stamp Office (Weiner 1969: 195), and funds were set up to support the families of those in jail. However, the penalties did little to deter the industry largely because involvement was motivated by ideological reasons, as reports of their court cases evidence, in addition to making money from sales. Eventually the sheer weight of numbers of these titles made the law practically unenforceable; unstamped newspapers outsold official titles tenfold to the extent that the *Weekly Herald* boasted in 1836 that 'a stamped paper now indeed is regarded as a curiosity, in Bath, Birmingham, Manchester, Liverpool, Newcastle, Hull, Portsmouth etc' (Hollis 1970: 124).

Therefore, while the debate around Stamp Duty was dominated by political arguments, underwriting it was the commercial success of the unstamped press, which challenged the prevalent business model for the official provincial newspaper. These political arguments centred around different conceptions of the educative potential of the newspaper. Those in favour of maintaining taxation feared the implications of extending knowledge to the masses because it would destabilize the established order; the middle-class radicals, conversely, suggested that abolishing Stamp Duty would enable 'responsible' papers to thrive and foster the 'right' sort of opinion, and so create a stable society. Additionally, it would thwart the unstamped press, which sought to constitute the workingman as an excluded class and threaten the established order. If 'the middle-class campaigners sought to change the law, the working-class radicals "sought to smash it"' – both of which positions horrified the conservatives' (Hollis 1970: 10).

Among those against the repeal was the Provincial Newspaper Society, which was formed in 1836 to represent the interests of the regional newspapers.

While it might be expected that the producers of newspapers would seek to free their industry from punitive taxation, instead the society employed arguments around 'respectability' to campaign for the preservation of Stamp Duty. The business model underwritten by taxation meant entry into the newspaper market was priced out of the reach of most; starting a daily newspaper would require a capital of some £40,000 in the 1830s, leaving the business in the hands of an established elite who had to think only of the narrow interests of a relatively small readership. In effect, it preserved what Hollis has termed a 'monopoly' (1970: 17) form of ownership whereby a small elite were largely free from the challenge of new entrants to the market. The provincial industry justified its opposition to the abolition of taxation with a discourse of preserving the public good. Whorlow's narration describes Stamp Duty as a state mechanism for protecting itself against 'unsavoury' press owners, who were seen 'as a suspected person, one to be feared and dreaded, as ever ready to asperse the characters of innocent men, and without honour, conscience or common decency' (1886: 8). But the financial pressures of newspaper ownership meant that 'unsavoury' could be equated with people of lesser financial standing who lacked the considerable amount of capital to enter the industry. As such, evidence suggests the men of means who made up the Provincial Newspaper Society were speaking from a position of self-interest.

> Country newspaper proprietors appear at that time, to have been haunted with the apprehension that the abolition of the impositions with which they had contended for so many years, and the soothing away of difficulties which their prosperity had surmounted, would open the door to a host of nobodies who would lower the tone of the press, and elbow the old-established concerns out of the field. … The effect of the measure would be to lower the character of the newspaper press in this country, by the competition for cheapness, and by the increase in the number of publications diminishing the means of incurring the large outlay made for every respectable journal, thus tending in reality not to cheapen but to enhance the cost of valuable information. (Whorlow 1886: 53–5)

In 1833 Advertisement Duty had been reduced from 3s. 6d. to 1s. 6d.; it was abolished in 1853 – the immediate effect of which was to increase the volume of advertising. In 1836 the 4d. tax on newspapers was reduced to a penny, which had prompted the Provincial Newspaper Society to attempt price fixing in an attempt the preserve the high-price, lower-sale business model. Advocates argued that this would preserve the quality of newspapers to the benefit of owners and readers alike. In 1849, however, the pressure for repeal grew with the formation of the Association for Promoting the Repeal of the Taxes on Knowledge, which numbered among its members those who had successfully campaigned for the repeal of the Corn Laws. Yet, when in 1850 the 114 members of the Provincial Newspaper Society were canvassed for their opinions, most of those who responded disagreed that owners would benefit from repeal; just a few said they would benefit from the repeal of advertisement duty. In 1852 a special meeting of the society resolved to call on the then Chancellor of the Exchequer Benjamin Disraeli to preserve the penny stamp. Despite this, it was abolished by the Whig government two years later.

Communities of interest and profit

With the loosening of state control, the business model for publishing newspapers changed. The taxes on knowledge had preserved the monopoly enjoyed by incumbent publishers, but high-cost, low-circulations and advertisement duty had the effect of limiting the revenues which could be yielded from them. Without taxation, however, the path was cleared for the provincial newspaper to revolutionize and become a mass-circulation, mass-produced product, with advertising revenues central to their profitability. The time was also ripe for investment in emerging technologies to make these papers; this meant that establishment costs did not fall, but such was the possibility of the mass-circulation newspaper that revenues rose. Between 1839 and 1844, for instance, the *Manchester Guardian* made an average profit of £6,777; in 1855 that had risen to £12,000 and between 1862 and 1865, to £20,000. As such, post-repeal the landscape for the provincial newspaper was far from homogeneous as publishers employed a variety of tactics as they sought to establish a foothold in what was to become a highly competitive market place.

Writing in 1871, newspaper worker James Grant catalogued more than 1,500 provincial papers to create a permanent record of the variety of forms these titles took. His detailed compendium demonstrates that publication frequencies differed between daily (morning and evening) and weekly or with some titles retaining the tri-weekly pattern of publication, which had originally aligned with the eighteenth-century postal service. These newspapers' papers were also priced at varying levels within a range between 4d and a halfpenny according to their 'class'; this meant that some locations such as Hereford were able to sustain a market that comprised a high-priced newspaper and a cheaper rival. Neither were the number of titles in a set locale specifically related to the size of the population; the Isle of Wight has nine titles, while Sheffield had only four and Wolverhampton none. The best-served county was Lancashire, which had no fewer than 101 newspapers.

There was also considerable variety in content. The *Middlesex County Chronicle*, one of the few provincial titles with proximity to London, functioned as a paper of record, carrying adverts and reports of county events. Some relied on regional business news to build a highly profitable advertising base, such as Birmingham's *Aris's Gazette*. A small number of titles were free and relied wholly on income from advertising; the *West Sussex Gazette,* founded in 1853, was among those to sustain a circulation based on free distribution. Even fewer newspapers appeared to be part-free and part-paid-for, such as the *Midland Counties Herald*, which Grant praised for the quality and quantity of its adverts. However, free distribution was the exception rather than the norm, and regional newspapers usually expected to generate around 50 per cent of their costs through advertising. A modern provincial newspaper makes more than 90 per cent of its revenue from the same source.

This increased reliance on advertising income did not displace the political labels of the early nineteenth century, and in 1860 provincial titles could still be classified accordingly. Members of Parliament in particular likened the circulation areas of provincial newspapers to constituencies, so that together they formed an interconnected network (Hobbs 2009: 23). To aid the cause, parties would send out material for inclusion in papers such as 'handysheets' to help editors write opinion pieces. Titles in a set locale would also be defined in terms of these oppositions, even using it as a marker of difference for sales purposes. In Leeds, the Tory *Intelligencer* competed with the Liberal[5] *Leeds Mercury;* the Liberal *Brighton Guardian* was opposed by the Tory *Brighton Gazette;* Newcastle had the Liberal *Tyne Mercury* and the conservative *Newcastle Journal;* on the Isle of Wight, five of the nine titles were aligned with the conservative interest. However, this political alignment was not absolute, and other titles proclaimed their independence or loyalties to local specialisms, such as agriculture or business. In Plymouth and Portsmouth, titles sought to provide information on the navy, while Oxford and Cambridge favoured university news. In Liverpool,

---

[5]   The Liberal Party was formed from an alliance of Whig and radical politicians in the 1850s. It won its first election in 1859.

religious affiliation trumped political affiliation because of the strength of the Roman Catholic community in the city.

Grant was himself the former editor of a regional newspaper in Elgin, Scotland. He recorded that he turned down the editorship of the newly founded *Salisbury Herald* because his Liberal beliefs conflicted with the Tory principles of the title. Politics also continued to underwrite the motives for ownership. Joint stock companies – which spread the risks associated with newspaper businesses by introducing limited liability – were set up with the specific purpose of a promoting a cause. These companies were able to raise the necessary capital of up to £200,000 to invest in the industry. In Leeds the *Intelligencer,* the forerunner of the still extant *Yorkshire Post*, was given a firm financial footing in the face of increased competition by the formation of the Yorkshire Conservative Newspaper Company, which issued 5,000 shares at £10 each. The company was set up to preserve the paper as a 'daily organ of expression' for Yorkshire and wider West Riding area, to promote Conservative Party and to link town and country and to see off competition from the Liberal *Leeds Mercury* (Gibb and Beckwith 1954).

In 1865 the political position of the *Carlisle Patriot* was formalized with the creation of the Carlisle Conservative Newspaper Company, which bought the copyright. The first object of the company was 'the associating together persons entertaining Conservative political opinions for the purpose of printing and publishing newspapers in Carlisle and elsewhere, having for their political object the upholding of Conservative political opinions' (Cumbrian Archive ref: DB20/42). Subclauses subsequently added enabled the directors to exclude through resolution any shareholder deemed not Conservative enough in their beliefs. Among the founding seven shareholders of the Carlisle Conservative Newspaper Company was a banker, a Conservative MP and a solicitor, and all were citizens of considerable standing in Carlisle. However, it seems evident that their political principle was tempered with a strong dose of commercial reality, and the company listed in its objects its other interests, including publishing, printing and book selling, and 'the purchasing, renting, or building houses and other premises for the purpose of carrying on the same'. Similarly, political conviction could be watered down, or even set aside, if it came before profit. Grant recalls that the political difference was not seen to be a bar to his editing the Salisbury paper because 'the proprietor sought to obviate this objection, by saying that the politics of the paper would be only moderately Conservative' (1871: 245). Similarly, while he consistently referenced the politics of individual titles, Grant also made it clear that it was not always evident in the columns of the newspaper how the avowed political stance translated into editorial content – even when titles were associated with high-status politicians. Examining the newspapers in Bristol founded by Peter Stewart Macliver, who went on to serve as Liberal MP for Plymouth, for instance, Grant was unable to distinguish any difference between the politics of the *Western Daily Press* and the weekly *Bristol Observer*, although they claimed to be different. Instead, in this instance, Grant understood the differences to be a matter of special interest content, so that one concentrated on literary matters, and the other on attracting a 'family' audience (1871: 271).

Newspaper ownership was a risky business; between 1867 and 1871 alone fifteen newspaper proprietors went bust, although the risk was on a level with other Victorian industries. But it must have had a lure of its own because entrepreneurs were willing to try – and often try again – founding serial titles until one was successful. That these papers had to make money was beyond doubt, and throughout the course of the nineteenth century, owners faced accusations of sacrificing principle and public interest for profit. As the commentator William Lovett remarked in 1838, 'The Newspaper Press, daily and weekly, is the property of capitalists who have embarked on the enterprise upon purely commercial principles, and with the purpose of making it contribute to their own personal and pecuniary interests. It is the course which is *profitable*, therefore, and not the course which is *just* which necessarily secures their preference' (Lee 1976: 49–50). When Archibald Prentice attempted to set up a radical liberal title in Manchester in the 1820s, he put principle before profit and ended up bankrupt; conversely the *Manchester Guardian* was successful, precisely because, though radical, it was not 'too political' and its editor would even drop editorial content to make room for late adverts if it meant making a profit (Turner 1991: 117). This emphasis on profit meant that there was not always an alignment between the apparent political dominance of titles and the political representation of an area. Grant notes that Oxford returned Liberal MPs without having a Liberal press; additionally he said that 'while Essex is generally regarded as a decidedly Conservative and Protestant county, the majority of its twenty-eight newspapers are either Independent, or Neutral or Liberal. I am unable to account for the fact; yet such it is'. For all titles in the county he noted that the most important issue 'no matter what may be the character of their politics' was agricultural news (1871: 288). Therefore, increasingly local interest trumped political labels when it came to commanding market share.

During this period chain ownership also became increasingly common, as owners, either individual or shareholder, founded or acquired serial titles. This analysis has already noted the advantages of cooperative working practices to the provincial newspapers of the eighteenth century, with publishers aligning their newspaper interests to those of others concerned with distributing products. In the nineteenth century, this alignment became increasingly specialized so that newspaper publishers began to co-own but also co-produce multiple provincial titles. Among the largest chains was that belonging to Mr W. E. Baxter, who held no fewer than twenty-four titles in the south-east of England. Mostly published weekly, and mostly priced one penny, the newspapers were all partly printed in Lewes. Shared production was also at the heart of the *Guardian* series of newspapers in the north west; based in Warrington,[6] the owner Mr A. Mackie, described as the 'most enterprising man in the newspaper world' of the 1870s, developed a unique and 'extensive system of stereotyping, and a mode of setting up types peculiar to himself, whereby he furnishes all his other papers with typographical facilities for prosecuting his journalistic enterprises' (Grant 1871: 347–8). Key to the success was the large amount of advertising secured because advertisers in one title would be included in all seven newspapers of the *Guardian* series. In this way Mackie averaged 900 adverts per week – while most of his competitors managed only 200. Joseph Cowen, who succeeded his father as the radical MP for Newcastle, adopted chain ownership to promote Liberal newspapers. Owner of the *Newcastle Chronicle*, Cowen was a rather eccentric character, who dressed similarly to the miners he employed – even when he was in the House of Commons. He turned the *Chronicle* into a mass-appeal morning paper, which gave a voice to the working people, but which also covered such pastimes as sport. With the biggest sports reporting team of its time, Cowen was criticized for his populist coverage by the then editor of the *Leeds Mercury*, Sir Edward Baines. However, by 1873 the *Chronicle* claimed a daily print run of more than 45,000 copies a day, compared with the *Manchester Guardian's* 30,000 and *The Times* of London's 60,000. It also championed causes at national and local levels, backing engineers fighting for a nine-hour working day and offering practical support through the ensuing nineteen-week strike. This operation ensured the *Chronicle's* survival where others fell. In his survey

---

[6] Warrington was also the home of Eddie Shah's *Messenger* series of newspapers. He was the first to invoke anti-union legislation introduced by Margaret Thatcher in a process explored in Chapter 7.

of papers of the north east, Milne charts how twenty-five newspapers were founded in Northumberland and Durham between 1855 and 1868; by 1868, nine had closed and by the turn of the century there were only eight.

Industrialization: Demarcation and news work

At the heart of the success of the *Newcastle Chronicle* was its organization, enacted by a demarcated, specialist staff working within established norms associated with newspaper production. As such its operation signals the increased maturity of the provincial newspaper as an industrial product, geared around both commercial logic and journalistic norms associated with content and production timetables. Its foundation was the dissemination of news, at local, national and international levels, collected and disseminated as quickly as possible. An infamous criminal was hanged at 8 am – the story hit the streets in a special edition timed at 10 am. In 1870 a reporter went to Canada to follow the exploits of some Tyne oarsmen; in 1873 they set up a London office with a special telegraph link to Newcastle to make sure they got the news they wanted. In 1974, when Cowen was elected as MP, he would send a daily letter to his readers informing them about Parliament. Accompanying this was the development of a rhetorical conceptualization of the role of the journalist as a professional, geared around the notion of the journalist as the guardian of the fourth estate.

In the early 1800s, Lee (1976) portrays the occupation of journalist as a lowly one, commanding poor salaries and little respect, largely due to the precarious nature of the business, and so the working life. Salaries were low when compared with other professions with an editor's salary similar to that of a clerk. In the provinces a reporter earned less than a bricklayer, although the former would have enjoyed a higher social status. It was this uncertainty which, Lee suggests, led many a journalist to drink. Black (2001) argues that the move to mass production necessitated a more sophisticated organization, which led to increasingly specialized roles, including business, foreign and parliamentary reporters, and the increased demarcation of production roles including the development of subediting. Therefore, in tandem with industrialization was the increasing segmentation of the provincial newspaper industry into demarcated roles as 'the task of gathering information outpaced the occupational structure' (Nerone and Barnhurst 2003: 437).

Therefore, in tandem with this demarcation is a shift in the status of journalism and the beginnings of what might tentatively be termed the professional journalist. Elliott charts one exemplar of an occupation's shift to a profession as being the ability of employees to make a living from it alone; at the beginning of the nineteenth century only a few high-profile editors could make a living from their newspaper work, and, indeed, the work of the journalist varied greatly in pay until the end of the century. However, the 'gentleman of the press' – and they were overwhelmingly men during this period – were increasingly able to draw on the prestige of the ideological position of the fourth estate to gain status through their occupation. This, despite the fact that some would sacrifice their principles for money, for instance by accepting bribes to keep information out of print. This increase in status was exemplified with the creation of professional bodies including, as previously discussed, the Provincial Newspaper Society in 1836; the National Association of Journalists in 1886, which gained a charter and became the Institute of Journalists in 1890, which controlled entry to the journalism and specified training, for instance shorthand; the Society for Women Journalists in 1894 (which was actually founded by man) and the National Union of Journalists in 1907.

The more poorly paid journalists of the provincial press could also enhance their earnings through 'linage', selling stories on to the London-based newspapers, often secretly to escape the approbation of proprietors (Elliott 1978: 172–4). However, technological developments, which meant papers could get news more quickly and could, in turn, get that news to their readers as fast as possible, contributed to its enhanced status as a sector. Among those in the vanguard of daily publications were the major cities including Manchester, Birmingham, Liverpool and Sheffield. In turn, the existence of these daily publications had implications for the non-daily provincial newspaper which had to compete without being able to publish news with the same frequency. The first daily titles were published in the mid-1850s, spurred by the abolition of Stamp Duty and the market for news about the Crimean War. The Manchester-based *Daily War Telegraph* was specifically aimed at this market, and other titles soon followed, including the *Manchester Daily Times* and the *Northern Daily Times* (Liverpool), none of which were very long lived (Milne n.d.: 21). During the 1880s the morning dailies were met with competition from the nascent daily evening press which became dominant by the middle of the decade (Lee 1976). The total number of provincial dailies continued to rise rapidly from 43 in 1868 to 121 in 1910. These numbers peaked at 172 in 1900, but the total decreased due to competition and amalgamation.

Steam power had been available to the printing process from 1814 onwards. This facilitated production at the rate of 2,500 copies an hour – fast enough to print a weekly paper's entire circulation under two hours – but its use was largely confined to major titles like *The Times* (Lee 1976). The real breakthrough in print speed came in the wake of the abolition of Stamp Duty with the introduction of the rotary press, which made use of paper on a roll rather than individually stamped sheets. By the 1870s this technique dominated newspaper productions. By the 1880s the cost of paper was reduced by its manufacture from wood pulp, rather than the cotton rags which had been used. This made newspapers more profitable. The provincial press was also in the vanguard of those using machines to improve composition – probably because these papers were not heavily unionized and so mechanization was not met with opposition. This was to pave the way for the highly successful Linotype machines which had been universally used by newspapers by the end of the century (Lee 1976).

Not only were these newspapers printing more copies, faster and more cheaply, they were also filling them with content gathered as quickly as possible. Lee contends that industrialization made speed an obsession for the Victorians, and newspaper proprietors were no different and that it was this aspect of production which made a mass press possible (1976: 59). The expansion of the railway network eased the transportation of news between the capital and the provinces, but it also enabled the London-based papers to be transported to the far reaches of the country, and by the 1870s special services had developed so the London press arrived in outlying areas by the afternoon. This may have been a driver for the expansion of the morning daily press in the provinces, as those copies had to hit the streets first in order to maintain their market share.

By 1870s the newspaper wholesaler had arrived – including the still extant W. H. Smith. This may have made distribution efficient, but Lee argues that they also had the potential to limit reader choice, for instance by their refusing to distribute halfpenny papers because newsagents thought that the profit margin was too slim. For this reason provincial newspapers also organized their own distribution methods, relying largely on cheap child labour – often the eponymous 'newsboy'. Copies reached rural areas via train and then milk cart, and cheaper papers were delivered to shops or sold by street sellers. To seal their competitive edge, the provincial newspaper industry exploited the advent of the newly nationalized telegraph and joined forces under the auspices of the Provincial Newspaper Society to create the Press Association in 1868 to ensure they received vital news – such as reports of parliamentary proceedings – as soon as possible, an innovation the society credited for sealing the industry's position in terms of growth and influence. Before the advent of the Press Association, only London and maybe two leading provincials carried full reports of Parliament, while the remainder carried summaries supplied by the pre-post office-owned telegraph companies themselves. In contrast, from the outset the Press Association sent out a full report of each sitting to up to sixty papers. This meant the reader of the local paper had a better service than those of the London papers, Whorlow contended, for 'in addition to strictly local intelligence – which is denied to readers of the metropolitan "dailies" – (he) finds a copious supply of every description of news which has been telegraphed during the previous 12 hours from all quarters of the globe' (1886: 103). Whorlow noted the impact of this on the rising number of titles so that 'the dwellers in provincial towns and rural districts are now in as close touch with current events as are the inhabitants of the metropolis' (1886: 84–5).

Alongside the rhetorical conceptualization of the role of the journalist as working in the public interest was the process by which the newspaper constituted itself as a 'civic institution'. As part of this process, newspapers began to inhabit landmark buildings so that their social status was seen to be central to the communities within which they placed themselves. In Reading the oldest title, the *Reading Mercury*, founded in the 1720s, inhabited the traditional heart of the town, the Market Place. By contrast, the *Reading Observer*, founded in 1873, made its headquarters in the up-and-coming part of town close to the County Hall and civic buildings, the library and museum. At the same time, the content of these titles was developing from the didactic towards the populist in order to accommodate the interests of a wider population. The usual fare of reports of local bodies, including councils and churches, was augmented by more titillating content, initially pioneered by the Sunday press, but gradually becoming the norm for many papers, including the cheaper halfpenny press. The *Shields Daily News*, founded in 1864 in North Shields, had an affirmed focus on local news – but it also included national and foreign coverage and focused on the bizarre and often gruesome aspects of news (Black 1987). Describing the development of the US newspaper, Nerone and Barnhurst have described this type of paper as adopting the 'master metaphor of the department store' which 'invited readers to browse through content organized in to departments – pages, then sections' (2003: 438). By the 1870s Lee also suggests that proprietors were diversifying the ways in which readers were targeted for advertising purposes, introducing features such as situations vacant. In an effort to maximize circulations, they were also attempting to make themselves as popular as possible by making innovations such as experimenting with formats and typefaces and carrying news on the front page (Black 1987: 7). What was not yet secured was the idea that these titles provided a diet of news about the local area. Studies of the *Preston Herald*, a biweekly newspaper serving north and north-east Lancashire, put local content – when defined as news of the town from which the paper is named – at around 25 per cent of total content. However, there could be as much as 35 per cent coverage of the surrounding area with non-local content amounting to between 10 and 38 per cent. Even this non-local content may well have originated from other provincial newspapers via the network of provincial reporters who supplied their copy to other newspapers and news agencies. Henry Lucy, for instance, became chief reporter of the *Shrewsbury Chronicle* in 1864 and was also the Shrewsbury correspondent for daily papers in London, Liverpool, Manchester, Birmingham, Sheffield and Leeds. Where one person owned more than paper, ready-made pages might also be shared, as in the case of William Saunders who owned papers in Plymouth, Hull and Newcastle and to whom he would distribute ready-made 'stereotyped' leaders (Hobbs 2009: 25–30).

Similarly, features would also move from paper to paper. This was true of specialist content aimed at women, and it is in this area that women as journalists make some inroads into the nineteenth-century provincial newspaper. Thus, 'a woman's letter to women' by Phillis Browne found its way from the *Liverpool Weekly Mercury* to the *South Wales Weekly*. It is acknowledged that there is little research into the role of women in the provincial press at this time, and early historians of the newspaper remarked on their presence as 'anomalous' (Onslow 2000). However, W. T. Stead predicted a rise in the profile for content aimed at women as newspapers sought new markets and the latter quarter of the century saw more specialist content aimed at women as the practice established in the United States crossed the Atlantic. In 1895 Stead foresaw that 'the Press of the Twentieth Century … will tend more and more to be homely, easy to read, commonplace, and full of pictures and stories. It will constantly seek to cater for fresh readers and for readers who will command advertisers. That is to say, it will tap the unreading ocean of womanhood' (Varty 2002: 3). It is likely that women produced this content for women – which encompassed such content as fashion, cookery, domestic 'economy', furniture, the 'toilet' and weddings –, not because men couldn't, but because they wouldn't. Personal connection played a part in women gaining employment in the provincial press, and until the 1930s, most women had worked as contributors or freelance correspondents. Because of less formal education and less knowledge about the workings of newspapers, women were also seen as 'amateurs' in comparison with male journalists. Writing in 1898, E. A. Bennett, editor of the magazine *Woman*, wrote:

> The female sex is prone to be inaccurate and careless of apparently trivial details because that is the general tendency of mankind. In men destined for business or a profession, the proclivity is harshly discouraged at an early stage. In women, who usually are not destined for anything whatever, it enjoys a merry life, and often refuses to be improved out of existence when the sudden need arises.

The answer was training, although that would not stop journalism being an 'exhausting' and 'disappointing' occupation (1898: 17).

The process of industrialization in effect created the market for more local content because it created more segmented and specialist provincial press. To differentiate themselves, the weeklies focused on targeted geographical areas, compared with the more regional reach of the dailies and more lurid content of the Sundays. Black suggests this segmentation enabled the weekly papers to become 'more truly local newspapers' in response to the more widely circulating, news-hungry, regional dailies. In turn the regional morning and evening papers invested in technology and staff to mirror the internal organization and developments of the London daily press. It was these similarities which made it easy for staff to move between provincial and metropolitan titles and so embedded what would be an established training route until the end of the twentieth century. The removal of personal ownership in favour of joint stock company enabled these industrial titles to position themselves as 'neutral' papers so they could maximize circulation and profit rather than to support the interests of a partisan owner. These 'neutral' titles could then be owned in chains, with elements of centralized production and control. In this way the market became stratified according to newspaper type, with a degree of homogenization aligned with each type in a development which would presage the dramatic shrinkage in the provincial press post 1918 (Lee 1978).

The good of the community and representation

The provincial press, then, may be said to have an ambivalent relationship with politics during this era, with ownership tied up with a desire for social status and financial success. As the business model changed and industrialized, so carving a strong position in a crowded market place entailed increasingly serving up for a mass market a varied diet of content and advertising, justified around the social function of a serving the public interest. News workers aligned themselves within the discourse of the fourth estate – a position which was refined by the provincial press to suit a localized market, and it is at this point that we begin to see the provincial press draw on the discursive position of serving the good of the community. This then marked a shift in the position of newspapers; at the outset of the nineteenth century, they were largely positioned within the overarching Victorian values of ministry and improvement. It is these values which informed the efforts of Robert Raikes Junior as he used his columns of the *Gloucester Journal* to promote the education of the working classes, and to ultimately found the Sunday School movement. Black contends that these 'paternalistic' newspapers promoted the values of 'polite society', justified by a position of moral improvement, and this informed a moderate position on many political questions. For instance, the *Leeds Mercury* supported factory legislation for children but not adults, opposed universal suffrage and defined reform as a way of advancing capitalism. Under Editor Christopher Kemplay, who took over in 1848, the Conservative-owned paper had increasingly focused on the 'social question' – roughly equating to improving the lives of the working population of Leeds. So in 1849 when the city was hit by a cholera epidemic, the newspaper campaigned for better sewage systems and housing and for the city to buy Woodhouse Moor as the 'lungs of Leeds'. He also co-founded the Society for Promoting Public Improvements in Leeds to clean up the city, which featured a 'casino', numerous beerhouses and was known as one of the dirtiest in the country.

These titles were owned by men of 'character' who sought to build and preserve their own social capital, along with the value of their businesses. As these men were significant members of their communities, their physical proximity with other businesses also cemented the relationship between newspaper and locality. The Provincial Newspaper Society's jubilee publication published in 1886 offers us a fascinating glimpse of those who owned the provincial newspapers during the first fifty years of its existence. Of the biographies of presidents offered, many were privately educated and involved in public life. Some were the latest in a line of newspaper men, suggesting an established link between newspapers and status. In 1886 the society's president was Peter Macliver, who, in addition to serving as MP, was a magistrate in Somerset. In 1851–2, the presidency was held by Henry Smith, editor of the *Cambridge Independent Press* for twenty-eight years. Educated at Bedford and Cambridge, he was a town councillor and alderman and eventually mayor of Cambridge. Similarly the president in 1849–50, Mr Bradshaw (no Christian name included), was both the editor and owner of the *Nottingham Journal*. A solicitor by profession, he bought into the paper in 1832, becoming sole proprietor and editor in 1841. Also a member of his town council, he wrote pamphlets, and passed the paper onto his sons in 1866 (Whorlow 1886). That the society campaigned for the rights of newspaper owners to be members of public bodies, including local councils and health boards, is testament to the value which the proprietors put in such positions (Black 2001: 102–3). By the end of the century, more than thirty newspaper proprietors had progressed to hold seats in Parliament; countless newspaper workers were involved in municipal affairs.

This shift has been theorized as marking a transition in the cultural position of the newspaper in relation to politics. Hampton (2004) conceptualizes this as a move away from the educative ideal of the newspaper described in the early parts of this chapter, towards one where the role of the newspaper was to represent the interests of the reader. This shift neutralized the didacticism of publications and instead enabled them to step aside from the political labels, at a time when these titles were increasingly refined for a commercial ideal. This, more than anything, curtailed the ability of the newspaper to inspire populations politically. Lee contends that as the nineteenth century drew to a close, the extension of the franchise by the 1884 Reform Act, after which two in three men could vote, meant papers were increasingly reflecting the views of voters rather than educating those who had no direct stake in the democratic purpose. However, equally Lee argues that the ability of the press to function as a fourth estate was compromised by the need to make money. In turn, Curran argues that this commercial, industrialized press was able to act as an agent of social control because its broad appeal 'emaciated and diluted the ideology of the earlier radical press to such an extent that it acquired a new and therapeutic value for the functioning of the social system' (1978: 71). As such, commercialization was more effective than taxation had ever been in stopping the spread of the radical 'unstamped' press.

Despite this, my analysis suggests that these twin drivers of representation and commercialism were not mutually exclusive but were part of a continuum in which politics was seen as a pillar of the business model of the newspaper because of the ideological value the association brought. As such, the titles continued to proclaim a political allegiance, even if it was, as they say, politics with a 'small p' rather than full-blown party political campaigning. Political stance was in this instance a position which could be employed in a variety of ways to construct and sustain a sound business model with allegiance just one instrument among many for formulating and attracting a readership. For the provincial press we can begin to trace a specific definition of politics which abandoned party labels in favour of local interest so that Asquith (1978) describes politics in the provincial press as a form of 'ministry' which influences opinion in local communities. O'Reilly (2014) has charted the way in which city titles covered the issues of the day – and municipal politics in particular – as a way of creating 'civic consciousness'. By doing so, these newspapers increasingly carved out their position as a local watchdog and promoted the interest of their areas. In Gloucester, Robert Raikes Jnr campaigned for conditions in the city prison; in Leeds, newspapers campaigned for parks; in Birmingham the *Post* worked with Chamberlain in a concerted effort to improve the public health of the city.

Thus increasingly political interest was stretched and sacrificed as it deployed for local benefit. For the Carlisle Conservative Newspaper Company, for instance, political position was best described as fluid. It was certainly no barrier to the development of the populist *East Cumberland News*, launched in 1890. However, that does not mean that this political structure was incidental or without use to the business model: specifically the clause which enabled directors to preclude shareholders on political grounds offered protection to the Carlisle papers which were able to resist acquisition by Rothermere's 'combine' in the early twentieth century. Further, correspondence held within the Cumbrian archives demonstrates that the Carlisle Conservative News Group was prepared to 'sell out' to Starmer's 'Liberal' *Northern Echo* rather than be subject to a hostile takeover by the acquisitive Rothermere. Similarly, when Charles Starmer rejected this approach, he did so not only on political grounds, but also because the price asked was too high. Despite the documented discussions with Starmer, it has remained one of the few newspaper publishers not to have been bought and sold in what has been a process of unremitting move to centralized ownership for the industry.

It is this fluidity, Curran (1978) argues, that enabled these papers to be 'therapeutic' to their communities – a role reinforced by the institutional role they created for themselves through such strategies as landmark buildings and involvement in staff in public life. They were equally able to draw on the increasing recognition of journalism as a practice in itself and, additionally, as a practice that was rising in status in some areas. This rising status was in no part due to the relationship with politics that the newspaper had been able to claim.[7] But as the nineteenth century waned, this position was in fact facilitated by a neutrality which enabled as broad an appeal as possible with a defined locale; additionally, this position was to the advantage of the business model by its potential inclusivity. As such we can see here the foundations of the notion of existing for the good of the community, which remains a professional notion for the provincial newspaper. It is this position which enabled the 'neutral' mass-produced local paper to create the monopolistic circulation patterns which typified the twentieth century.

---

[7] See a full discussion of this process in Conboy's *History of Journalism* (2004).

4

The Impact of 'New Journalism'

The emergence of 'news'

The paper consisted of four vast pages and its main use to its readers was the
supply of local news, especially the local shipping and business news. There
was no other morning paper in the town, and since in those days no workman
bought a penny morning paper, its readers consisted almost entirely of the local
business men and shopkeepers. Most of these, as I soon discovered, hated it,
for with few exceptions they were staunch Conservatives, and its politics were
advanced Radical. They took it because they had no option.

(Spender 1927: 34)

When J. A. Spender found himself at the helm of the *Eastern Morning News* in
Hull in October 1886, he realized that he was in charge of an ailing business.
The politics of the paper, owned by his uncle, campaigning Liberal William
Saunders, who also owned the Plymouth-based *Western Morning News*, was
alienating its readership. Nevertheless, they depended on it as the only source
of information about local commercial issues. Spender, aged just twenty-four,
dare not challenge his uncle's political position; instead he found the answer
by championing local causes so that 'he plunged head over ears into the local
dock and railway struggles' (ibid.: 36) and mapped the poverty of the city's
expansive slum areas. Spender, who enjoyed a brief spell as the assistant editor
of the metropolitan *Pall Mall Gazette* and a more successful tenure as editor
of the *Westminster Gazette*, was part of a rising tide of newspaper workers
who understood that profit did not lie in partisan allegiances. This prompted a
process by which the provincial press shifted from a product focused on political
information to one in which content and presentation were increasingly refined
for a local audience. This process has been understood within the context of
New Journalism, which describes innovation in the range of editorial content,
concomitant with the development of the presentation of news. The titles were

developing into sophisticated commercial products which superseded the political classifications described in Chapter 3.

New Journalism used here is the 'neutral description of social and political conflicts' as 'Journalistic routine', which is made possible by political and economic conditions in the United States from the 1860s. As such, it changes the position of newspapers and journalists in society, by shifting the emphasis on content from that that aimed at education or political influence to one focused on sales. It is no coincidence that New Journalism originated in the United States and the United Kingdom – the two countries where the press industrialized the fastest (Chalaby 1996). Therefore, the provincial newspaper described here was in the process of change, in terms of its relationship with the reader, and reasons for, and shape of, ownership, as it developed into a form in which the business of selling newspapers came to the fore.

This period saw a shift in the number of provincial newspapers, so that the market for readers became increasingly competitive, with titles competing within the same town not only with papers of the same form but also with other forms. In 1880, for instance, there were twelve towns with one morning paper, but nine towns had two, five had three and one had four morning titles all competing with each other. In the same year the number of towns with evening titles also grew rapidly so that twenty had one evening paper, eleven had two and five had three. Just six years later those same figures had increased so that twenty-five towns had one paper but sixteen had two. The figure was higher still in 1900 when thirty-six towns had one evening paper and twenty-one had two competing evening titles. At the same time there were still twenty-five towns with one morning newspaper and seven with two (Lee 1976: 288). This rapid increase in the number of daily titles in particular to 1900 was followed by a period of consolidation during which titles closed and amalgamated. In 1900 there were 70 provincial morning titles and 101 daily titles in England. By 1914 this had dropped to forty-two and seventy-seven respectively; this meant fourteen towns now had one morning newspaper and five had two, while thirty-two had one evening title and nineteen had two. The number of other, mainly weekly, papers, had remained largely stable at 1,304 and 1,326 (Lee 1978: 121). At the same time, the national news market saw the advent of the halfpenny *Daily Mail* in 1896, which sparked a bitter circulation war between rival titles. As such, provincial newspapers were operating in a highly competitive commercial environment with a reliance on advertising for profit to the extent that most titles had a London office to facilitate advertising business. Writing of this structure in

1893, Walter Wellsman, London manager of the Middlesborough-based *North Eastern Daily Gazette*, said: 'The necessity for advertising is now so obvious that to expatiate upon its advantages would be pure waste of time. … The Proprietors of successful Newspapers which are of the utmost use to advertisers are the most businesslike of men; they maintain their circulations and the importance of their Newspapers by the exercise of constant care and forethought.' These titles could also yield substantial revenues, for instance the *Liverpool Daily Post* reported a profit of more than £40,000 a year between 1900 and 1905 (Lee 1976: 174).

This increasingly commercial context also marked a watershed in terms of the emergence of key professional conventions for editorial workers within the provincial press, including objectivity – or perhaps more accurately of the associated notions of impartiality and fairness – and the inverted pyramid style of news presentation, which has come to define, and normalize, the practice of the journalist (although in its own turn it is now changing with the online development of more open and long-form narratives for telling stories). These values in turn informed and influenced other aspects of journalism practice, such as presentation and content, to produce the style of newspaper which becomes known as 'New Journalism'. The emergence of these professional conventions, which persist within the industry today, can therefore be mapped against the development of the provincial newspaper as a highly industrialized product. This process of stylistic development has been theorized as the emergence of the 'news paradigm' by Hoyer and Pottker (2005), who focus on the development of the norms which govern how news is produced in order to track changes in those norms. Therefore, they can track values which underpin those norms to interrogate the cultural position of journalism. The decisions journalists employ when they produce news are governed by this paradigm, which itself consists of five elements: the event, news values, the news interview, the narrative structure of the inverted pyramid and journalistic objectivity. The adoption of these practices varies as these professional norms are 'diffused' between practitioners in different contexts.

The rise of the techniques of New Journalism in America has been attributed variously to technological (the telegraph), social (the increased need for speedy, telegraphed news caused by the American Civil War in the 1860s) and economic (the need to sell more papers) reasons.[1] Pottker (2005) argues that

---

[1] These differing hypotheses are contested and debated in detail in Hoyer and Pottker's *The Diffusion of the News Paradigm, 1850-2000*.

the timing of the emergence of the convention of the news pyramid in the New York press makes it too late to be wholly influenced by technology and, significantly, more likely to be as a result of journalists working to improve the communicative quality of their work. What seems certain is that the impact of New Journalism in America was widespread and significant as increasingly competitive newspapers focused on speed, news and scoops in their fight for domination in what Wiener described as a 'creative frenzy' of newspaper development (1994: 63). Additional defining characteristics of the new form of newspaper writing included the interview and human-interest story, adding up to a 'democracy of print', which signalled a broadening of culture as well as growth of information. Though it is hard to chart exactly the shift of influence from one side of the Atlantic to the other, Wiener does find evidence of a journalistic 'brain-drain' which saw US journalists move to Britain as well as UK-based journalists spending time abroad in order to brush up on modern techniques (1994: 70).

Therefore, the development of New Journalism by the provincial press in England was not sudden but was a gradual process as journalists in different environments adopted these techniques as they became 'the norm'. J. A. Spender arrived at an *Eastern Morning News* where local news was 'disposed of' so that attention could be paid to 'high politics': 'The London letter came in a parcel by train about eleven and was supplemented by late paragraphs which were telegraphed. But our chief material was reports of public speeches, which poured in a detestable "flimsy"' (1927: 36). The journalist's job was to either supply the speeches on thin chemically treated sheets of tissue paper – the 'flimsy' – which were interleaved with carbon sheets to enable reproduction – or to handle them at the newspaper end, editing and emphasizing accordingly. While they may have been cut to fit, the speeches were not rewritten or fashioned into narrative but reproduced verbatim. However, as newspaper content developed, the news report replaced the recount; this fashioned information into a specialist form of communication, produced by an increasingly 'impartial' journalist, perhaps writing sensationalized 'eye-witness' accounts of events in order to attract as many readers as possible. In line with this, both the content and design of newspapers changed; features, such as gardening, gossip and 'ladies' pages, were introduced as were larger, bolder headlines and illustrations to replace the 'tombstone' layout of monotonous column inches.

The development of news presentation as a sales technique

These changes in newspaper content were contextualized by the prioritization of norms – including the shape of ownership – which favoured the industrialized process of newspaper production. This decline is exemplified by the operation of the newspapers associated with the Rowntrees, which were initially funded in support of the Liberal cause. At their zenith the Joseph Rowntree Social Service Trust and fellow Liberal newspaper group, Starmer's North of England Newspaper Company, owned more than twenty morning and evening titles including the *Birmingham Gazette, Yorkshire Observer, Northern Echo* and *Nottingham Journal.* The subsidies were considerable; having paid £5,000 for the Darlington-based *Northern Echo*, the trust subsidized the title to the tune of around £66,000 between 1904 and 1939 – most of which was spent before 1918, despite a rise in circulation from 30,000 to 80,000 during the course of the First World War (Gliddon 2003). The titles were to form the basis for the Westminster Press newspaper company created in 1921, but only after a 'massive' £250,000 investment from Weetman Pearson, Viscount Cowdray, a Liberal politician and highly successful businessman, who had amassed a considerable fortune from construction.[2] It was named after the *Westminster Gazette,* which was part of the original group; in 1928 the loss-making title was merged with the *Daily News,* and the resulting share interest was later sold to the News Chronicle so that the Westminster Press had no London-based holdings. The group paid its first dividend to shareholders in 1935 – only after the *Westminster Gazette* had been closed and the number of titles rationalized with the sale of the Sheffield Independent Company in 1931 to Allied Newspapers.[3]

Gliddon suggests that political subsidy was abandoned as a strategy when profit-making newspapers failed to realize political success; in an echo of Grant's analysis, discussed in Chapter 3, political titles were not always aligned with the political representation of an area, and Dawson's (1998) study of the ownership

---

[2] The group took its name from the *Westminster Gazette* which was part of the original group. It was merged with the *Daily News* in 1928 and the resulting share interest was later sold to the *News Chronicle* so that the group had no London-based holdings.

[3] Allied Newspapers was formed in 1924 by the Berry brothers, Lord Kemsley and Viscount Camrose, and Lord Iliffe. It originally comprised of the Hulton papers sold to them by Lord Rothermere but went on to acquire a range of provincial titles in Britain. In 1928 the group acquired the *Daily Telegraph*. In 1937 the company was split up with the provincial papers going to Lord Kemsley, to be held by a company of the same name.

of newspapers in the south west of England concludes that influence was at best 'subtle'. Similarly, it seems that the profitability of these titles had as much to do with the prevailing economics of newspaper ownership – which demanded increased investment to fund industrial production methods – as with politics, so that the structure and nature of ownership was altered. Therefore, profitability was just as important as influence, and this emphasis was to change the very nature of newspaper content as economic factors increasingly disrupted the concept of the newspaper as a political organ.

For Pottker (2005) this commercial context is a key driver in the development of the use of the inverted pyramid[4] as a norm for the presentation of information in newspapers. His compelling contention is that it developed as a journalistic technique employed by an increasingly specialist staff to improve the ability of papers to reach readers – and so increase sales. Pottker argues that its emergence is based on a convention, whereby journalists prioritize what they see as the most important information, which became prevalent in US journalism from 1875 and was established practice twenty years later. Concomitant with the rise of the inverted pyramid were other changes in newspapers, including the inclusion of more, shorter stories; the use of headlines and illustrations and the clearer organization of news into defined sections. These techniques improved the 'communicative' power of the news story and enhanced the commercial position of the newspaper. At the same time, the production values enabled newspapers to be produced more quickly and efficiently, enhancing their ability to be timely – and the capacity for increased sales.

The emergence of New Journalism is then, as a watershed in the development of journalism, marking the shift between the pre-modern and modern newspaper. Both commercial and linguistic characteristics change as a definable 'news discourse' emerges, characterized by factual reporting of news, rather than its being attributed to a third party, and an identifiable newspaper style, which has become known as the inverted pyramid, to structure news content. Matheson (2000) charts the evolution of this process over a fifty-year period from 1880 (with the birth of the halfpenny evening

---

[4] The inverted pyramid is a narrative structure, usually for the hard news story, whereby the key information (the fives Ws) is included at the top. This makes it easier to read – and to subedit – as the least important information can simply be cut from the bottom.

papers in London), but argues that it forms a cohesive historical period for newspapers not only because of technological and economic changes, but also because of discursive developments. Journalists frame information within the context of the newspaper story by editing, summarizing and contextualizing – and thereby creating the modern news story as information in itself rather than the representation of information disseminated by a third party. The newspaper develops from a mere transmitter of information to become a 'communicative event'.

Typical of this shift is the collection of connected events into one story – as exemplified by the reports of a night of storms in 1895. The *Yorkshire Post* brought together disparate paragraphs on the events into one story, rather than leaving it to readers to make links between paragraphs distributed about the pages as they arrive. The report of the Great Thunderstorm fills more than a column on page four of the edition of Thursday, 27 June 1895, and is signposted with headline and two sub-decks – including the dramatic 'Visitors to the Royal Show killed by lightening'. The varying reports of the effects of the storm in the region were unified by the top introductory paragraph.

> The sultry weather which has been experienced during the past few days gave place yesterday to a violent and prolonged thunderstorm, which was experienced over the whole country and also in Ireland. Great damage was done to crops by the heavy rain and hail, and many buildings were struck by lightning and damaged. Unfortunately this is not the full tale of disaster, for at least four lives have been sacrificed. ... A detailed account of the painful incident will be found in our report of the Royal Show in another column. Another dreadful occurrence is reported from Normanton. ... Reports from Halifax, Sheffield, Hull and other centres show that in those places the full violence of the storm was experienced. (*Yorkshire Post*, 27 June 1895: 4)

This new 'egalitarian' mode of writing, which moved away from the conventions of reporting authority, was increasingly recognized as a specialist way of presenting information as news, which emerged during the evolution of the mass-circulation newspaper. Critically it differentiated between opinion and fact and so paved the way for the provincial newspaper to become a mass-circulation product because it enabled information to be presented as independent and impartial. The inverted pyramid emphasized the presentation of information as 'factual' and, therefore, and more contentiously, 'objective'. Chalaby notes that as early as 1858, British journalists prized 'accuracy' above all else in relation to the information they published (1996: 305). However, while objectivity has been prized by US journalists, and has formed part of their professional codes, in Britain, we might more usefully look at connected terms such as 'fairness' and 'impartiality', and Hampton argues that UK journalists are happy to present 'the facts' from a partisan point of view (Hampton 2008). Writing his *Handbook of Instruction and Counsel for the Young Journalist* in 1894, John Mackie put independence above all other qualities for the reporter. 'He must never permit private and personal interests to warp his judgment or affect his impartiality. … As a reporter, he is expected to take no side, to keep out of all party contention though he may be surrounded by it on all hands, and to be always, and above everything, strictly loyal to fact and fair play.' Significantly for Mackie, this impartiality extended to political reporting: 'He fails conspicuously in his professional conduct who fails to extend a fair and full hearing to opponents,' he said, for it was this which would bring 'financial stability'.[5]

The influence of New Journalism on content and production

Alfred Harmsworth is widely credited with modernizing the newspaper with his innovative approach to both owning and editing the *Daily Mail*. Both Chalaby (2000) and Conboy (2004) argue that Harmsworth's journalism became less partisan and more anodyne in a bid to attract as many readers as possible. Thus New Journalism was a product of the commercial logic, manifest in a new-look newspaper both in terms of content, such as an increased emphasis on human-interest stories, sport, crime and entertainment, and layout with the inclusion of headlines and illustrations.[6] This analysis has already charted the increasingly

---

[5] For Schudson (2005) it is the self-articulation of the importance of these values which cements their normative influence on the profession. He posits that objectivity had not been established as a professional norm in US journalism until the 1920s. For objectivity to have the status of moral obligation on the journalistic profession, it is necessary that there is more than just news which appears to be presented in an objective way; what is needed to cement that status is both a moral imperative saying you must produce objective news and the accompanying condemnation when you do not measure up to that professional standard. So, while the profession began to champion 'fact-based' reporting from the 1870s – typified by interviews and the inverted pyramid – it was not until after the First World War that the profession began to debate and adopt the notion of objectivity, including it in codes and text books (Schudson, 2005: 29).

[6] Conboy defines the characteristics of New Journalism as including changing layout, such as using crossheads, shorter paragraphs, larger headlines and more illustrations; news on the front page, encouraged by evening papers which were hawked on the street and on news stands and so needed a visible 'sell'; changing content, such as stop press and parliamentary sketches which replaced the lengthy verbatim reports; and more emphasis on news, as opposed to comment, often presented in short snippets and not contextualized by explanation (2004: 121).

ambivalent relationship between politics and provincial newspapers, which sought commercial success in a crowded market place. Baylen (1972) goes so far as to argue that the roots of New Journalism can be found in the regional press with the campaigning style of W. T. Stead, then editor of the *Northern Echo*. Stead became editor of the Liberal title in 1871, despite being only twenty-two, having already established a relationship with the editor of the title, Jonathan Copleston. Stead had at first been unpaid by the *Echo*, which, as a new paper with a small staff, was grateful for additional help. It was Copleston though who persuaded Stead into journalism by telling him he could use it as a vehicle for furthering his reformist beliefs. As an editor, employed for £150 a year, Stead set about improving the *Northern Echo*, 'giving it a sense of purpose and urgency, which most of the British daily press lacked, and made it one of the most readable newspapers in Britain' (Baylen 1972). Stead's success was part 'brilliant timing' and part acute journalistic perspicuity; he focused on reformist and popular causes and told them via the lenses of people, telling one young reporter that 'nothing that is human is foreign to the press'. The causes he supported were both at home and abroad and nothing seemed out of bounds. One successful campaign he backed was the repeal of the Contagious Diseases Act, which sought to curb the prevalence of sexually transmitted infections among military personnel by confining prostitutes. Considered an unsuitable topic for papers by some, Stead published a typically forthright editorial on 18 July 1876, urging 'north country' members of Parliament to support the repeal of what he termed 'immoral legislation', because it 'violated the liberties of half the human race'. A month later in August he launched another campaign – this time calling for action in the wake of the 'Bulgarian Horrors', which gained national prominence after Liberal politician and former prime minister William Ewart Gladstone highlighted the massacre of 15,000 Bulgarians – many of them women and children – by the Ottomon Empire. In addition to an editorial outlining reaction in the north, Stead included a lengthy and detailed eyewitness account of the discovery of the attack at Batak, which, he said, was enough 'to make the blood run cold'.

The *Northern Echo* of this era was also a highly readable paper in terms of its production values. When it was founded in 1870, Milne (n.d.) describes it as a 'fairly small' (17-and-a-half by 15 inches), four-page halfpenny paper. Content was shared between an average of ten columns of adverts, two columns each for editorials and commercial information and ten for news. There was hardly any feature content and just half a column of sport in the form of racing tips.

By 1873 Stead had managed to extend the page depth by an additional three-and-a-half inches. The space brought additional adverts and increased revenue so a London office could be opened. After four years as editor, Stead had built a circulation of 13,000; by 1877, it had grown again to 15,000 and the paper had invested in a new press capable of producing 40,000 impressions an hour. Milne suggests that while Stead was ambitious in his copy, his design remained largely conservative while at the *Echo*. However, extant copies reveal a quality paper and evidence small flourishes which are perhaps precursors to his later innovations, including, for instance, the use of a ship imprint as a decoration for shipping news.

Stead, who trained Harmsworth, extended this style during this time as editor of the metropolitan *Pall Mall Gazette*, which saw him take up moral crusades, often in an 'indisputably sensational and often prurient manner' (Lee 1976: 125). These causes enabled him to reproduce testimony and eyewitness accounts from those in the thick of the controversy. This was demonstrated by his notorious Maiden Tribute campaign against child prostitution – during which he procured a child virgin, an action which ultimately led to his imprisonment – in the course of which he included interviews with key players in the story. At this time the interview was considered an innovative approach to journalism; yet Stead was sure enough of his audience to include testimony amounting to a thousand words or more. Just as he had drawn on first-hand accounts of the atrocities in Bulgaria, in the Maiden Tribute, Stead published the personal testimony from those involved in prostitution; in this way the voices of brothel keepers, procurers and prostitutes were all brought to the readers of the respectable title. And all this at a time when interviewing itself was seen as a highly controversial practice, verging as it did, on the intrusive, and transgressing socially entrenched norms to do with challenging authority because rather than accepting what was said, journalists would ask questions and investigate. Stead's experimentation with content was extended to innovations in layout, including the use of cross heads in headlines, characteristics which earned the moniker New Journalism. His use of voyeuristic headlines, such as the The Violation of Virgins, further served to sensationalize the subject matter being presented.

Stead's legacy, argues Lee (ibid.), was a style which was a commercial success 'when free of the political mill-stones with which Stead had sought to encumber it'. Ornebring (2006: 8) argues that Stead's innovation was to bring the attributes of the popular press – including more sport, sensation and 'entertaining' content, written in a straight-forward style – to the 'respectable'

Pall Mall Gazette. But his innovations were far from universally acclaimed, and prominent among those to attack his approach was Matthew Arnold, who is said to have coined the term New Journalism in an article criticizing Stead in 1887 (Marzolf 1984: 530). Nevertheless, it seems likely that the adoption of New Journalism by national titles would have presented challenges for the regional press and probably encouraged them to adopt the emerging characteristics of the popular press. Andrew Walker (2006a) suggests that it had the effect of slowing the growth of the provincial press in terms of circulations as the new popular national titles presented themselves as economic rivals. As a result, these provincial titles adopted not only new ways of presenting information, but also a much wider range of content, in order to preserve their market share.

This analysis has demonstrated that provincial newspapers had always included coverage of sensational content in their columns; early titles in the eighteenth century had covered notorious trials, and had even supplied detailed accounts as separate publications in pamphlet form during the era of Stamp Duty, perhaps building on the tradition of the chapbook. High-profile Victorian cases such as that of Jack the Ripper, therefore, contributed to the creation of an appetite for more salacious content in the reader – something which was largely exploited by the more populist Sunday press but which can be found across the range of provincial newspapers of this time. Benson (2009) draws on the coverage by the *Wolverhampton Express and Star* of the arrest, prosecution and acquittal of a well-known local businessman Edward Lawrence for the murder of his mistress to demonstrate that it was not just the metropolitan titles which exploited the techniques of New Journalism. He classifies the *Express and Star* as a 'typical', local daily paper of its time, and it was undoubtedly successful; by the advent of the twentieth century, it had a daily circulation of more than 40,000. What Benson finds atypical – or at least surprising – is the extent to which the *Express and Star* deployed the discursive strategies of New Journalism, at that time considered the preserve of the popular press. The court reports concerning Edward Lawrence draw out the human-interest angle taken on these stories, and it is clear that flamboyant reporting of personal details was a key feature of the coverage. It also moved away from a verbatim report of the court proceedings and put the reader on the spot, relating scene-setting details, including that the defendant was 'attired in a smart brown costume, with a chic picture hat of the same shade' (*Express and Star*, 1 February 1907). As such, the court case humanized the characters within it, portraying them as 'individuals in whom their readers would be interested' (Benson 2009: 839).

The story of the origins of the *Express and Star* resembles the origins of such newspapers from Chapter 3 – rooted, as it was, in political partisanship. It was founded by Scottish-born Thomas Graham with the backing of multimillionaire industrialist Andrew Carnegie, who owed his fortune to the American steel industry. Graham, who had made his money curing bacon and who had already been active in civic life, holding the posts of magistrate and town councillor, supposedly met Carnegie on a train in the 1870s. Carnegie aspired to owning a chain of Liberal titles in Britain, and twenty years after their first meeting, the pair realized their dream of opening a reformist title in the industrial heart of the Midlands. They bought the *Evening Star* with partner Samuel Storey – the Liberal MP who founded the *Sunderland Echo* in 1873. They created the Midland News Association with shareholders to raise funds and in 1884 bought the Conservative-leaning *Evening Express* for £20,000; the two titles were merged by July to form the *Express and Star*.

Carnegie withdrew from the title in 1902, by which time, Graham had been striving to be commercially successful. In particular, Graham had set his sights on being first with the sports news, and employed imaginative tactics to be so, for instance, by employing carrier pigeon to bring back results. He booked a phone line to ensure communication of the results of the 1908 FA Cup between Wolverhampton Wanderers and Newcastle United played at Crystal Palace. The *Express and Star* was also among the first provincial papers to produce a special sports edition – called the 'green 'un' because of the colour of the paper it used. By 1910 the paper was probably selling around 60,000 copies a day – despite competition from papers in Birmingham and beyond (Rhodes 1992). The first audited figures in 1927 attested to a sale of more than 74,000. This philosophy of giving readers what they wanted was later honed by Thomas's grandson, Malcolm, who joined the business and learnt on the job. Malcolm Graham introduced pictures – even becoming a photographer himself – and set up a library and by March 1927 the staff included 25 editorial personnel out of a total of 121.

The adoption of New Journalism by the British newspaper has been linked with its foundations in America. Both Graham and Stead shared direct contact with transatlantic newspaper practice, where an emphasis on speed, informality, human interest and the use of interview to question had led to an increased focus on the newspaper as an active – if popular – voice in the democratic process

(Weiner 1994). The path between America and Britain was a well-trodden one for journalists – and indeed the nature of international news itself depended on the employment of British-based journalists as 'stringers' for the US papers or depended on US nationals, who worked as London-based correspondents. Alternatively, British-trained journalists would find themselves working in US titles. The *Daily Express* was originally founded as the halfpenny *Morning* in 1892 with an American editor, Chester Ives, who introduced such 'un-English features' (ibid.: 73) as news on the front page. Although Stead had not physically visited America until the 1890s, he corresponded with a variety of practitioners, and the Maiden Tribute affair was closely followed across the Atlantic, usually reported in the international news columns.[7] Similarly, the US-based Carnegie would correspond with Thomas Graham about the form of the nascent *Express and Star*. Later, Graham's grandson Malcolm would travel to Montreal to learn the profession of journalism. Ironically perhaps, Stead was lost with the *Titanic* as it travelled from Southampton to New York in 1912.

The provincial newspaper was also extending the range of content included in its columns; specialist interest such as gardening became more common place alongside what called be termed 'feature' content. Children were also targeted in an extensive programme, which extended beyond content to societies and networks, which solidified the attachment of reader to title. The Dicky Bird Society, set up by the *Newcastle Weekly Chronicle* in 1876, built up a membership of 50,000 in five years. Others followed suit, including in the 1880s the Sunbeam Society in the Dundee *People's Journal*, Golden Circles in the *Leeds Times* and *Northern Weekly Leader* and a Kind-Hearted Brigade in the *Sheffield Weekly Telegraph*. In the next two decades societies were opened by newspapers in Birmingham, Cardiff, Nottingham, Portsmouth, Hull and Bristol, so that by 1914, forty-three newspapers had started societies. The aim was, the *Bradford Weekly Telegraph* said, to 'meet the tastes of the widest circle of readers' (Milton 2009).

The coverage of sport was to be a key area of development for the provincial press, used to promote 'localness', and so differentiate between the popular national press and provincial publications, but also as a marketing strategy with the development of specialist sporting supplements. Not unsurprisingly, sport was most widely covered in urban areas where established teams thrived,

---

[7] Nerone and Barnhurst (2012) suggest that the US fascination with Stead was part of a wider flow of reformist thinkers between the continents; at a time when the US press was also striving for political independence, Stead signified the possibility of 'Government by Journalism' (ibid.: 110).

especially in the area of football, which saw gates of up to 20,000 a week. Typical of this was the approach by the *Sheffield Telegraph*; with two teams, Sheffield Wednesday and Sheffield United, in the league from 1895, the paper's coverage was diverse ranging from match reports to expert comments from the pundit 'Looker-on', photographs, cartoons and features. So important was sport deemed to be that by 1907 this had developed into a specialist sporting newspaper, the *Green 'Un*, which boasted a circulation of up to 120,000 (Jackson 2009: 73). Walker notes that sports coverage also grew, albeit on a smaller scale, in rural papers between 1870 and 1914; his analysis of newspapers in Lincolnshire shows how sports coverage focused on the local and grew from items in the news columns to a dedicated section of publications. In this way it not only reflected the increased leisure time of newspaper readers, and the growth in amateur sports, especially football, but it also served to promote local pride and, ultimately, a sense of local community (Walker 2006b: 458–9). Lee (1976) also cites contemporary reports from the turn of the twentieth century, which proclaimed the sporting press to be the reading matter of choice for the working classes in Lancashire.

New Journalism and the *Midland Daily Telegraph*

This evolution of newspaper practice was neither equal nor sudden, but a gradual process of transmission between people, techniques and production processes. The characteristics of the developing newspaper, including the writing style and layout, were, therefore, linked to other facts including its commercial positioning and the changing practice of journalism itself. An analysis of the content of the *Midland Daily Telegraph*, the forerunner to the still extant *Coventry Telegraph*, suggests that, at this time, this paper was increasingly constructing a special relationship with the reader as a community member, which would help the provincial press mark out its unique selling point when set against the national press. An analysis of the presentation of news stories in terms of the extent to which they adhere to the inverted pyramid demonstrates that this aspect– and others – of New Journalism gained prominence within this newspaper within the comparatively defined period of 1895–1905. Contextualizing this process within a wider analysis of the development of newspaper content and layout (including advertising, inclusion of features and sport, and organization and labelling of that content) reveals those factors which may influence, and be influenced by this process – including ownership, competition and commercialization, and the professional values of those working in these newspapers.

The *Midland Daily Telegraph* was founded by William Iliffe, and Henry Sturmey (of bicycle brake fame) in 1885 in Coventry. Iliffe was the son of a bookseller and printer, based in Hertford Street – the home of the paper until the Second World War. In 1879 he launched *The Cyclist* at a time when Coventry was at the heart of the cycling industry and bought *Bicycling News* in 1885. In 1879 Iliffe bought the weekly *Coventry Times*, and in 1891 he expanded into daily newspapers, launching the *Midland Daily Telegraph* with £2,500. With a population of around 52,000, Coventry was a competitive newspaper market, served by five papers (the Coventry *Standard*, the *Coventry Herald*, *Coventry Reporter*, the *Coventry Times* and the daily *Birmingham Evening Mail* which circulated in Coventry). Iliffe set himself apart from the competition with a dedicated evening paper for the city, and the *Midland Daily Telegraph* was first issued on 9 February 1891. By 1905 (the first year for which figures are available), circulation was put at 10,000. The *Midland Daily Telegraph* cost a halfpenny, which put it firmly in the camp of the 'popular', mass-market evening paper. As such, sport was a significant factor in the newspaper, and a specialist 'pink' sports paper was launched in July 1891 in addition to an extra 8.00 pm sports edition on Saturdays (Rhodes 1981).

The development of modern news techniques can be seen via an analysis of the title between 1895 and 1905. Four editions were published each day; this analysis concentrated on the final edition of the newspapers from the first week of February in each year. For most of this time, the paper was set across seven columns until a new press in 1904 enabled it to be set across eight columns. By studying the few still extant copies of the paper at the Coventry History Centre, it has been possible to ascertain that the paper was first 20 inches by 24 inches, with each of the seven columns measuring 2.5 inches (*MDT*, 1 February 1899). At some point, the paper then increased in size slightly to 22 inches by 26 and ¼ inches (*MDT*, 5 July 1910).

The newspaper of 1 February 1985 was typical of most titles at this time by carrying display adverts on the front page (see Figure 4.1). More than four columns of adverts were carried on page two and non-advertising content – the editorial comment in this instance of the Queen's speech on the occasion of the opening of Parliament – first appeared on the fifth column. There were no illustrations in the paper, although typography was sometimes used to simple illustrative effect. Page three was the main news page, headed Latest News

Figure 4.1 *Midland Daily Telegraph*, 1 February 1895, p. 1. Newspaper Image © The British Library Board. All rights reserved. With thanks to The British Newspaper Archive (www.BritishNewspaperArchive.co.uk).

and This Day's News, which included national and international content. Of note was the length of all the stories – all one paragraph – most had a separate headline and many concerned crime and court reports. Sources were sometimes acknowledged, such as the report of an escaped lion, supplied by a telegram from Dalziel's international news agency, which had a reputation for sensational stories. These items were presented in a most recognizable 'news' style, and it has been suggested that telegraphed news was the reason why such a style became widespread, although criticized (see Hoyer and Pottker 2005).

The first, and therefore the most prominent, news item (the equivalent of a modern front-page lead) was about a shipwreck which was first covered in the previous day's paper. The second lead was the weather (there was widespread snow) with a national angle (a death in London), and the death itself was not mentioned until the fifth paragraph (*MDT*, 1 February 1895: 3). Page three included more local content, headed 'District news' shared between news, social (a ball at nearby Warwick Castle) and sport. This was a paper which was using a range of content to target a mass audience; the wide variety of content presented in this one issue ranged between national and local politics, court reports – both criminal and inquests – police reports, fires, international, national and local sport, serializations, agricultural market prices and local share prices, comment, and a wide array of display and classified adverts.

Typical of the type of story favoured was the report of an affair between a married man and teenaged servant, a tale which combined a prurient interest with criminal proceedings and which was placed under a four-deck headline to give it prominence.

THE ALLEGED BEDWORTH

ELOPEMENT.

A CHRISTMAS HOLIDAY.

PRISONERS BEFORE THE MAGISTRATES.

A young man and woman left Bedworth about a month ago under circumstances which created a good deal of stir in the little mining town. There was considerable interest taken in the case when the couple were brought before the county magistrates sitting at Coventry this morning. (*MDT*, 1 February 1995: 2)

Within one title there was also a noticeable difference in reporting styles between local news and telegraphed items; this suggests a profession in development and one which not yet has a unified 'house style' which governs presentation across all pages. The 'Bedworth Elopement' was reported chronologically, after the style of the court hearing rather than according to the conventions of the inverted pyramid; similarly, its very inclusion was justified on the grounds that it caused 'considerable interest'. The paper also justified its use of the interview, which was still emerging as a form of journalism practice at this time and which provoked controversy in terms of the extent to which questions could probe their subjects. Its use in this edition of the paper was in fact for advertising purposes, as a testimonial for Dr Williams' Pink Pills (*MDT,* 1 February 1895: 4). This inclusion of advertising copy in the editorial columns was common practice at this time for newspapers with such snippets as 'Venus Soap washes white and pure, all fabrics, Venus soap saves rubbing' used to fill column inches (*MDT,* 1 February 1895: 3). The next day the interview was used in an editorial section, but was self-consciously referenced by the journalist who used it.

> Tramps seem to me becoming more numerous on the Queen's highway. Whatever doubts I may have had on the point were dispelled in the course of an accidental 'interview' I had the other day with 'one o'the'reg'lare perfession' as he admitted himself to be. (*MDT,* 2 February 1895: 2)

Local content was also growing in prominence during this period, and by 1897 the *Midland Daily Telegraph* was organizing and labelling its editorial copy to signify its relationship with its circulation area. Page two saw the introduction of reader's letters and Coventry increasingly appeared in headlines. This was coupled with changes in layout to improve readability, so that headlines got bigger and more white space was used. Dr Williams Pink Pills was now promoted via a display advert. The main story in the edition of 1 February 1897 was a sensational local report of a fire at Foleshill (a district of Coventry). The headline has five decks and the story is split with dramatic sub-decks including 'Enveloped in Flames' and 'His Wife Arrested'. In the paper of 1 February 1899, even the Latest News lead story on page three concerned a Coventry story – that of a local man found dead in Northampton. Innovatively this paper also included the advent of a 'late news' space in the fourth column, 'reserved for news received after going to press' – in this instance carrying a sole football result (*MDT,* 1 February 1899: 3).

Alongside local content was an increased variety of specialist interest content, such as gardening, not least of which was sport. In Friday's edition of the paper (*MDT,* 5 February 1897), a literary serialization gave way to previews of the next day's sport, and in the final edition of Saturday's paper all of page three was dedicated to sporting news. This focus on sport was clearly an editorial and commercial priority for the *Midland Daily Telegraph*. By 1898 the paper had been heavily promoting its 'football edition' and proclaiming its role as the foremost paper for local and national sporting news. It also seems likely that the paper had started to sponsor a local football league with the promotion of the Telegraph Cup Ties (*MDT*, 1 February 1898: 2). This use of sport was featured alongside other sales strategies within the titles' own columns; included was a coupon for readers to have their photographs taken in the form of *Midland Daily Telegraph* 'craotint' portraits (*MDT*, 1 February 1898: 2).

A key event, the death of Queen Victoria, in 1901, shows an increased correlation between the writing styles of telegraphed copy and that produced by the staff of the Coventry title. The death of the monarch was actually reported in the papers of Tuesday, 22 January and Wednesday, 23 January in editions featuring the traditional black gutters as a mark of respect. However, more interesting for the purpose of emerging reporting styles was the edition of February 1901, which featured extensive reports of the funeral itself drawn from national and local sources, which are presented in similar styles. Thus we have a report of scenes in London – 'The City of the Empire wore a weird aspect this morning at a time when the whole of another busy day is usually inaugurated. Of business life there was no sign. Shops that usually drove a thriving trade before breakfast remained firmly closed. The early wagons and market carts were conspicuously absent' (*MDT*, 2 February 1901: 3). Turning to the reports of the scenes in Coventry, which, one supposes, could only have been provided by staff reporters, the copy reads:

> The day in Coventry was indeed of a gloomy character. Following a light fall of snow during the early morning covering the face of the city with a white pall the aspect changed, with falling sleet, giving a muddy, somber appearance to the streets. The closing of the business houses and factories was general. Flags were at half-mast upon the churches and public buildings, while the mourning boards of the shopkeepers and drawn blinds at private houses testified to the local share in the national grief. (*MDT*, 2 February 1901: 3)

This convergence of writing styles can be seen in other local stories in the *Midland Daily Telegraph*. It is also notable that in tandem with this development in writing was the increase in the proportion of space to dedicated adverts, which grew to take up nearly all of page four. These adverts were varied, including a striking advert for Veno's Lightening Cough Cure and large display advert set across four columns for Ogden's cigarettes. Other adverts include local traders, as well as classified adverts covering 'wanted', 'situations vacant and wanted', 'lodgings and apartments', 'cycles for sale', 'miscellaneous' and 'musical instruments for sale or exchange'. Significantly the paper proclaimed its own worth as a commercial product at the same time as its news presentation was developing. 'No other paper can possibly offer the same facilities to advertisers as the *Midland Daily Telegraph*, the only daily newspaper published within a radius of eighteen miles and thousands search the Advertising Columns daily. Please cut out and keep for future reference' (*MDT*, 5 February 1902).

By 1903 the internal organization of the employees around commercial and editorial divisions was evident in the columns of the paper itself, as the paper set up structures to manage the amount of business coming its way.

> Letters regarding news and coming events should be addressed to the Editor. Letters containing, or having reference to advertisements should be forwarded to the Manager.
>
> In order that attention be given to forthcoming meetings and that this journal may be represented by a reported, it is essential that early intimation of these should be sent to our office.
>
> To avoid delay, letter being upon news or other matter for the paper, should not be addressed to individual members of the staff. (*MDT*, 2 February 1903: 2)

A year later the *Midland Daily Telegraph* invested in improved production methods; it boasted in its heading, 'This paper is set up by Linotype machines and is printed, folded, cut and counted at the rate of 24,000 copies per hour by electric power' (*MDT*, 1 February 1904: 2). By 1905 the paper had also matured into an established commercial advertising medium, set across eight columns and using a new sans serif font. The adverts on page one included promotions for the paper's own value as an advertising medium. The content was increasingly diverse, and presented in line with the style of the 'inverted pyramid', which has come to define news discourse. In parallel was a development in the amount of space devoted to advertising and the increasing self-definition of the paper as an advertising medium. This suggests that this was an important period of commercial development for the *Midland Daily Telegraph*; coupled with this are indications that the paper had organized its staff along the division of advertising and editorial and had invested in improved production methods. At the same time, this period had been a stable one for the cover price (one halfpenny), indicating that advertising revenues had played a key role in funding investment in the product. Within the context of the *Midland Daily Telegraph*, the emergence of the dominance of the 'inverted pyramid' is in parallel with the rise in the percentage of space given to adverts. This suggests a strong commercial imperative for the dominance of this presentation of news both in terms of making the paper more attractive to readers, in line with Pottker's hypothesis, and it seems reasonable to suggest that the techniques of New Journalism were not only adopted because of a transmission of practice between external sources of news and home-based reporting, as suggested by the coverage of the funeral of Queen Victoria, but also because of the physical constraints on space, which demanded a succinct presentation of news.

Commercial success as an organizing factor

By the time John Mackie described the working life of the journalist in his 1894 handbook, he was describing a profession not dissimilar to the one experienced by reporters on local papers in the pre-internet days of the late twentieth century. The reporters – who needed to be bright, happy to miss meals and good at shorthand – were not only the 'eyes and ears' of the newspaper, but also its 'hands and feet' (1894: 29). Mackie also describes a recognizable newspaper organization, including a chief reporter who ran the newsroom diary. The subeditors were at the heart of the organization, keeping in touch with all the departments and with responsibility for the telegraphed copy, which was a significant source of content. The editor, who had oversight of everything, was embedded in society but also independent of it so that he could 'open his columns impartially to all sides, or individuals that are striving for the public good' (ibid.: 95). Therefore, alongside the development of the discursive construction of news, we also see the discursive construction of the professional journalist, based on an ideology which valued accuracy and, above all, impartiality, and which was, in turn, dependent on its commercial worth. In the words of Mackie, 'No institution occupies a position of great independence than the modern English newspapers. Its business interests protect its integrity' (ibid.: 124).

The wages for a beginner district reporter – a 'learner' – would be £1 a week. A reporter on a good weekly would expect £2 a week, while a junior reporter on provincial daily could receive £120–£130 a year, rising to £400 for the chief reporter. In comparison, in 1910 a clerk (a similar non-manual profession) could expect to earn £150 a year (Hampton 2005: 148). A similar wage range for subeditors would see a junior sub (usually a reporter) on £150 a year rising to an annual salary of £500 for the chief sub. Provincial editors could expect up to £1000 a year. Importantly, Mackie charts the foundation of the journalists' first professional body, the Institute of Journalists, which was inaugurated in 1889 for the 'elevation and protection' of the profession. Among its innovations were entrance exams and a campaign to improve the legal status, for instance by guaranteeing access to certain meetings. However, unlike the professions of law or medicine, journalists did not seek to form a 'closed' profession where examinations were the gatekeepers; this was a world where talent and hard work would win professional recognition. Mark Hampton's review of contemporary material at the end of the nineteenth century builds a picture of the journalist as a tough character, who needed tenacity and a strong constitution to withstand the rigours of the profession. He does not distinguish between journalists working at a national and local level, but many of his sources are contemporary accounts of those working in provincial papers and are drawn from a wide variety of social and political backgrounds, united in a rhetoric which seeks to establish a professional identity by the commentary they themselves provide of their working lives. Discursively, this claim to openness supported claims by journalists to be committed to the public sphere – a 'politics by public discussion' (Hampton 2005: 144).

A journalist was now a content producer, as opposed to a newspaper owner, who was 'born' to the profession and may well have fallen into courtesy of talent and opportunity. Both W. T. Stead and Sir Thomas Wemyss Reid, who rose from being a reporter on the *Newcastle Chronicle* to be editor of the *Leeds Mercury*, believed they were following a vocation (ibid.: 142) and felt it was impossible to train to be a journalist, despite the recognition that shorthand was increasingly useful. Although education was deemed to be useful, it did seem that this was largely because of the class allegiance it signified, so educational background was related to the newspaper journalists could work for; Oxbridge graduates worked on the 'quality' titles like the *Pall Mall Gazette*, while 'ordinary' journalists were more likely to be found towards the bottom of the profession.

The rigours of journalism, with long hours and low wages the norm, were cited as the reasons for the formation of both the Institute of Journalists and the National Union of Journalists (founded in 1907). While life on a provincial paper was 'varied and exciting', there was also 'little rest'. The speed of work required also meant it was stressful and the requirements to be first with the news put constant pressure on the worker, who might be required to work twenty-four hours a day when necessary. These claims to rigour not only contributed to the journalists' claims to occupational status, but also meant that the profession became categorized as one more suited to men – and often unmarried ones at that. The changes characterized as New Journalism have also been largely understood as a 'feminine' style of journalism, with aspects shaped by the interest of women and so increasingly written by them. As such, it also brought a closer attention to the diurnal concerns of women, and so brought them into the journalism workforce, albeit segregated in terms of producing content for women (Hampton 2005: 150). In this way the content of newspapers was understood as gendered: the work of male journalists, concerned with impartial reporting of the affairs of men, was considered neutral, whereas the work of women – particularly at this stage when it was strongly connected with female consumers – was considered 'feminine'. 'Women were associated with – and assigned to – journalistic styles and topics widely deemed as outside 'serious' reportage. The emergence of "women's pages" ensured that women journalists played a central role in feature writing and stories aimed at women. ... Beyond that, women's role in mainstream journalism was producing sensationalism and human-interest stories' (Chambers et al. 2004: 14). Even when women did venture into areas of 'harder' newspaper content, it was in relation to the emerging practices of interviewing and the 'human interest' angle.

Journalism was, as with most occupations of this time, also intensely hierarchical. The Institute of Journalists, which represented editors, managers and publishers of newspapers, did not admit female members at all, although the National Union of Journalists did. The Society of Women Journalists was founded in 1894 by Joseph Snell Wood, who published the magazine, *The Gentlewoman*. However, the end of the nineteenth century also signalled an improvement in the social status of women with legal changes which improved the rights of women within marriage and education. There was an increased recognition that women made decisions over domestic purchases and were also gaining financial independence as more took paid employment outside of the home. In 1918 women in the UK were given the vote. These changes were both subject matter and context for those women who wanted to work in newspapers. Flora Shaw was the first woman to gain a permanent position on *The Times* in 1892; she also worked for the *Pall Mall Gazette* and the *Manchester Guardian*. Other women drew on their personal contacts to break into journalism, which was perceived as one way in which women could go beyond the domestic confines of the home, and this progress was undoubtedly facilitated by the changes discussed here. Emillie Peakcocke was encouraged into the profession by her father John Marshall, then editor and co-proprietor of the *Northern Echo*. Despite her apparent ability, her career path was not smooth, and she was turned down for a position as a subeditor on the *Yorkshire Daily Observer*, because 'we cannot possibly see our way to offering a position as a sub-editor to a lady' (Chambers et al. 2004: 25). In a similar vein, Mary Stott was offered a job on the *Leicester Mail* in 1925 by her uncle, who was chief subeditor, only to be made editor of the women's page – a move she felt was an insult. To this extent women working in newspapers at this time were 'ghettoised', although the content they produced was actually a key component in commercializing these titles and preparing them for mass readership.

Following the path of the emergence of New Journalism and its impact on the provincial press in Britain, therefore, enables us to chart the emergence of three key factors of professional journalism practised at a provincial level, which have lasted until the beginnings of the twenty-first century: first, the emergence and dominance of the presentation of information as 'news', organized according to the professional conventions of the inverted pyramid; second, a greater variety of content designed to attract a wider audience; and finally, the increasing characterization of the audience as a 'community' against which the paper itself is defined as a supportive champion. In doing so we are charting the development of an industry from one often promoted and subsidized for political gain to one geared around commercial efficacy. In this context, the commercial imperative became the driver for innovation, as evidenced by the organization of staff, the use of illustrations (overwhelmingly applied to adverts) and even the use of new fonts to save editorial space when column inches were at a premium. Despite the pressures on space, titles like the *Midland Daily Telegraph* were still willing to devote space to adverts for their own worth as a promotional medium in order to maximize their commercial success.

This marks the emergence of a mass-produced newspaper, on an industrial scale for a mass readership – produced by an increasingly demarcated and specialist workforce, which found new ways of balancing its commercial and social functions. These 'new' newspapers presented an increasingly wide range of content, itself specialized and produced by specialist writers, made accessible to a wide audience by its manner of presentation. At the same time, they used their presentation of content to define and establish both an audience – the 'community' of readers – and a role for themselves as community champion. In this way the ground was prepared for the circulation battles and company consolidations which were to typify the immediate future of a mass-circulation newspaper industry.

Marzolf suggests that 'the modern general interest newspaper noted for its independence, its journalistic enterprise and entertaining reading matter had attained its precarious balance between commercialism and social responsibility' during this period (1984: 691), and it is this financial independence which enabled the provincial newspaper to construct a particular narration of its own social role. The metropolitan newspaper was able to claim the role of 'fourth estate' because it was able to take a position of editorial independence from any political party (Hampton 2008; Chalaby 1996). Additionally, the power of New Journalism in the hands of practitioners like W. T. Stead demonstrated the possibility of 'Government by Journalism' (Nerone and Barnhurst 2012: 110). For the provincial press this independence from political influence was established as a component of commercial success by titles like the *Manchester Guardian*. These papers were early adopters of the strategy which favoured the well-being of its readership over any particular political party, and it is this specific relationship with the reader which came to underpin the raison d'etre of the provincial press.

Therefore, this particular branch of journalism was constituting its readership as a 'community' on whose behalf it should campaign and whose interests it should promote, in a continuation of the process noted previously. It is a stance exemplified by *Cambridge Daily News* in its coverage of the 'Spinning House Case', a battle between the university authorities and the town over who should police prostitution. A four-page newspaper with a mixture of content designed to attract both Town and Gown, its allegiance was unequivocal when it came to the Spinning House Case, which had seen a townswoman imprisoned by the university under an arcane law which gave it jurisdiction over the streets of Cambridge after dark. The paper campaigned to overthrow the law and was rewarded with letters of support from the community, which it published in its columns; as such it defined itself as the champion of local causes by its ability to give a voice to those citizens (Taylor 2006). This editorial stance as a local champion can be equated with that of serving the good of the community; the newspaper will exploit the interests and issues facing its local community for popular support, so that those interests and issues come to define what the newspaper sees as 'news'. Not only does the newspaper construct a 'community' to represent, but it also uses that community as a constituent of what it defines as news – that is as the source of a news value (Taylor 2006: 412).

In this process provincial journalism took the notion of the fourth estate and refined it to create its own distinctive normative ideology – that of functioning for the good of the community; this same relationship had developed a discursive prominence by the time of resurgent interest in the provincial press in the 1960s and 1970s, as exemplified by works by Jackson (1971) and Cox and Morgan (1973). These provincial newspaper workers replaced the politically didactic with the role of community champion in a move which was not only precipitated by, but facilitated by, the commercial imperative of the new news style of New Journalism.

5

The Corporatization of the Provincial Press

The growth of chain control

The plan was to have an intelligent group [of newspapers] by serving the area with first, a daily newspaper giving the 'hot' news, international news, national news and the principal local news; second a strong county weekly newspaper in *Berrow's Worcester Journal* and then third the town papers giving a more intimate local news. We also had a sports newspaper published on Saturdays. We have been very successful in most ways, particularly in satisfying the public. The effect of the amalgamation was that throughout we achieved a greater efficiency internally, a better staff which gave us better quality contents; we had a stronger business organisation and in every respect I think it was in the interests both of the proprietors and of the public we serve.

(Ivor Griffiths, Berrows Newspapers Ltd,
Evidence to the Royal Commission, 1947)

The unremitting process of commercialization in the twentieth century, signalled by the process of New Journalism, was to have a dramatic effect on the shape of regional newspaper industry in England. Big profits meant that increasingly big players in this market sought to consolidate their holdings and reorganize their titles in a way which enabled them to make the most of their assets. This business approach, outlined above in relation to newspapers in Worcester, was based on building strong circulation areas for different 'types' of newspaper in order to maximize income from advertising. The first thirty years of the century saw the rise to ascendancy of the mass-circulation regional daily evening newspaper, which was able to yield substantial profits from a combination of sale and advertising revenues (Political and Economic Planning 1938). Such was the significance of advertising to revenue streams that this is the era in which circulations began to be audited and published. It is also the one in which ownership of different forms of regional newspapers were increasingly brought together within one commercial structure, which could, therefore, enjoy the benefits of scale from combined operations. Their success was measured by those who sought to justify this process as serving not only the interests of the financial organization of the business but also the interests of the 'public' in the form of the reader. Outside of London this period is, therefore, characterized by the growing domination of the provincial newspaper market by a few, huge commercial enterprises in a relentless process which was interrupted only by the Second World War. Ivor Griffiths had overseen such a process in the city of Worcester when he had bought a 100 per cent shareholding in the well-established Berrow's Newspapers Ltd and amalgamated two competing evening titles which were 'indulging in the most ruinous competition in sales and in advertising' (*Royal Commission Evidence* 1947: para 11,011) to create one profitable newspaper. This consolidation was, therefore, marked by a shift in the pattern of availability of newspaper titles in favour of an increasingly monopolistic presence within circulation areas.

Among those at the forefront of this process were key figures in the newspaper industry, who were themselves part of publishing dynasties and who enjoyed the privilege and title that this success had brought. These included the Lords Rothermere and Iliffe and the Viscounts Camrose and Kemsley. Their unremitting quest for domination prompted substantial resistance from newspaper owners, workers and even readers who sought to remain independent of, what was at times, a brutal process, underpinned by cut-throat competition. Concomitant with this shift was the rise of an increasingly unionized workforce which was often in conflict with the increasingly remote corporate owners. The factions within the industry increasingly positioned themselves within formal organizations – the Newspaper Proprietors Association and the Newspaper Society for the owners, versus the Institute of Journalists, largely for the editors and managers, and the National Union of Journalists and the printers' unions for the workers – which lobbied to promote their views. Attempts to resist and question these changes, expressed as anxiety about the effect of these changes on the role of the press as a fourth estate, were expressed at parliamentary level, with reference to the implications for the ability of the press to function as a part of the democratic process. This concern resulted in three Royal Commissions into aspects of the newspaper industry in fewer than thirty years (1947–9, 1961–2 and 1974–7). These inquiries highlight the tension between the role of the press in the democratic process[1] and the

---

[1] The significance of this conception to those producing newspapers, as evidenced by the NUJs campaign for the Royal Commission of 1947–9, is discussed below.

view of newspapers as a purely commercial product. In the latter conception, put forward by the owners themselves, newspapers were owned to make money alongside ventures in mining or oil. As such, leading industrial figures – epitomized by Viscount Camrose, a Berry brother, owner of the *Daily Telegraph* and a former partner in the Allied Newspapers Ltd provincial newspaper group – defended the giants of the industry (Camrose 1947). This strife ended only after the industrial disputes which surrounded the introduction of new technology into the industry in the 1980s. This dominance of the commercial ideal has led Lee (1976) to characterize this period as a shift away from the philanthropic, educative ideology underpinning the operation of the Victorian press so that newspapers increasingly focussed on what readers wanted – rather than what they were supposed to want. The result of this is the foundation of a popular press which was highly contested by contemporary commentators who define its products varyingly as either displaying improved production values made possible via the investment from chain ownership (Camrose 1947: 8–9) or 'dumbed down', to satisfy the needs of shareholders and advertisers – to the detriment of journalists and readers alike.

Murdock and Golding cite this as the era in which 'national' papers as they are understood today become established, with the result that the provincial press contracted in the face of the dominance of those London-based titles (1978: 130).[2] These titles were able to make incursions into the regions by virtue of improved communications. New 'liner' trains were introduced in the 1890s to ensure that national papers could be transported to the regions overnight, and these papers also began printing regional editions in places such as Birmingham and Manchester (Packer 2006). Among those in the vanguard of improving distribution was the *Daily Mail*, launched in May 1896; by 1899 it had been selling more than 700,000 copies a day. The sale was aided by its ability to distribute across Britain by breakfast – enabled by simultaneous printing in London and Manchester, which also facilitated the distribution of papers in Scotland. This practice was established by the *Daily Mirror* with a successful Birmingham-based edition in 1926, and by some major provincial titles too, including the Leeds-based *Yorkshire Evening Post* and *Yorkshire Evening News*, both of which published a South Yorkshire edition in Doncaster from 1925 (Herd 1927).

For these businesses, circulations and profits grew almost without faltering for the extended period of 1914–76, despite the strictures of the Second World War, which are discussed at length in Chapter 6. However, although total provincial circulations remained buoyant, the number of titles which were on sale fell. In

---

[2] See Chapter 1 for a discussion of the national/provincial dichotomy.

1900 there were 196 local daily papers and an estimated 2,072 weekly papers (Curran et al. 2003: 33). But as newspapers became increasingly reliant on high circulations and high advertising revenues to break even, this number reduced, falling to 169 in 1920. In 1921 there were forty-one morning provincial titles and eighty-nine evenings; by 1937 these had dropped again to twenty-eight and seventy-five, respectively. This reduction translated into a loss of choice of newspaper for many as towns lost one of two competing titles (in 1921, thirty-three of sixty-five towns had two titles, but this had dropped to twenty by 1947 and of those twelve were owned by the same company). Local monopoly had become the dominant order of the day for the provincial newspaper (Murdock and Golding 1978: 132). Between 1937 and 1976 overall circulations for the provincial papers increased by 50 per cent – from 4.4 million to 6.3 million for morning titles and 8.6 million to 12.3 million for evening papers. Concurrently, the industrialization of newspaper production – necessary to produce high-circulation titles within a short space of time – restricted new entrants into the industry due to the capital required. The potential gains from advertising revenues were also substantial. A by-product of these rising costs, and potential profits, was a process of consolidation of ownership, often within companies for which newspapers were just one revenue stream among many.

Significantly, in addition to the rise of the dominance of the evening press, this period also sees the emergence of a new class of newspapers – the 'freesheet' or free weekly, which challenged the traditional role of 'purchaser' and 'buyer' by selling readers to advertisers, rather than content to readers, in order to secure advertisers (Franklin 2006b: 151). Initially dismissed as a transient form, these papers were thought to pose no threat to the established industry, which failed to foresee a rate of expansion in the 1980s and 1990s, which challenged the status quo. This reshaping of the provincial newspaper industry was the result of a combination of factors: first, the impact of industrialization on the economic structure of the newspaper industry, which promoted the process of consolidation of ownership by making large capital sums necessary to enter the market: second, changes to business law which made it easier and more common to form partnerships to fund such capital investment; third, an unwillingness – and increasingly an inability – by owners to subsidize those more costly newspaper businesses for political gain; fourth, high potential returns in the form of advertising revenue, which made owning newspapers worthwhile, and fifth, increased competition from the metropolitan (London) press, which prompted cooperative agreements between companies to create monopolistic circulation areas.

The consolidation of ownership: Pattern and process

This book has already charted how the 'early adopters' of the newspaper had an entrepreneurial attitude to their business, geared around the opportunities for synergy mastering distribution chains brought. These people ran multiple titles as well as associated businesses, and in London in particular, by the mid-eighteenth-century group ownership was the norm rather than the exception for papers. This pattern of complimentary interests was sustained into the Victorian era where newspapers were held alongside other interests, particular weekly titles, which though profitable, yielded lower returns. Of 216 newspapers listed in Charles Mitchell's Newspaper Press Directory in 1847, 115 of them had accompanying business interests, the most popular combination being the familiar 'Bookseller, Stationery and Patent Medicine Vendor' developed in the preceding century (Roberts 1972: 15). As the nineteenth century progressed, this pattern of ownership was extended, as documented in Chapter 4, and was to be found in the growing daily newspaper market; typical was Andrew Carnegie, who came to control eight dailies, including for a time the Wolverhampton *Express* & *Star*, and ten weeklies (Curran et al. 2003: 39), motivated by the desire to establish a chain of Liberal daily newspapers (Rhodes 1992).

Consolidation had become easier following legislative changes in the nineteenth century, including the abolition of Stamp Duty; additionally reforms to business law in the latter half of the nineteenth century extended the concept of limited liability to shareholders – and effectively enabled the limited company. This meant shareholders were only liable for the debts incurred by a company to the value of the shares held, which effectively broke the link between business failure and personal ruin (Lee 1978; Loftus 2002). Telegraphy was also nationalized under the auspices of the post office and promised a fixed rate for twenty-word messages despite the distance travelled. The service ran at a loss and was, therefore, described as a 'subsidy' to the newspapers who took advantage of it (Briggs and Burke 2002: 140). During and just after the First World War,[3] consolidation intensified – especially with reference to the provincial evening newspaper – with the rise of four principal newspaper groups: Northcliffe Newspapers, Kemsley Newspapers, Provincial Newspapers and the Westminster

---

[3]   During the First World War the costs of publishing increased 'dramatically' (Silberstein-Loeb 2009: 786) because of rises in newsprint and plant costs, and of building and sustaining circulations. It is discussed in Chapter 6.

Press. These groups would dominate the industry for fifty years (Duncum 1952), and their influence persists today. Unionization also impacted wages with printing staff in particular becoming the best-paid artisans in the country (Political Economic Planning 1938: 138).

For the provincial newspaper industry, the period of consolidation of ownership was most rapid between 1921 and 1929; by the time of the outset of the Second World War, the main groups in the newspaper industry had been formed as a result of mergers and acquisitions. By 1948 nearly 43 per cent of all newspaper titles had been in the hands of the top five chains in the country (see Table 5.1). These figures were fairly stable till 1974, as Tables 5.1 and 5.2 demonstrate. Between 1921 and 1974 there was also a marked change in the number of titles in existence and the dominance of newspaper forms with the rise of the evening paper and the demise of the morning paper. The number of provincial mornings in Britain fell from forty-four to nineteen during this period, most rapidly before 1937 by which time thirteen of the nineteen titles cited had closed, most likely casualties of a bitter turf war fought between factions which sought to established profitable evening titles. The effect of this was to limit most towns to just a single morning title, which enjoyed a monopoly circulation and enhanced advertising revenues. In the same period sixteen evening titles closed, again mostly between 1921 and 1931, reducing further the number of towns with a choice of evening titles from twenty-six to eight. Seven of these evening

Table 5.1 Chain ownership of newspapers 1921–48

Newspaper group	Total titles (1921)	Total titles (1923)	Total titles (1929)	Total titles (1937)	Total titles (1939)	Total titles (1948)
Berry: Kemsley	2	2	26	22	20	22
Northcliffe; Associated	9	14	14	14	11	11
Westminster	9	11	13	14	14	14
United: Provincial	3	3	9	4	4	4
Harmsworth	2	2	4	4	4	4
Total in five chains	25	32	66	58	53	55
Total in the country	167	158	149	136	130	128
Total controlled by chains as percentage of total	14.95	20.24	44.29	42.65	40.76	42.96

Source: Royal Commission on the Press 1947–9. Appendix IV. Newspaper types counted include national mornings, London evenings, provincial mornings, provincial evenings, Sundays.

Table 5.2 The National Chain Publishers' shares of provincial morning, evening and weekly newspaper circulations in Great Britain in 1937, 1947, 1961 and 1974

		Associated Newspapers Group/Harmsworth Newspapers	Iliffe family interests	Thomson Regional Newspapers/Kemsley Newspapers	United newspapers/ provincial newspapers	Westminster Press	Total national chains
Provincial mornings	1937	1.7	n.i	50.8	–	12.9	65.4
	1947	1.8	n.i	49.9	–	10.9	62.6
	1961	3.6	4.1	25.8	–	5.5	39.0
	1974	3.6	3.1	20.0	8.0	5.7	40.
Provincial evenings	1937	13.7	n.i	22.3	6.6	7.5	50.1
	1947	9.7	n.i	20.2	6.7	7.7	44.3
	1961	13.3	8.7	14.3	6.6	5.4	48.3
	1974	14.8	8.6	14.3	10.0	9.0	56.7
Provincial weeklies	1937	1.4	n.i	0.6	1.0	4.3	7.4
	1947	2.2	n.i	0.9	1.3	3.6	7.9
	1961	2.6	1.3	1.6	2.0	5.2	12.7
	1974	4.4	1.8	3.3	3.2	11.7	24.4

Sources: 1937, 1947 – Royal Commission on the Press 1947–9, report, Appendix VI, Table 2. 1961, 1974 – Royal Commission on the Press 1974–7 (Hartley et al. 1977: 44).

Notes: n.i = not included.

papers which faced competition from another in the same town were owned by the same company, and the closures were mostly the result of horse-trading between groups which agreed to demarcated circulation areas in a bid to create one paper which could charge a substantial price for advertising. In most cases between 30 and 50 per cent of the closed title's circulation was lost. However, in all but one case, the closed title also had the highest advertising rate, implying that the company strategy was one of preserving the market share of advertising rather than building sales numbers (Hartley et al. 1977: 61). Healthy advertising revenues were also a key factor in the launch of new titles, and while a further nine titles closed between 1971 and 1974, eleven new papers were created, seven of which were in the commuter-rich south-east of England. Most unaffected was the number of Sunday provincial papers, which decreased by just one between 1921 and 1974.

Less easy to quantify is the effect on weekly titles during this period – largely due to the difficulties of defining individual titles, some of which may only be an edition of a main paper. The 1977 Royal Commission concluded that the decline followed a similar pattern to that of daily newspapers; the biggest losses occurred between 1921 and 1937, followed by a period of stability to 1948 during the Second World War, followed by a steady decline. Significantly, when compared with the shape of ownership of weekly titles, the 1977 analysis also noted a change in the organization of weekly titles, with closures, mergers and amalgamations all accounting for the change in numbers. This may in some part be accounted for by the rise of chain ownership of these types of newspapers and their subsequent subjugation within more generalized publishing centres. In 1961 there were about 460 publishers of weekly newspapers; by the time of the 1977 Royal Commission on the Press, this figures had been drastically reduced to just 180. A significant incursion into this market was the free sheet, and by September 1974 there had been 9.4 million free newspapers circulating, compared with 11.2 million for the traditional paid-for weekly. Although the origins of a few experimental free titles have been discussed elsewhere in this work, most of those 150 newspapers in existence in the 1970s were launched in the first half of the 1960s. This newspaper form was reliant on incomes from classified and recruitment advertising; this made it vulnerable to economic factors which would impact on those revenue streams. As such, they were largely cyclical in nature and individual titles would come and go. Among owners of these titles were, perhaps predictably, the large corporate owners; Westminster Press owned the most – but owners also included local printers or independent entrepreneurs, many of whom had papers with circulations of fewer than 40,000. This was not a newspaper form to be easily dismissed, and their growth was to accelerate in the 1980s to a peak circulation of 42 million in 1989, enabling them to 'effectively undermine the local advertising monopolies enjoyed by the traditional press' (Franklin 2006b: 153) in a process which is examined later in this work.

Murdock and Golding (1978) highlight the death of Alfred Harmsworth – Lord Northcliffe – in 1922 as speeding the shift to chain ownership, possibly because a small group of newspaper magnates were vying for the position of top owner. To this end, the history of consolidation includes instances where newspaper groups were bought – only to be sold on to another member in the top five, and it is not until the post-Second World War period that new players in the game, such as Rupert Murdoch, began to the challenge the status quo. Significantly this period was a watershed for the understanding of the motivation for newspaper ownership to increasingly put profit before politics in discussions around the operation of the industry. This shifted some of the residual political values out of newspaper ownership. Packer describes how the Starmer Group's strategy for establishing a newspaper in its market – one of dropping the cover price, investing in modern machinery to lower costs and modernizing the design of the product – made titles dependent on high circulations to justify the capital investment. This meant principles like a ban on betting tips, enforced in the *Northern Echo* until 1910, were set aside (Packer 2006: 418). Similarly, when the group took over the *Lincolnshire Chronicle* in 1914 it did so solely for financial purposes, and its strategy was indistinguishable from that employed by Rothermere in his quest to establish a chain of populist *Evening Worlds* explored below. As such, the Starmer purchase was a 'harbinger of the commercial ... future that lay before provincial newspaper groups' (ibid.: 423–4).

By 1938 Mitchell's Newspaper Press Directory listed 24 morning papers in the English provinces, 70 evening, five Sunday titles and 896 weekly papers. Together they sold more than 7.5 million copies a day (5.2 million of which were provincial evening titles). The impact of the London press was evident in the geographical spread of these titles; just three towns within 100 miles of London – Brighton, Ipswich and Leamington Spa – had a provincial daily paper, and these were all morning titles which may have retained a time advantage over their London rivals. By that time, in most cities titles were in monopoly positions due not only to competition but also to inter-group cooperation, which saw areas delimited between them. This is perhaps due to the nature of the profitability of the evening newspaper, which did not need ever-increasing sales, but instead found its profitability in the amount it could charge for advertising in relation to that sale (Political Economic Planning 1938: 85). Just Birmingham, Leeds, Manchester, Sheffield, Newcastle and Nottingham had two morning papers, and only Birmingham, Bristol, Leeds, Leicester, Liverpool, Manchester, Nottingham and Shields retained markets consisting of multiple evening papers. Certain morning titles were seen to wield great influence, especially the *Birmingham Post*, the *Yorkshire Post* and the *Manchester Guardian*, the latter of which was seen as the Liberal foil to *The Times* (Political Economic Planning 1938: 48). By 1977 the monopoly situation had increased so that just Sandwell experienced competition between two evening titles (the Wolverhampton *Express* & *Star* and Birmingham *Evening Mail*).

Between 1921 and 1937, the top five companies – Beaverbrook Newspapers, Associated Newspapers, Daily Mirror Group (later Reed International), News of the World (later News International), Kemsley Newspapers and Odhams Press – increased holdings in terms of percentage of all titles (both national and provincial) owned, from 15 per cent to 43 per cent. This was done, Murdock and Golding suggest, by 'weeding out' (1978: 135) the weaker titles, which left them with a larger share of remaining circulations and so reinforced their market dominance. Although these figures had remained fairly stable until the 1960s – largely because of the continuity in the number of titles – the market share in terms of percentage of circulations actually rose from 43 per cent in 1948 to 63 per cent in 1974, because of the fall in overall circulations for the top three groups (ibid.: 135).[4] However, by looking at both national and provincial ownership together, Murdock and Golding disguise shifts in the relative dominance of the provincial newspaper ownership alone (see Tables 5.3 and 5.4 below). This is particularly marked in the field of weekly newspaper ownership. The top two groups (Westminster Press and Associated Newspaper Group) remained dominant in terms of the percentage of circulations of titles owned between 1961 and 1974; we also see the rise of significant newcomers including F. Johnston and Company (to become Johnston Press), which accomplished its expansion largely by the acquisition of weekly titles (Riley 2006: 26). With the exception of the Iliffe family, each of the national chains more than doubled their share of the weekly newspaper market between 1937 and 1974, with the

---

[4]   Overall circulations fell, in part at least due to rises in cover prices which saw the price of national titles double between 1960 and 1970 and again by 1975.

Table 5.3 The largest ten publishers of provincial evening newspapers in 1974 and their share of the total circulation of provincial evening newspapers in the UK in 1961 and 1974

	1974			1961		
	Rank	Number of titles	Total circulation ('000)	Rank	Number of titles	Total circulation ('000)
Thomson Regional Newspapers	1	11.5*	1,069	1	8	1,156
Associated Newspapers Group	2	12	922	2	13	894
United Newspapers	3	6	625	5	4	445
Westminster Press	4	10.5*	559	7	8	363
Iliffe family interests	5	3	533	4	4	586
The Guardian and Manchester Evening News Ltd	6	1	376	3	2	604
The Midland News Association	7	2	314	11	1	209
Liverpool Daily Post and Echo Ltd	8	1	307	6	1	412
Scottish and Universal Investments/ George Outram and Company	9	2	253	8=	1	234
Portsmouth and Sunderland Newspapers	10	3	218	10	3	225

Source: Royal Commission on the Press 1974–7 (Hartley et al. 1977: 40).

*Half the circulation of the Slough Evening Mail, launched jointly between Thomson Regional Newspapers and Westminster Press in 1969, has been allocated to each of them in 1974.

biggest rate of change between 1961 and 1974 (Hartley et al. 1977: 43). The weekly newspaper may have been the 'medieval fiefdom' of 'minor press barons' (Riley 2006: 26), but they were also likely to be fairly uneconomical to produce because of the combination of high first-print costs typical of the newspaper industry and smaller circulations. As such, the reorganization of the industry into consolidated publishing centres probably improved profitability. Even so, in 1977, statistics produced for the Royal Commission show that weekly newspapers were still considerably more expensive to produce than evening

Table 5.4 The largest ten publishers of provincial weekly newspapers in 1974 and their share of the total circulation of provincial weekly newspapers in the UK in 1961 and 1974

	1974			1961		
	Rank	Number of titles	Total circulation ('000)	Rank	Number of titles	Total circulation ('000)
Westminster Press	1	94	1,234	1	50	603
Associated Newspapers Group	2	33	467	2	19	298
Thomson Regional Newspapers	3	39	383	4	27	227
United Newspapers	4	31	333	3	19	228
Scottish and Universal Investments/ George Outram and Company	5	20	323	27	3	73
News International/ News of the World Organisations	6	33	297	15	15	95
Home Counties Newspapers	7	14	252	7	11	145
British Electric Traction Company	8	28	215	8	114	111
F. Johnston and Company	9	20	214	67	13	39
East Midland Allied Press	10	13	214	5	16	202

Source: Royal Commission on the Press 1974–7 (Hartley et al. 1977: 42).

papers, with a total average cost-by-copy of 22.5p, compared with 9.6p for an evening (Hartley et al. 1977: 23).

Lord Rothermere: Ambition and resistance

Perhaps the most notorious accelerator of efforts to consolidate ownership was Lord Rothermere, founder of Northcliffe Newspapers Ltd. His bid to create a national chain of evening newspapers set a standard for aggressive marketing techniques and sowed disquiet among members of the industry, who fought to oppose his quest for domination. Rothermere was reported to have been driven by a wish to be the largest newspaper proprietor in the country after the ascendancy of Allied Newspapers, the partnership between the Berry brothers (the Viscounts Camrose and Kemsley) and Lord Iliffe. In 1928 he formed Northcliffe Newspapers Ltd with the intention of founding opposition titles to theirs in key cities, including Newcastle, Bristol and Cardiff. He also targeted existing titles, acquiring, among others, the *Grimsby Evening Telegraph*, the *Gloucestershire Echo*, in Cheltenham, and the neighbouring *Gloucester Citizen*, the *Derby Daily Telegraph* and the *Hull Daily Mail*. Rothermere's first new launch was the *Newcastle Evening World*; employing some 300 people at the aptly named Northcliffe House, it was formally opened in May 1929 by former prime minister and then leader of the Liberal Party, Lloyd George, who broke his election campaign trail. Rothermere used his other titles to promote the event.

> Mr. Lloyd George wished to take advantage of the opportunity to inspect the most up-to-date and lavishly-equipped newspaper office in the North of England. … The actual ceremony was simple. Mr. Lloyd George, standing at a point where the mechanical conveyors deliver the papers in the Publishing Department, pressed a control button. Instantly a section of the giant presses sprang to life, and a continuous stream of paper, as though by magic, leaped up from the machine, traversed the ceiling of the press room, and poured out on the bench to be distributed among the guests as souvenirs. (*Gloucester Citizen*, 4 May 1929: 1)

Even at this early stage, it was clear that Rothermere was prepared to invest substantial sums, not only in establishing these businesses but also in promoting them. The Newcastle title's inception coincided with the North East Coast Exhibition – a regional version of the Great Exhibition of Victorian times designed to counter regional economic depression; the paper sponsored a pavilion and offered a £100 diamond as a prize. In 1930 the *Bristol Evening World* has its 'own' plane, which flew the family of Amy Johnson – the first woman to fly solo from Britain to Australia – from Hull to Bristol for an air pageant (*Derby Daily Telegraph*, 30 May 1930: 1). These stunts were typical of strategies employed by newspaper groups at this time at both national and regional levels as a way of building readerships; enticements ranged from giving away substantial 'free gifts' to running subsidized insurance policies, a strategy which resulted in Westminster Press devising its own insurance products. By December 1929 Rothermere's *Newcastle Evening World* was claiming a 'record-breaking' circulation of 174,000 copies per day – double the sale originally envisaged for it. The *Bristol Evening World*, the second of what Rothermere would hope would be eight titles around the country, was printing 100,000. 'Northcliffe Newspapers has a wonderful future before it,' he told the editorial staff at a celebratory dinner in January 1930. 'There never was any newspaper enterprise in this country which had more money at its disposal, more technical skill, more understanding of the public taste, and more zeal on the part of every member of its staffs' (*Derby Daily Telegraph*, 6 January 1930: 5).

One strategy employed by Rothermere was the instigation of verified circulations of his titles, and he required each Northcliffe newspaper to publish a 'net sales certificate' (ibid.). Publicly, his aim was to counter the inflated claims of his competitors for advertising share by making available a circulation figure which was verified by chartered accountants. However, it also followed criticisms by Lord Camrose (first Sir William Berry, then later Viscount Camrose) that the *Newcastle Evening World's* circulation was overstated. When titles took up the practice of publishing verified circulations, they would advertise it – with the *Derby Daily Telegraph* making it front-page news (see Figure 5.1). Two years later the practice was formalized with the creation of the Audit Bureau for Circulation in 1931. Similarly, Rothermere did not merely found new titles, but also acquired existing titles and created others through merger and consolidation. Sometimes the acquisition was outright, sometimes a shareholding was acquired and sometimes single titles were created by the combination of others, such as the *South Wales Daily Post* in Swansea. This title was formed by the merger of an eponymous title with the *Cambria Daily Leader* and the existing facilities modernized with new production equipment, because 'it was decided that the interests of that important area could best be served by one really up-to-date newspaper' (*Gloucester Citizen*, 26 September 1930: 7). An acquisition was the *Leicester Mail* in 1931; 'the *Leicester Mail*, will, on Monday next appear in a new and enlarged form, and during the next few weeks it will be steadily improved', its sister paper the *Derby Daily Telegraph* reported (23 April 1931: 1).

Rothermere's progress was not without opposition. Bristol was the site of a fierce battle between Allied Newspapers, owners of the Bristol Times and Mirror Ltd, which sought – unsuccessfully as it happened – an injunction to stop the nascent *Bristol Evening World* from poaching staff, and in particularly canvassers. The legal judgement delivered by the Chancery Division of the High Court rested on whether the *Evening World* had sought to 'seduce' workers to break their contracts with the direct intention of putting the rival title out of

Figure 5.1 *Derby Daily Telegraph*, 12 August 1929, p. 1. Newspaper Image © Mirrorpix. All rights reserved. With thanks to The British Newspaper Archive (www.BritishNewspaperArchive.co.uk).

business, targeting Allied Newspaper titles in Newcastle as well as Bristol. 'They have endeavoured to lower the credit of my clients, not as a newspaper, but as persons of financial stability. In fact, they have utilized every device in their power to cause deliberate damage to my clients as rivals,' argued Sir Patrick Evershed, King's Counsel for the plaintiff in a lengthy report published in the Bristol-based *Western Daily Press* (26 October 1929: 8). Instead, countered Mr Wilfred Green for the defence, all was fair in love, war or establishing a rival newspaper staff. 'It was quite obvious there was intense trade competition, a newspaper was entitled … to use any method it pleased to get together as good as staff as it could even if it did so by inviting members of the rival concern to join it' (ibid.).

During these bitter times, other titles looked at business structure as a way of protecting themselves against takeover; such was the antipathy of the owners of the *Cumberland Evening News*, the Carlisle Conservative Newspaper Company, to Lord Rothermere that they were able to exploit their independence and offer their holdings to Allied Newspapers instead. When that came to nothing, they approached Liberal Charles Starmer, of Westminster Press and publisher of the *Northern Echo*. In Birmingham Lord Iliffe created a trust to protect its morning title, the *Birmingham Post*, an anti-competitive structure which meant it was not publicly traded and which lasted until 1964. Similarly, the Scott Trust was established in 1936 to own the *Manchester Guardian* and the *Manchester Evening News*. The Birmingham paper also sent practical support to Bristol when a rival evening title was founded in protest not only at the actions of Rothermere but also of Allied Newspapers. In 1928 the city had four independent newspapers, two morning and two evening. Allied Newspapers bought control of two when it acquired control of the *Bristol Times and Mirror* to combat the actions of Northcliffe Newspapers Ltd. The ensuing competition was described as a 'war' with the first casualty the *Bristol Evening News*. But what followed was a truce whereby the two conglomerates carved up the remaining titles between them and two more newspapers closed instantly. The reaction of staff who had lost their jobs and prominent citizens was almost instant—a subscription was set up to scrape together enough money to found the *Bristol Evening Post*, 'the paper all Bristol asked for and helped to create' (Belsey 1992: 3). The title had held onto its independence until 1934 when a new company, the Bristol United Press, was formed to run both the *Post* and *Evening World* titles, although separate management boards ensured a degree of separation between them.

Northcliffe Newspapers reached its zenith in 1931, by which time the titles within the its stable included ten evening papers: the *Bristol Evening World*, the *Derby Daily Telegraph*, the *Gloucestershire Echo*, the *Gloucester Citizen*, the *Grimsby Daily Telegraph*, the *Hull Daily Mail, Lincolnshire Echo, Newcastle Evening World, South Wales Daily Post* and *Staffordshire Evening Sentinel*. The amount needed to sustain this trajectory was substantial. The company had been launched in 1928 with a debenture issue of £3 million. Yet as early as September 1930, the company was running a loss of nearly £200,000, and in December 1932 it went into voluntary liquidation. Its assets were transferred to Associated Newspapers, which together formed the Daily Mail and General Trust. Northcliffe Newspapers had retained an identity as the overarching structure of the company's regional titles until its holdings were sold to Local World in 2012. But its future progress was largely organized around cooperation and merger rather than rabid competition.

The Political and Economic Planning report of 1938 into the business of newspaper publishing suggested that cooperative working arrangements became common between newspaper groups, both in terms of practices – for instance agreeing not to publish on Christmas Day and Good Friday and maintaining stop-press times – but also for negotiations with the workforce via established organizations. Consequently, it is not surprising that when faced with the increasing costs of circulation wars, companies agreed a truce and delimited the areas in which they operated. Northcliffe Newspapers Ltd made a conscious decision not to launch titles in some areas inhabited by Allied Newspapers, including Cardiff and Sheffield, despite its ambition. By the time of the post-war Royal Commission on the Press of 1947, these cooperative practices, which operated between both regional centres and those centres and London offices, were entrenched to the extent that much of the enquiry focused on their impact on the independence of those titles. Speaking for Northcliffe Newspapers in 1947, Managing Director William McWhirter described how the regional titles could look to London for management support and specialist input for in terms of London news and legal cover. But he looked back on the *Evening World* days with a degree of apology.

> In the early days we made a lot of mistakes, and I think we learnt from them. We did not realise how we had to make each papers as individual and local as possible. The editor-in-chief in London had a certain amount of authority over the local papers. In the last 10 or 15 years that has vanished. Now we have a London editor but he has no control. He is only a service man, a supplier. (*Royal Commission Evidence*, 1947: para 5393)

Newspaper costs as a driver for consolidation

The raw materials of paper and ink formed a substantial proportion of a newspaper's costs – set at more than one third by the funding model for a newspaper drawn up by the PEP (1938). Technologically, printing equipment had developed and the Linotype and monotype machine had become ubiquitous as the method of typesetting. Developments were also made in the area of graphics. In 1906 the *Glasgow Evening News* was produced on seventeen Linotype machines, and printed at a rate of 123,000 copies in eighty-one minutes on five three-deck Goss straight-line printing presses (Carlaw 1906). This meant a sharp increase in the costs of setting up papers. Drawing on a national example, James Curran states that Northcliffe estimated £0.5 million as required to establish the *Daily Mail* in 1896, compared with start-up costs of £20,000 in 1855 and £50,000 in the 1870s. Yet in 1837 the *Northern Star* was founded with just £690 (Curran et al. 2003: 27–8). By the time Conservatives in Cornwall wanted to set up a local paper in 1922, they thought the cost prohibitive at £50,000 (Dawson 1998: 210). The founders of the *Bristol Evening Post* hoped to raise £60,000 to start their paper in the early 1930s but were only able to manage on £40,000 because of donations, hire purchase agreements and a large overdraft. By 1976, it was thought that £2 million would be needed to found a title from scratch, including the purchase of land and buildings; this explained why most new daily titles were founded by existing newspaper companies who not only enjoyed economies of scale in terms of production but who also had the capital necessary to support the investment needed to establish a title (Hartley et al. 1977: 64).

The continued rise in the costs of labour and materials created an economic context which was to be a driver for innovations in new technology in the 1980s. Between 1920 and 1977 the costs of paper rose from £11 to nearly £230 a tonne (Royal Commission on the Press 1977–49: 57), with the British newspaper industry reliant on imports from Scandinavia. Yet the British were avid consumers of newspapers; in 1936 the nation had the largest estimated consumption of newsprint per head at 59.38 lbs, compared with 57.5 lbs for Australasia, 57 for the United States and only 18.1 for France. The newsprint industry was therefore significant and the owners of newspaper companies also held interests in newsprint production. In contrast, the relative costs of the elements of newspaper production as a proportion of the overall costs remained fairly stable. Both the Political and Economic Planning report of 1938 and Hartley's investigation for the Royal Commission in 1977 offer

Table 5.5 Distribution of costs of newspaper production 1938 compared with 1974–7

	Daily Newspaper 1938 (percentage)	Daily Newspaper 1974–7 (percentage)
Newsprint and ink	34.6	31.1
Editorial	23.1	24.7
Production	23.1	33.6
Circulation and distribution	15.4	11.8

Source: Political and Economic Planning 1938: 71; Hartley 1977: 21.

a picture of the various elements involved in newspaper production and distribution. While based on a differing methodology,[5] comparable figures are presented in Table 5.5.

To balance the risk, the newspaper companies branched out not only into allied industries, including magazine and book publishing, film and paper companies, but also further afield. Writing in 1947 in a pre-emptive strike against the Royal Commission of the same year, Viscount Camrose described how, in addition to its core newspaper business, Associated Newspapers owned £1 million in government securities, the Empire Paper Mills and more than 900,000 shares in the Anglo-Newfoundland Development Co Ltd, whose interests included mining (1947: 56). By the 1960s this eclectic pattern of company interests was in ascendancy in a position embodied in Lord Thomson who told the 1961 Royal Commission: 'My purpose is to run newspapers as a business ... to make money. That is what you do business for' (Murdock and Golding 1978: 142).

By the time of the Report of Royal Commission of 1977 it was evident that this strategy had given commercial benefit to the top chains, who had managed to preserve trading profits – or at least experienced a smaller decline – in the face of a harsh economic climate caused by an 8 per cent fall in advertising revenues (Hartley et al. 1977: 25). By this point the organization of the chains was no longer led by the titles owned, but instead by the publishing centres from which they were produced. For the Royal Commission this new unit formed the focus of study, because it was simply too difficult to disentangle

---

[5] The Political and Economic Planning model was based on a fictional 1d. daily newspaper, whereas the Royal Commission surveyed actual newspapers to come up with its findings.

aggregated costs such as management from shared centres of publication; this marked a change from the surveys carried out fifteen years before. By 1974 the top ten newspaper groups controlled nearly 81 per cent of total evening newspaper circulations (up from 74% in 1961) (ibid.: 39). In most cases they owned the only title in a town, and these monopolies were grouped along geographical lines so that particular newspaper companies formed contiguous monopolies . For instance, by 1977 the Associated Newspaper group had extensive holdings in the south west, publishing five evening, two morning and weekly newspapers in Cornwall, Devon, Somerset and Gloucestershire.

Such organization enabled businesses to share costs in management, production, editorial and advertising sales, and between 1961 and 1975, thirty-five of the sixty-seven printing centres owned by the national chains were closed (although two new ones were created on greenfield sites). However, it also meant that groups could probably afford to pay over the odds for existing titles because of the potential savings, as well as profits, which may have accounted for the large decrease in independent ownership of profit-making titles (ibid.: 85).

Consolidation of ownership: Royal Commissions

A continual theme of this period is the obsession with the effect of the consolidation of ownership on a newspaper's ability to act as a democratic organ. The three Royal Commissions form extensive testament to this, but though full of facts and figures, they offer few concrete conclusions. Read in tandem, though, the three government-sponsored reports can be seen as narrating a long road to realizing the full impact of the dominance of big business on newspaper ownership. The first Royal Commission of 1947–9, while admitting that the provincial press had been most affected by changes in ownership, still maintained that consolidated ownership had had little impact. As early as 1938 the left-wing think tank Political Economic Planning's report had concluded that while a limit was advisable, consolidation in itself was not detrimental to newspaper freedom. In fact, the report concluded, it could offer a way to harness capital for the benefit of the Labour movement, as with the *Daily Herald* newspaper. The report had though got to the core of the question which was to test the industry for nearly half a decade; when should a limit be put on group ownership of newspapers and how should that limit be imposed? What all seemed to agree on was that the newspaper industry was special.

> The Press, however, cannot and does not exist on a purely commercial footing. Almost every newspaper to some extent consciously performs a social function, although its performance is moulded by its proprietor's and its editor's views of what the public wants, their ideas of what is ethically, socially and politically desirable, and its resources of ability and technical equipment. (Political Economic Planning 1938: 256–7)

The debate polarized the two factions, which were increasingly aligned along party political lines with the election of the post-war Labour government. As previously cited, the owners, embodied in Viscount Camrose and Thomson, proclaimed that they owned newspapers for their business potential only – and not to wield undue influence over the readers. Opposing them were those who produced newspapers – an increasingly unionized workforce which criticized the power exerted over them by capital. The result was an 'us and them' relationship between those who owned the papers and those who produced them.

At the same time as the motivation for newspaper ownership narrowed, so the operation of those newspapers became increasingly demarcated, continuing the process described in the preceding section. With increased demands on both speed and standard of production, roles within newspapers were increasingly specialized. These changes formed the backdrop to the anxiety which is manifest in the motion of the National Union of Journalists in calling for the first Royal Commission, and in the motion before the House of Commons calling for the commission itself. This increasing demarcation of newspaper production also meant that owners and workers were increasingly separated with each section represented by its specific union. While the owners were represented by the Institute of Journalists, the National Union of Journalists explicitly excluded proprietors (Lee 1978: 127). By the census of 1931 of 9,000 journalists and photographers employed in newspapers, some 6,600 were members of the NUJ and a further 2,700 were members of the Institute of Journalists. Print shops, employing 29,000 men, were nearly totally unionized, usually via membership of the London Society of Compositors or the National Society of Operative Printers and Assistants (Natsopa), which was affiliated to the Printing and Kindred Trades Federation (Political Economic Planning 1938). These organizations campaigned for improved pay and conditions for their members, and it is worthy of note that newspaper sellers, who remained outside of the Labour movement, continued to be the worst-paid sector of the newspaper industry. In contrast a 1935 survey by the Ministry of Labour showed that printing was one of the best-paid artisan occupations in the UK. A total of 24,000 men earned 110s. 9d. a week, compared with textile workers' wages of 36s. 4d., 53s. 2d. for those in the metal industries and 61s. 10d. for the chemical industry workers. The popularity of the printing trade, therefore, meant it was a hard one to enter with friends and relations taking priority among new entrants.

Journalists' wages had also increased. It had been considered a poorly paid profession, and an NUJ survey in 1911 showed that average wage of a reporter in the provinces was 33s. a week and for subeditors, 35s. a week. By 1921 an agreement between the Newspaper Proprietors' Association and the NUJ set provincial minima within a range from £5 5s. for journalists on daily newspapers in large towns to £4 7s. 6d. for those on weekly newspapers in small towns, payable at the age of twenty-four after four years' experience. London journalists were assured nine guineas a week – a wage structure which reflected, and reinforced, the significance of the provincial press as the starting point and training ground for London-based workers. Therefore the industry also gave rise to organizations which represented the interests of the employers with the creation of the Newspaper Proprietors' Association (later to become the Newspaper Publishers Association) in London in 1908, the continuation of the Newspaper Society for provincial owners and editors, and the formation of the Joint Industrial Council to negotiate with the unions. It was also recognized that the printers' unions were in a very strong position, because of their ability to paralyse production this may explain employers' willingness to support high wages.

The Political Economic Planning report (1938: 239) also evidences that the further the provincial newspapers were from London, the more dominant their position was in a market. Evidence from the National Executive Committee[6] of the NUJ also suggested that an increased concentration of ownership of provincial newspapers in particular was cause for concern, and it was a resolution passed by the NUJ which led to the formation of Royal Commission on the Press 1947. The minutes couched the argument in terms of the need to preserve the freedom of the press and concentrate on the reputation and

---

[6] The minute books examined here are within the holdings of the Modern Records Centre at the University of Warwick.

operation of journalism; to this end the NUJ was also active in campaigning for appropriate training and worked with the Newspaper Society to create a 'national council' to oversee it. One aim was to arm journalists with the power to resist interference from owners; the minute books document instances where reporters were asked to act against the values they associated with their practice as journalists – for instance by being told to trail celebrities of the day, having been specifically asked not to by their targets – in the pursuit of newspaper sales (NUJ 1947: 182).

Alongside the anxiety about the effect of consolidation on the role of the press as a fourth estate, there was a party political aspect to this debate. The unionized press workers feared that capitalist-owned newspapers would not support the post-war Labour government. This stance was backed by a report by the Labour Research Department, which was commissioned by the NUJ, into 'the ramifications and profits of newspapers' (NUJ 1946: 125). The substantive argument of the report was clear from its title, *The Millionaire Press* (1946):

> These tendencies [of chain ownership], dangerous at any time, are of particular concern to the Labour movement today. The Labour Government, elected with a clear mandate, stands confronted with, in the main, a bitterly hostile Press … which reflects not the interest and the aspirations of the British people or of any considerable section of it, but purely those of large-scale capitalism. (Labour Research Department 1946: 3)

The pamphlet concentrated on unpicking the complex ownership of the national and provincial press in Britain. Adding weight to calls for a Royal Commission, it argued that the industry was so complex that only a commission could 'go behind' the complexities of ownership and advertising pressures facing newspapers (Labour Research Department 1946: 17). In calling for a government-led inquiry, a deputation from the NUJ laid out its arguments in a resolution before the lord president of the council. Significantly the resolution was supported by key provincial NUJ chapels – including those in the Kemsley Federated Group Chapel, Withy Grove (Thomson) Chapel and the Manchester Trade and Periodical branches – and explicitly drew on the discursive position of the press as a fourth estate to legitimize their position.

> The freedom of press we claim from the Government of the day must not be choked by the concentration of the country's newspapers in the hands of two or three powerful commercial groups. Control of any commodity necessary to the community by a few persons who may succeed in cornering it is bad, but such a

control of our commodity is particularly deleterious because we are concerned with the mental and cultural needs of the people. (NUJ 1947: 63)

The arguments then transferred to Parliament via the MPs – whose number included members of the NUJ – who moved the motion in the House of Commons to convene the inquiry in 1946.

The debate into the need for the Royal Commission, as recorded in the official Parliamentary record of Hansard, draws directly on the NUJ's call for an inquiry. The motion was introduced by NUJ member and MP Haydn Davies (St Pancras, south west), who clearly stated the perceived incompatibility of profit and community interest. The Liberal MP also expressed the concern felt by journalists about the erosion of their integrity by the pursuit of profit. Proposing the motion, Mr Davies said: 'We have watched the destruction of great papers. We have watched the combines come in, buying up and killing independent journals, and we have seen the honourable profession of journalism degraded by high finance and big business. Worst of all, as a result of this, we have watched subservience replace judgment, and we are worried about the position' (Hansard 1946: vol. 428 cc452456). This trend in provincial newspaper closures was cited by parliamentarians as necessitating an inquiry into the shape of newspaper ownership in the aftermath of the Second World War. Mr Davies encapsulated the arguments when he told his fellow MPs:

> What is wrong is not so much the private ownership of the Press, but the use that is being made of that private ownership in order to pile up dividends. It is claimed, for example, that these big, powerful combines do not influence local opinions – that they are free. But what kind of freedom is it? There were four papers in Sheffield; they buy four and kill two. There were four in Cardiff; they buy four and kill two. I wonder whether the killing of these papers was really done in the interest of the freedom of the Press, in the interest of the people of those towns, or in the interest of that blessed word 'efficiency', which means dividends. (Hansard 1946: vol. 428 c457)

These arguments failed to win over the Royal Commission convened as a consequence. Preceding the commission by nine years, the Political Economic Planning report of 1938 suggested that alternative business models, such as cooperatives, would add variety to the newspaper market and even went as far to suggest that a newspaper works should be publicly owned to make production affordable to alternatively funded publications. The Royal Commission of 1947 though concluded that the free market was the best preserver of the free press.

It remarked that consolidation was unlikely to continue at the pace already seen and that, at its current level, it was 'not so great as to prejudice the free expression of opinion or the accurate presentation of news or to be contrary to the best interests of the public' (1947: 176).[7] The next Royal Commission, while echoing this tacit support for consolidated ownership, recognized that competition between newspapers had become fiercer and entry costs more prohibitive. It also acknowledged that one of the perils of chain ownership was the loss of a local paper's local character (1962: 116). The commission did suggest the creation of a Press Amalgamation Court to consider the effect of future mergers and from 1965 significant mergers were referred to the Monopolies and Mergers Commission. The final Royal Commission report (Vol 1 1977: 231) would go on to recommend that the circulation at which mergers were considered should be dropped from 500,000 to 200,000.

Commercial practice and the good of the community

Writing of the regional press in the interwar years, Bromley and Hayes (2002) suggest that the commercial context described at length above acted as a liberating force for journalism, creating a 'democracy of print'. The interwar years in particular coincided with a 'golden age' for local government and enabled regional papers to offer '*the ubiquitous civic voice*: vital yet distanced from partisanship'. The consolidated titles may have created – and exploited – urban markets for advertising revenues, but this commercial position did not preclude an editorial stance which influenced the creation of civic identity. The priority given to local content, commercially as well as editorially, was outlined in evidence to the Royal Commission of 1947, by William McWhirter, of Northcliffe Newspapers Ltd.

> We give preference rather in this order: first of all local public notices, such as notices from the Town Council or the Ministry of Health; then the classified advertisements, or what are called 'smalls'. We attach great importance to these 'smalls' because they are part of the life of the community. … Thirdly we put the local display advertisements, for example, by the local draper or the furniture

---

[7] It did recommend that a press council be created to 'safeguard the freedom of the Press; to encourage the growth of the sense of public responsibility and public service amongst all engaged in the profession of journalism' (ibid.: 177), and this resulted in the first manifestation of press self-regulation, the General Council, in 1953.

man. After that, and very far after it, we carry the national advertising because we consider it to our duty to five as much publicity to the local community as is possible. (Evidence to the Royal Commission 1947–9, para 5379)

Contrary to the 'subservience' outlined by Haydn Davies, McWhirter suggested that those journalists working in the commercialized press were able to act independently of political partisanship. This meant they could position themselves as serving the interests of their community, scrutinizing and holding to account those in power, while simultaneously negotiating the working conditions of an increasingly consolidated industry. This position was also codified in the training route into journalism, which was organized around a 'start' in the regional press before the best progressed to Fleet Street. The National Council for the Training of Journalists was formed in 1951 following long debates over training standards (National Council for the Training of Journalists 2011). Thus, when Richard Stott recalled his early days as a reporter at the *Bucks Herald* in Aylesbury in the early 1960s, it was this key relationship between journalist, reader and local decision-makers which was brought to the fore.

Nevertheless, it was a concern with the triumph of profit over public benefit which formed the backdrop for research carried out by Ian Jackson and published in the early 1970s, writing as he was against the background of an increasingly monopolistic pattern of ownership for titles described here. At the time of writing, he suggested that around 55 per cent of daily and 25 per cent of weekly regional and local titles were owned by 'chains' – by which he meant the News of the World Organisation Ltd, Associated Newspapers, United Newspapers, The Thompson Organisation and the Westminster Press Group. Following from the Royal Commission of 1947–9, Jackson expressed concern that these owners would elevate the profit motive above all others, which would result in a 'world of candy floss and puff' content favoured by 'consensus-seeking market journalism'. Therefore, while the notion of the local press as serving the good of the community might have been 'an essential part of its public legitimacy' (Conboy 2004: 127), increasingly the extent to which a highly commercialized local press, was able to fulfil this role, was called into question. This concern has come to the fore again when speaking of the legacy local newspaper in the digitized twenty-first century, faced with falling revenues and circulations. In this process, the pressure of profits reduces the proposition that communal life depends on this form of news reporting to an ideology of news production which serves the economic interest of the localized provincial newspaper industry (Franklin and Murphy 1991: 56). The idea that the journalist serves the good of the community is reduced to a 'functionalist' notion which serves the organization of the moneymaking title, rather than any higher purpose which might give value to the journalist's work. And this is possible precisely because the relationship between paper and community is primarily ill-defined and opportunistic and, therefore, open to exploitation for profit.

> Central to it is the idea of a community, a social unit of indeterminate size united by a common set of interests and worldview which differentiate it from the wider social world which constitutes its environment. There is then a definitional equation between the life and events of the people in that community and its institutional structure, so that the version of events promulgated by powerful individuals within this institutional order become the established truth of communal life. The market, in the form of the circulation area of the newspaper, is also identified with the community so that even if they are not definitionally identical, the two are at least in a mutually supportive relationship. And the role of the journalist is formulated precisely in functionalists terms; to provide a record of the community to make people publicly accountable who should be; to participate in the system of social control; and to do this in the context of a set of relationships, with 'contacts' chosen by their roles in the institutions which they themselves and the newspaper identify as the defining structure of the community. (ibid.: 58–9)

This conflict embodied the reasons for the first Royal Commission in 1947–9, and its discussion has implications for the ideological posturing that the provincial press exercised then and continues to exercise in contemporary discussions around its future. In particular, the good of the community, rather than being the guiding principle for the press, becomes an idealized standard promoted by the discourse which expounds the value of the provincial press. This conflict between the ideology of community champion and the business imperative began to show during this period of consolidation, when individual provincial newspapers began to lose the distinctive character which had bound them to their locale (Lee 1978: 128). At the same time, the ideological values of editorial staff were increasingly tested by the same commercial context which reduced their titles to anodyne units in a chain of linked products. In this view, as the period under consideration drew to a close, the scene was set for a period in which the nature of the provincial newspaper was to become increasingly homogenized as companies stripped out editorial resources, to maintain shareholder profits. This was possible only after pitched battles to defeat collective bargaining, and, in doing so, disempower journalists.

6

The Provincial Press in Wartime

Conflict is good news for newspapers

In his analysis of Manchester's newspapers during the city's blitz, Guy Hodgson observes that 'war, generally, is good news for newspapers. What is being reported has an increased significance, readers have a greater stake in what appears in print, and, correspondingly, circulations rise' (2015: xii). This is particularly true for the provincial paper in the Second World War to the extent that the effect on its business model was so profound as to be described as 'abnormal' by the post-war Royal Commission. This abnormality reached far into the structure of the industry, affecting content, materials and staffing; but its combined effect was to maintain, and even increase, the profitability of these businesses so that, over all, the provincial newspaper industry might be said to have had a good war, despite the hardships it endured. In particular, the Second World War interrupted the unremitting march to consolidation, which typifies the newspaper between 1914 and 1976, by promoting cooperative working arrangements which triumphed over business rivalries to ensure that titles were produced. At the same time this cooperation was justified, not in terms of enabling newspapers to continue trading but in terms of facilitating their service to their readers. Therefore, it is during this period that we see the provincial newspaper consolidate its construction as steadfast community champion, a role which it publicly promoted and proclaimed as it did its best to provide continual publication in a move which also maintained profits.

Such was the demand for newspapers that between 1937 and 1947 circulations rose from 1.6 million to 2.7 million for the provincial morning paper and from 4.43 million to 6.78 million for the provincial evening. The circulation of weeklies and biweeklies nearly doubled during the same period from 7.42 million to 14.2 million. This rise in circulations was accomplished despite severe restrictions on the raw material of newsprint, imposed incrementally during the course of the conflict, which at worst reduced the amount of paper to just 20 per cent of the pre-war levels. Systematic rationing meant that titles could choose to print more, small papers, or fewer copies, with higher paginations. Circulation wars to achieve a high sale to attract advertisers, which had typified the preceding decades, were, therefore, out of the question; more significantly smaller papers made such competitive practices unnecessary because demand for advertising was greater than the space available. The pre-war practices epitomized by the *Evening World* chain, designed to give titles supremacy in a market, were made redundant, and instead competing titles cooperated to ensure that print runs were maintained – producing each other's papers when print works were damaged by bombing and even sharing skilled manpower. In effect this meant that the normal rules of competitive practice were suspended for an industry where demand for sales and advertising space outstripped supply. This situation lasted beyond the end of the war due, in turn, to continued shortages of, first, the raw materials to make paper and, second, the national wealth to afford imports. Its effect was to prolong the life of those poorly performing publications which might have otherwise folded and also to restrict new entries into the market which was already grappling with scant resources.

The BBC has been credited with being the lynchpin of morale for the British civilian population during the Second World War (Curran et al. 2003), and this period is one in which the broadcast industry in the form of the BBC gained ascendancy over newspapers as a form of mass communication. However, an analysis of the provincial press at this time demonstrates how it positioned itself as being key to the war effort in the areas it sought to serve and as being recognized as vital in keeping the information channels open by the Ministry of Information (McClaine 1979: 134). Such was the emphasis placed on their continued ability to publish that in key areas likely to be bombed – including Plymouth and Newcastle – standby print works were created. Contemporaneous accounts also highlight the importance to a population of seeing their local paper on the streets after destructive events, such as air raids. This is typified by the *Midland Daily Telegraph*, the daily paper for Coventry, which was on sale the morning after the city sustained catastrophic damage in one of the worse German bombing raids of the Second World War – including the destruction of the newspaper's own offices and printing presses. 'In its blackest days', wrote Sir William Bailey, president of the Newspaper Society for the duration of the Second World War, 'the Provincial newspapers carried into every one of the millions of homes of the Provinces messages that inspired hope. … Government, industry and commerce learned to appreciate the Provincial newspapers at their proper worth. They placed their trust in the Provincial Press, and that trust has not been misplaced' (Fletcher 1946: 6). This evidence suggests that during the Second World War the discursive construction of the provincial newspaper as serving the good of the community was solidified as the industry made claim to bolstering the local population through times of crisis; not only did this position chime with the discourse of the war effort, and specifically the 'blitz spirit' which came to dominate discussions of how the UK population fared during the conflict, but it also justified an anti-competitive cooperation among newspaper owners that enabled them to continue to make substantial profits during a time of national crisis.

The provincial press and the community in the First World War

The operation of the provincial press during the Second World War was largely shaped by systems which had their origins in the first conflict. This was the time in which the provincial press – the sole source of news for many of its readers – learnt to capitalize on the commercial potential of war, drawing, in turn, on lessons learnt by covering the Boer War at the end of the nineteenth century in a way which helped these titles cement their relationship with a specific community. The system of censorship and government intervention into newspaper coverage of the second war also built on the operation of the first. The relationship between the provincial press and censor was such that the industry was able to draw on a multitude of sources to create a complex picture of the conflict from a specialist community-based focus. Finn suggests that the significance of the provincial press increased for its readership during the First World War – largely due to the recruitment of forces around local regiments. Coverage was, therefore, able to include testimony both via personal and written contact with both the paper and its readers in order to 'provide a locally-focused, community-oriented narrative of what the war represented' (2002: 27). In the provincial press, this extended to reporting the deaths of local men and carrying obituaries, often in the form of a simple picture and statement of name, regiment and place and date of death.

At the outset of the conflict, these titles met a demand for war news by increasing paginations; special editions were also published on Sundays – a traditional 'day off' for the provincial daily in 1914. As much war news as possible was included, drawing on a variety of angles, many of them particular to its circulation area. These included news of local regiments, and recruitment services and areas were proud of their efforts in joining up. When Barnsley was able to raise 150 men more than the first battalion needed, the Barnsley Town Council agreed to raise a second – a fact proudly reported by the *Sheffield Evening Telegraph* (1 December 1914: 4). Alongside the domestic stuff of war, uncompromising reports of battles involving local regiments were included. '"I have lost my right leg," Private W Hartness told readers of the *Barnsley Chronicle* on 15 July 1916. "It is something awful … I am very sorry to say that the Barnsley lads have caught it. It was like hell let loose, and I never thought I should get through it alive"' (Finn 2002: 206). A Coventry Soldier was able to give first-hand testimony to the horror of the front line having been sent home, injured.

> We were in the thick of it Monday night, all Tuesday night, and Wednesday. It was raining heaven's hard. I got wounded on Wednesday morning. I crawled about eight miles before I got picked up and I was in great pain. Just before I advanced to the firing line on Wednesday I could see a lot of chaps falling down so I made my will out to you. … Why we have lost so heavily is because there are too many Germans for us to tackle. If we shot one down there were a dozen to take their place. (*Midland Daily Telegraph*, 1 September 1914: 5)

This soldier provided graphic details of the experiences of his fellow soldiers, 'Coventry and Leamington chaps' (from Leamington Spa, nearby), many of whom would have been members of the local Royal Warwickshire Regiment. The report is graphic: this man was injured as the man beside him died; he reported seeing dead women and children and villages burnt. But in common with most of the reports, this man was not disheartened by his experience. 'I am ready to have another pot at them [the enemy forces] if they send us out again,' he continues, 'and I hope and please God I only get off wounded again' (ibid.). Focusing on the experience of the 'Royal Warwicks', a report on 5 September describes how the regiment was among 3,000 men caught in the Battle of Mons. The paper reports a 'conversation' with one of the men who said, 'We found ourselves in a slaughterhouse. … We were so overwhelmed by the German forces that we were ordered by our officers to look after ourselves. I don't know how I got away from it' (*Midland Daily Telegraph*, 5 September 1914: 5).

These titles were passed back and forth between the front line and the local population so that they served as a palpable conduit of information between community and serving soldier. Papers were sent out by readers but also as part of a shipments of warm clothes and other 'comforts' collected via appeals run by the papers themselves. A letter from the skipper of the HMT Daimler, then anchored in Lowestoft, in the *Hull Daily Mail*, attested to this habit. 'May I, once again, thank our unknown friend for papers etc received. I am distributing them amongst any other fellow-townsmen I happen to meet here' (18 December 1914: 4). A particularly poignant demonstration of this connection was appeals for information placed by families who had not heard from their loved ones, such as Mrs Clarke, of South Street, Coventry, whose husband had been reported missing. 'Any comrade who can state what has become of him is urgently asked to forward the information and relieve Mrs. Clarke's suspense' (*Midland Daily Telegraph*, 28 October 1915: 2). In December 1915, Mrs Johnson, of Norden, Rochdale, appealed via the *Rochdale Observer* for news of her husband, a member of the Lancashire Fusilliers who had last written to her in the previous July. 'If this is seen by any reader of the "Observer" at the Dardanelles or at home, who knows anything of Sergeant Johnson, we shall be pleased to hear from him,' the paper wrote (*Rochdale Observer*, 15 December 1915: 2).

The government of the day exercised control over these press reports via a combination of voluntary and statutory methods. As early as 1912, organizations representing the provincial press had been included in the establishment of voluntary mechanisms of censorship, set by press and service representatives in what became known as the Joint Committee. As a founding member of the Joint Committee (Admiralty, War Office and Press Committee), the Newspaper Society pledged its own membership would abide by decisions over censorship as issued by the committee, and this voluntary collusion ensured that the British Expeditionary Force was in France before news of its departure was published. At the outbreak of the war, cables and telegraphs were censored, and the Defence of the Realm Regulations (DORA) created the Press Bureau to control the flow of news via dissemination and the use of the D Notice system to prohibit publication. The provincial newspapers were also among those who welcomed the institution of the Press Bureau in August 1914, and when it was up and running, it provided facilities for newsmen from both London and regional newspapers as well as news (Cook 1920: 47). The bureau operated according to the requirements of DORA in order to 'prevent the leakage of militarily useful information to the enemy'; this act also made it an offence to 'spread false reports, spread reports likely to case disaffection to His Majesty or prejudice relations with foreign powers, prejudice recruiting or undermine public confidence in banks or the currency' (Gregory 2004: 22). The bureau issued around 700 instructions to guide editors on what content should be submitted for censorship, although its operation was heavily criticized by contemporaries who claimed it served to conceal from the public the full horror of the conflict in its first year (Haste 1977: 31). This criticism of newspaper coverage that it was pandering to official guidelines rather than truthfully reporting in the public interest was to be reprised in the Second World War.

Embargoed information was released to the provincial press well in advance via post so that it could meet the same publications times as the London press (ibid.: 50). This supply of 'official' news came to restrict the localized service which dominated the coverage of the early part of the First World War. This was exacerbated by the shortage of newsprint, which was described as a 'serious crisis' by the Newspaper Proprietors' Association (Cabinet Paper GT3783, 28 February 1918: 239). The weekly press, in particular, was supplied with a supplement of content by the War Aims committee, which claimed to reach a million readers (Cabinet Paper GT4354, April 1918: 174). But the system was also riven by infighting and dissatisfaction. As early as 1915 the Metropolitan newspapers complained that the censorship of the provincial press was more lenient than that levelled at the London-based papers; no devolved regional system of censorship was ever comprehensively established, so the London titles submitted far more copies for review because of their physical proximity to the censor. In turn, provincial titles complained that they suppressed reports which then appeared in lesser publications such as parish magazines, and editors would inform the censor about stories published in rival titles, which they saw as contravening the system. Underpinning this attitude was a notion that the authorities in Berlin were scanning the pages of every local newspaper for a hint of significant information; it was the strength of this image that persuaded editors to continue to self-censor to the extent that some suppressed reports of the physical damage and human costs of air raids, while others thought they were too extensive and obvious to ignore – despite D Notices telling them to do so (Lovelace 1982: 104). The result was a form of a war reporting which subsumed the truth of the conflict to the interests of national security and continued recruitment. This cooperative form of a censorship was probably made easier by the close ties between newspaper proprietors and the political class (Gregory 2004: 19), and its institutionalization via legislation sowed the seeds for the professionalization of government communications and the eventual founding of the Ministry of Information (Haste 1977). By February 1917, the system of information control had been centralized under a Department for Information, and this organization was refined again to form the Ministry of Information in March 1918, which was to take centre stage in the Second World War.

Publishing in the face of the adversity of the Second World War

If the provincial press had been significant to the war effort during the First World War, by 1939 it was more so. Aggregate circulations for newspapers are hard to establish before the era of audited sales figures in the 1920s; but even so, evidence related to profitability suggests that there were more sales, in spite of fewer titles, by the time of the outbreak of the Second World War. At this time there were 25 morning papers in England, Wales and Scotland, 77 evening papers, 6 Sunday titles and more than 1,300 weekly papers. These figures remain stable from 1937 through the duration of the Royal Commission from 1947 to 1949. Circulations for all newspapers rose largely in the periods 1937–9 and 1946–7 because of the impact of newsprint rationing on the intervening period. The circulations of the national morning papers had also increased by 55.9 per cent, from 9.9 million to 15.4 million, the provincial morning circulations had risen by about 70 per cent for the same period and the provincial evening circulations by nearly 53 per cent (Royal Commission 1947–9: 80).

Sir Walter Layton, chairman of the Rationing Committee of the Newsprint Supply Company, ascribed the increased demand for newspapers in 1939 to 'the stirring events of the war and the dispersal of family units to the Forces or to munition factories' (Layton 1946: 12). The effect on the morale of a press which was voluntarily supporting the war effort was also recognized (Curran and Seaton 2003: 63), and Clampin (2014), in his discussion of advertising in newspapers, suggests that the press was seen as 'crucial' to sustaining morale. For the provincial press, a key contributor was seen to be its ability to publish in the face of adverse conditions. Speaking in October 1939, Sir William Bailey said on behalf of the provincial press, 'It is now a matter for each and everyone of us to see that, unless circumstances make it impossible, our papers come out for the continued information of our readers and the sustaining of their morale in what may prove to be a long struggle' (Fletcher 1946: 5).

To the government it was, therefore, vital that an industry of such import was managed via censorship. Drawing on the experience of the First World War, the Ministry of Information was created on the outbreak of war in 1939, having been previously planned and used to disseminate information about the pre-war political situation. Its advisory board numbered representatives from the provincial newspaper industry including Lord Iliffe, owner of the *Midland Daily Telegraph*, Lady Denman, of Westminster Press, and Sir William Bailey, then chairman of the Newspaper Society (Larson 1941: 417). The ministry came to be under the leadership of Lord Camrose, owner of the *Daily Telegraph* and co-founder of Allied Newspapers. Censorship forbad all British citizens from publishing information which might be useful to the enemy; it was also an offence to publicize military matters. This meant the ministry scrutinized all copy and photos which had the potential to be militarily sensitive, and failure to comply could give cause for the publication to be closed (Williams 2010: 175). Both national and provincial titles were subject to censorship and, unlike the system during the First World War, the organization of the system took account of the regions via a series of offices in Bristol, Cardiff, Birmingham, Glasgow, Manchester, Leeds and Belfast, specifically to serve the needs of the provincial press (Fletcher 1946: 13). In all, around 1,700 volunteers in the regions supported the official machinery, and submission of material to the censors ensured that editors were safe from potential prosecution should something be published which breached security rules. Provincial editors were also invited to monthly meetings in London, and these events formed the basis for the formation of the Guild of British Newspaper Editors, the forerunner to the extant Society of Editors, in 1946 (Pratt Boorman 1961: 16).

As in the First World War, cooperation was to be the key to the partnership between government and provincial press during the Second World War, to the extent that the system of censorship during the second conflict has been described as one based on a series of 'nods and winks'; the cooperative relationships between ministers and newspaper proprietors who shared a cultural background were characterized as 'the British way of censorship' (Williams 2010: 173). This voluntary collaboration was revealed to the readership by the *Coventry Evening Telegraph* once war was over, as it unveiled the secrets of the 'shadow factories' which had been hidden in the city (Fletcher 1946: 14). Some 40,000 workers had been employed at the former Coventry car manufacturers making Spitfires and Lancasters. The city produced nearly 19,000 aircraft – or 15.8 per cent of the country's total wartime output (*Coventry Evening Telegraph*, 11 May 1945: 2). As such, the factories could hardly have been secret from a large number of the paper's readership. 'For nearly six years the British Press has held a tremendous responsibility. Many of the most vital secrets of the war have been placed in its keeping, and those secrets have been as safe as if they had been locked in the Chancellor's despatch box' (*Coventry Evening Telegraph*, 31 May 1945: 3). The Ministry of Information was disbanded in 1946, but such was the recognition for the role of information services that its legacy was the Central Office of Information (Franklin 1991: 76).

James Curran (Curran and Seaton 2003: 56) argues that the most significant power in the structure of censorship was Regulation 2D which gave the home secretary the power to ban anti-war publications. Although opposition from within and without Parliament was successful in tempering the tenor of the regulation, the Communist *Daily Worker*, which had campaigned about a lack of appropriate air raid shelters, and the *Week* were closed on January 21, 1941. This was despite the small circulation of the *Daily Worker*, which stood at less than 1 per cent of the total circulation for all daily newspapers, a sale attributed to its sports coverage – including a successful horse race tipster (Williams 2010: 175). The *Daily Worker* was allowed to reopen eighteen months later, and Williams argues that its closure was part of a wider campaign to curtail the press.[1] The *Daily Mirror* was also subject to widespread pressure, because of its criticism of the government, and Williams argues that censorship did shape war coverage – for instance by glossing over the extent to which the Allied forces were defeated at Dunkirk (2010: 176). The material effect of censorship at provincial level was to delay news about the weather and to anonymize reports of attacks on regional towns; thus the Nuneaton-based *Midland Daily Tribune* could not name its own town in reports of a raid which killed 100 people and damaged more than 10,000 buildings (Fletcher 1946: 48).

The government professed the value of the provincial press as a conduit for communicating with people. Advertising placed in the regional press grew to promote the work of no fewer than twenty-four departments, including the Ministry of Food. Among these, the weekly Food Facts served an information purpose but were also designed to boost morale by 'showing that a besieged nation could feed itself adequately and sometimes even pleasantly' (Ogilvy-Webb 1965: 59). Interesting things to do with carrots, recipes using dried egg which 'taste every bit as good as if they were made with shell eggs' (*Tamworth Herald*, 2 September 1944: 4), were published in the pages of provincial newspapers until well after war's end. The Newspaper Society quotes a survey that showed that 91

---

[1] Research carried out as part of the AHRC-funded project into newspapers and the Second World War at the University of Aberystwyth suggests that the national press did not support the *Daily Worker* at this time (Nicholas 2014). The title had though been highly critical of those London-based papers which it saw as colluding with government and not telling the truth about war.

per cent of readers read the Food Facts and that 27 per cent of readers actually cut out and kept them (Fletcher 1946: 13). Similarly, the editorial director of the National Savings Committee, which ran adverts to promote saving in support of the war effort, said in 1941 of provincial papers,

> They go into every home. They are read by every member of the family. They are, in an enormous number of cases, afterwards posted to relatives or friends in all parts of the country, of the Empire and of the world. They are sent to our soldiers, sailors, and airman. They play a vital part in the civic, religious, industrial and social life of the nation. (Fletcher 1946: 13)

While papers might have been in demand, so too were those people employed in producing them, and during the Second World War, there was a near 80 per cent fall from the 90,000 people employed in the newspaper industry. This was partly due to titles shrinking their operations in line with the fall in availability of raw materials, but also because of the depletion of staff due to the call up. Editors were able to apply to the War Office to keep staff, if they could demonstrate that they were essential to the continued production of the newspaper. But even so, losses were great and the Provincial Newspaper Society notes that one larger title lost more than 400 members of staff to the services (Fletcher 1946: 10). One editor in charge of three weekly papers recalls how his total staff of twenty-three had joined the armed forces. He was producing the papers with 'outside help' including three formerly retired members of staff, two of whom were aged seventy and one was aged eighty-three. Another weekly editor catalogued how he lost his entire dispatch department, his advertising and circulation managers and a third of his printing workforce – when he used to have a staff of fifty.

> The rotary press, which trade union regulations stipulate shall be manned by four men, is now in the charge of one man, and he aged 67. He is assisted by a C3[2] van driver and a man drawn from the retired ranks of labour and who sweeps the floors during the greater part of the week. This rotary printer has also to see to the stereotyping and plate casting, and to help him out we borrow a stereotype from an associated office on publishing day because their day of publication is different from ours.
>
> This borrowed man works all day and half the night on his own paper, goes home to wash and rest for about two hours, travels 50 miles and works from 9am to 10pm on our publication day.

---

[2]   This refers to the British Army medical categorization. A 'C' classification meant fit for home service only.

> The type setting department consists of two men approaching 70 years of age, one operator with an artificial leg, one just recovering from an operation, one gassed in the last war, one apprentice with cardiac trouble, one other adult.
>
> There is an apprentice approaching 18 whom we expect to lose in two months' time. (Fletcher 1946: 10–11)

New machinery and spares were impossible to come by, so that the newspapers practised the make-do-and-mend philosophy they preached (Fletcher 1946: 11) while contributing to the 'will to win' by supporting war charities such as fighter funds or 'comforts' for the forces (Fletcher 1946: 16). Not least among preparations were the arrangements made between rival papers to cooperate should one be put out of action. These were foremost in risk areas, including the port cities of Hull, Liverpool and Tyneside, and were enacted so that papers were able to continue publishing. Following raids on Plymouth, the *Western Morning News* and *Western Evening Herald* had been printed in Exeter until replacement premises were created on Dartmoor. When the Exeter paper suffered a similar attack, it moved to the tennis courts at the Earl of Devon's seat at Powderham Park, seven miles away. Such were the demands of the press that special power lines had to be installed. The *Newcastle Journal* and *North Mail* had a second production centre in the pithead of a former coal mine at Heddon, eight miles from their primary city base. Among the worst hit was Southern Newspapers Ltd, which lost its *Southern Daily Echo* offices in Southampton in 1940 and those of its sister paper the *Dorset Daily Echo* in Weymouth two years later; for 13 months three papers were produced from the company's remaining offices in Bournemouth. Cooperation was also evident between competing companies; in Bristol the *Evening Post* and *Evening World* shared offices and even an edition during raids on the city. Locally titles also organized themselves to mitigate the risk of damage; delivery vans were no longer kept in one place, and after the *Birmingham Daily Post* lost 868 tonnes of newsprint in one air raid, it dispersed stocks under the protection of tarpaulin.

The business of newspaper publishing in wartime

Government control of newsprint had been imposed incrementally from 1939 and lasted until 1956, firstly as a result of the enemy attacks on merchant shipping, and latterly due to the country's need to balance its economic deficit. Before the war, the British were the largest consumers of a newsprint per head

(Layton 1946: 5), but because of the industry's reliance on imported paper – or imported wood pulp from which to make the paper – the industry was crippled by the war which put a near-stop to the international trade. Before the outbreak of war, 2.5 million tonnes of paper and pulp were imported each year; this fell to a low of 0.5 million tonnes in 1943 and was only gradually increased in 1946. Its effect was to dramatically cut the availability of paper to all newspapers. In 1938 the average pagination of a provincial daily and evening paper was thirteen pages; by 1946 this figure stood at four broadsheet pages (Layton 1946: 8).

In 1940 members of the provincial newspaper industry joined with their national counterparts to form the Newsprint Supply Company to introduce a rationing system; the initial membership included Associated Newspapers (publishers of the *Daily Mail, Evening News, Sunday Dispatch*), *Daily Mirror* and *Sunday Pictorial Ltd*, the Westminster Press (publishers of the *Birmingham Gazette* and *Bradford Argus*), Southern Newspapers Ltd, London Express Newspapers Ltd, *Manchester Guardian*, News of the World Ltd, The Daily News Ltd (*News Chronicle* and *Star*), The *Yorkshire Post*, the *Birmingham Post* and the *Bristol Evening Post*. This organization gained government consent to oversee imports of newsprint, introduced a single price for the product and shared it out relative to circulations of each paper, which had the effect of 'pegging' circulations at a set amount. This process set circulations at their 1940 and 1941 levels and paper was shared out accordingly. But some titles argued that this discriminated against papers in those towns where sales had been affected by the blackout and evacuations; this position was particularly taken by coastal titles. Despite this, These 'pegged' circulation levels persisted beyond the end of the war and were only relaxed incrementally. Newspaper pages also became smaller and lighter in weight, and titles supplied numbers of copies according to the numbers ordered in an effort to stop wastage through 'sale or return'. This limited choice for the reader, who could only buy a paper if it had been previously reserved.

In reality, for the daily provincial newspaper, this meant smaller papers, firstly reduced in size by reducing the number of pages, and then moving to a tabloid format so that more, smaller pages could be printed. At the same time, newspapers had to preserve a mix of content and advertising so as to preserve an air of normality for the reader. The *Birmingham Daily Post* was typically a sixteen-page pre-war title (and twenty on Saturday); by 1940 it had reduced to six pages, and by 1941 to just four pages with two Saturday six-page editions per month. When the *Midland Daily Telegraph* took the decision to shift to a more economical format in May 1940, it felt it necessary to justify its decision. The change, which included the use of a new font, was so dramatic as to warrant an

Figure 6.1 *Midland Daily Telegraph*, 6 May 1940, p. 1. Newspaper Image © Mirrorpix. All rights reserved. With thanks to The British Newspaper Archive (www. BritishNewspaperArchive.co.uk).

explanation on the front page (see Figure 6.1, *The Midland Daily Telegraph*, 6 May 1940: 1) and a comment in the editorial section.

> 'The Midland Daily Telegraph' appears to-day in a new form, made necessary by the drastic rationing of newsprint consequent upon the desirability of conserving British Shipping, further aggravated by the German attack upon Norway. ... Smaller newspapers are thus the general order of the day, and must be accepted by publishers and readers alike as one of the lesser inconveniences of the war.
>
> In order to meet this position, 'The Midland Daily Telegraph' is being produced in a form which makes the maximum use of every inch of paper passed through the machines. Slightly smaller type of the most modern design has been introduced, photographs will be smaller, and advertisements restricted. We shall make every endeavour to maintain popular features in modified form, but these must of necessity take a secondary place to the full service of war news, which must remain the chief function and responsibility of newspapers in war time. We hope to maintain that responsibility to the full. (*Midland Daily Telegraph*, 6 May 1940: 6)

As the war progressed, papers squeezed as much as possible into their pages, reducing the size of headlines, carrying few illustrations and cutting more feature-type content, such as specialized columns for women or children. Cover prices were also increased. But the hardest hit by space restrictions were the advertisers. As papers were smaller in real terms, there was just 8 per cent of the pre-war space available, and Fletcher (1946) describes how provincial editors shared out advertising space between national and local sources. At the same time, papers were also under pressure to find space for government advertisements. Demand for space for classified adverts also increased 'out of all proportion to pre-war usage of this newspaper feature', as readers scoured the 'smalls' to access goods which had become scarce during wartime, and traders denied space for display advertising also turned to the classified columns. Clampin suggests that the most draconian controls on advertising came under the Control of Paper (No 48) Order of March 1942, which set ratios between advertising and editorial; this limited advertising in morning and Sunday titles to 40 per cent, to 45 per cent for evening and to 55 per cent of total space in weeklies in titles, which were already smaller due to the restrictions described above. The move was intended by government to maintain the 'readability' of titles rather than to allow them to be swamped with commercial content.

Newspaper production then became a balancing act as titles struggled to maintain a façade of normality within the context of reduced resources. The pre-war *Portsmouth Evening News*, for instance, had been a twelve-page penny newspaper which still carried adverts on its front page. Owners Southern Newspapers were among the founder members of the Newspaper Supply Company, and by September 1939, they had modernized to include news on page one. When pagination was reduced to six pages, the title still squeezed in a wide variety of content. The edition of 1 September 1940 included public notices, letters, radio listings and the opinion column on page two. Page three was more than half-filled with display adverts, while page four – the favoured place for the prominent Food Facts adverts – carried sport, news and numerous cinema adverts. Page five was totally given over to classifieds (so a sixth of the total space available), and page six carried news, some adverts and the stop-press column. Two years later again, in the wake of the Control of Paper Order (No 48) cited above, the paper was redesigned and turned into an eight-page, reduced size, paper set across six columns, rather than seven as before. It is likely that this gave the impression of more news – now carried across pages one, three, four, five and eight – although in reality the proportion would have been fairly stable. Similarly two pages of the revised format were given over to classified adverts. What was significant in these papers was the pattern of content; there may have been fewer features and sport, but this content still appeared on a regular basis – alongside adverts for leisure pursuits and goods. This clearly made sense commercially but also accorded with efforts to maintain a sense of normality via the columns of the newspaper.

In spring 1940 the Newspaper Proprietors' Association recommended a 25 per cent increase in advertising rates, but the result of the restrictions on overall advertising levels was such that income from advertising dropped from 58 per cent to 43 per cent for the provincial evening newspaper market (Royal Commission 1949: 82). Profit margins were maintained by an increase in cover price – such as that exhibited by the *Midland Daily Telegraph*. With a guaranteed sale, this made wartime a highly prosperous period for the newspaper industry, and the Royal Commission report of 1949 notes that profits doubled between 1937 and 1946. There were also fewer individual titles running at a loss when the same two years were compared (18 per cent of all titles compared with 3 per cent in the post-war period) because even those less popular titles were able to retain a healthy share of advertising (ibid.: 81). [3]

Relaxation of these restrictions began in September 1946 when a short period of 'free sales' – unsullied by strategies to boost circulations – was aimed at letting 'natural circulations' re-establish themselves. This return to normality had to be

---

[3] At a national level, Williams (2010: 74) argues that this resulted in more news in the popular press because there was less need for it to chase readers. Curran argues that this economic structure enabled a more radical press to flourish and resulted in a re-politicized press which supported post-war social reforms (Curran and Seaton 2003: 64).

controlled due to a lack of supplies and a lack of foreign currency with which to pay for them; at the same time a threefold increase in price of newsprint, from £10 to £30 a tonne, brought about by the shortage, meant that papers could only have got much bigger if cover prices had increased. Thus the austerity of newspapers lasted beyond the conflict itself, and the producers of those newspapers perfected the art of publishing in shortened formats by learning the 'art of compression' (Layton 1946: 19). The ending of these restrictions was also painful for some titles which disappeared altogether in the face of the resumption of competition both from other newspapers and from the burgeoning commercial television industry, whose advertising revenue grew from zero in its founding year of 1955 to outstrip all that spent in national newspapers by 1958 (Williams 2010: 174). In all there were eleven fewer newspaper titles in 1961 than in 1948 – with the biggest fall in numbers among the provincial morning class of newspapers (see Table 6.1).

Table 6.1 Number of newspapers published in the UK in 1948 and 1961

	At 31 December 1948	At 31 December 1961
National morning	10	11
National Sunday	10	8
London evening	3	2
Total	**23**	**21**
Provincial morning		
England	18	12
Wales/Monmouthshire	1	1
Scotland	6	5
Northern Ireland	3	3
Total	**28**	**21**
Provincial evening		
England	63	63
Wales/Monmouthshire	3	3
Scotland	9	8
Northern Ireland	2	1
Total	**77**	**75**
Provincial Sunday		
England	4	3
Wales/Monmouthshire	–	–
Scotland	2	2
Northern Ireland	–	–
Total	**6**	**5**

Source: Royal Commission on the Press 1961–1962 Report: 171.

The provincial press and morale

The operation of the provincial press in the Second World War may be criticized on two connected counts; first, in an echo of criticisms levelled at titles in the First World War, is the contention that journalists prioritized their role of preserving morale over that of providing an 'objective' news service. In this reading, newspapers – including the provincial press – favoured a way of reporting which supposedly bolstered the communities they sought to serve by creating a 'myth of fortitude under fire'. However, a second connected criticism is that these titles prioritized their business over their readers; thus, their biased editorial stance, justified by their discourse of public service, actually preserved the status quo both between themselves and between publishers and censors and facilitated their continued trading at a time of guaranteed profit. Whether this reporting was actually of benefit to a beleaguered reading public is open to debate.

Wartime created a specific context in which the ideal value of serving the good of the community could operate for provincial news workers. During this time of conflict, it was allied with the notion of morale and, in the British context, the 'blitz spirit', a construction contemporary with the Second World War, which drew on the heroism of the First World War 'Tommy' to construct the myth of a nation which can take it (Calder 1991: 16–18). The blitz spirit is a purposeful construction of the nation as resilient and defiant by the elite (including propagandists and politicians), embodied in Churchill's now-legendary rallying cry, quoted at length by Calder: 'We shall not flag or fail. We shall go on to the end … we shall fight on the beaches, we shall fight on the landing grounds, we shall fight in the fields and in the streets, we shall fight in the hills; we shall never surrender' (ibid.: 110). It is epitomized by the phrase 'we can take it', at first applied to London and then widely adopted by provincial victims of the bombing. Heartfield (2005) traces the origin of the phrase to a Ministry of Information film, *London Can Take it* (1940).

This London-centric message, argues Kelsey (2010), became the model for the nation, and was perpetuated by the provincial press, despite the reality of the situation in cities around the country. Provincial journalists had even been given tours of the blitz-stricken capital, during which the ability of Londoners to 'take it' was emphasized in order to drive home the message (Calder 1991: 128). In this way the provincial press became part of the construction of this myth, presenting coverage of disaster in its own area in a way which propagated the perspective, which 'could now be transferred *en bloc* to any other city' (Calder 1991: 128). This transference was, therefore, allied with a set of interests external to those areas in which these titles were circulating. These newspapers then echoed this stance in their own reports of the impact of war and were more often reporting devastation on their cities in terms of the ability of plucky populations to resist disaster, rather than a factual account of the hysterical conditions which followed bombing raids. At the same time, they heroized their own ability to continue a reporting service in a process which cemented their discursive position as contributing to community well-being.

This stance is epitomized in the reaction of *the Midland Daily Telegraph* to the bombing raid on Coventry in November 1940. So bad was the damage on the night of 14 November 1940 that the attack coined the verb 'to coventrate' – to destroy by indiscriminate bombing. An estimated 1,000 people died – and were buried in mass funerals – and 32,000 homes destroyed. The offices of the paper in Coventry were damaged, and the presses and library were also destroyed, but by sending staff initially to Birmingham, and then to Nuneaton, the paper continued to publish (Fletcher 1946: 43). Based in Hertford Street in the city centre, the offices of the paper were hit, and the presses and library were destroyed. The paper had in place an emergency agreement with the *Birmingham Gazette*, 18 miles away, to shift production should the Coventry centre be put out of action. This had already been in used in the days leading up to the night of 14–15 November when smaller raids interrupted power supplies to the city to the extent that the Linotype machines could not be used (there was not enough gas pressure to melt the lead used in typesetting). On the morning of 15 November, the entire staff moved to Birmingham, with the exception of reporters who were left behind to cover the story of the devastation, working out of the post office where a room and a phone line were provided.

The claim by both producers and the Newspaper Society was that the paper went on sale that day – albeit not in Coventry city centre itself, not least because there were no newsagents left. This did not prevent the title from proclaiming its ability to continue to serve its community by publishing even in the face of such wholesale destruction. This claim was, though, disputed by the Communist Party, which had a strong membership among the factory workers in the city. Instead, it said it was its own publication, the *Daily Worker*, that had been the only paper to be on sale thanks to the efforts of members who had brought them from London and then sold them on the street (Hinton 1980: 95). This counter-action has done little to dent the way in which the Coventry title mythologized its own service so that it draws on this unstinting record of service to this day. This heroism underwrote publication in Bristol under similar conditions. A one-page emergency joint edition was produced by newspaper rivals the *Evening World* and *Evening Post* following raids in the city. It drew on a reference to a statue of a rampant lion in the doorway of a wrecked shop 'defiantly challenging entrance' to epitomize the defiance of the city (Fletcher 1946: 37). Again, in 1942 when the *Yorkshire Evening Press* and *Yorkshire Herald* were produced from Leeds for six days after their own base was damaged, the proprietor wrote: 'In a spirit of determination ... the men, women, girls and boys ... have toiled and sweated practically and continuously in dirt and filth to turn chaos into disorder and then disorder into production. ... Day after day, night after night, they never flinched or complained or swerved their purpose' (Fletcher 1946: 62).

It was in this vein that the paper in Coventry reported the attack on the city. In addition to headlining the 1,000 casualties and the destruction of the cathedral, it declared, 'The people of Coventry bore their ordeal with Great Courage.' The next day the paper reported that 'Crippled Coventry carries on' and 'swift measure to restore normal life'. The king came in person to witness the damage and 'was met with cheers and frequent shouts of such slogans as "We can take it"' (*Midland Daily Telegraph*, 16 November 1940: 1). The paper also provided essential information; the coverage of the blitz was, therefore, not just limited to what was destroyed, but it stated what was still functioning: the damaged hospital was still open and feeding centres were helping those made homeless (*MDT*, 15 November 1940: 1). The *Midland Daily Telegraph* of 16 November told the population there was no power, but that the postal service should be back up and running in a day. Citizens were advised not to use the phones unless absolutely necessary, to use their cars to assist with transportation and to open up their homes, if undamaged, to as many people in need as they could. This service developed over the ensuing days as different organizations were faced with reaching different people. 'Did you work for Owen, Owen, the department store which had been bombed?', one advert asks. 'All instructions to staff will be published through the columns of this paper' (*MDT*, 19 November 1940: 2). The same edition carried a warning from the Ministry of Health about the danger of typhoid due to extensive damage to the sewers.

The newspaper did not though dedicate space to its own story of continued publication. The only indication given of the *Midland Daily Telegraph's* predicament was a brief mention of damage to a 'newspaper office' within one story (*Midland Daily Telegraph*, 16 November 1940: 1). An earpiece advert on the front page of Monday, 18 November says the Hertford Street office was 'open for business as usual'. By 22 November, the paper reported its phone line has been restored, 'a tribute to the Post Office engineers'. Another indication of the disruption was the changing public notice stating where the paper was printed. So, 15 November – printed by the Birmingham Gazette Ltd, Corporation Street, Birmingham. By 9 December the paper had found a new home at the offices of the Nuneaton Newspaper Ltd in the nearby market town. The exception is via the comment piece, 'A Warwickshire Man's Diary', which appeared regularly in the paper. In the edition of 30 November, it carried a tribute to the *Midland Daily Telegraph* from 'an old journalistic friend'. 'The city has reason to be proud of the fact that despite all that a fiendish enemy could do, your paper has surmounted every conceivable obstacle and has not for a single day suspended publication' (*Midland Daily Telegraph*, 30 November 1940: 6).

In a very practical sense the local newspaper was vital to communication in the aftermath of such attacks, and the content outlined above shows the very utility of the paper. For this reason the Ministry of Information recognized the importance of newspapers in providing information, and the Regional Information Officers saw reviving the press in bombed areas as a 'vital task' because it alleviated any sense of isolation (McClaine 1979: 134). This may have been even more so in Coventry; contemporary Ministry of Information reports suggested there was a hiatus in official communications in the immediate aftermath of the bombing due to a lack of preparedness by official organizations (McClaine 1979: 131). However, there is also evidence that beyond this practical utility, the construction of a defiant community put forward by the paper may have been counterproductive to the people who read it. It is certainly at odds with evidence from the Mass Observation reports of the city in the aftermath of the attack and also the dissenting voice of the *Daily Worker*. Mass Observation was an ethnographic survey which began in 1937 in an attempt to supply accurate observations of everyday life. After the outbreak of the Second World War, the organization geared its attempts towards the war effort and began a wide-scale observation of the reaction of communities to the blitz, including that in Coventry (Harrison 1976: 11–15). The reports left by the unit contradict the 'blitz spirit' embodied in the paper to the extent that it is worth quoting at length.

The investigators found an unprecedented dislocation and depression in Coventry on Friday [the day after the bombing]. There were more open signs of hysteria, terror, neurosis, observed in one evening than during the whole of the past two months together in all areas. Women were seen to cry, to scream, to tremble all over, to faint in the street, to attack a fireman, and so on.

The overwhelmingly dominant feeling on Friday was the feeling of utter *helplessness* [original emphasis]. The tremendous impact of the previous night had left people practically speechless in many cases. And it made them feel impotent. ... On Friday evening, there were several signs of suppressed panic as darkness approached. In two cases people were seen fighting to get on to cars which they thought would take them out in the country, though in fact, as the drivers insisted, the cars were going just up the road. (Mass Observation 495: 2)

Official reports indicated that morale was similarly poor in other provincial cites subjected to widespread devastation. In Bristol, people felt let down by the government, Portsmouth suffered from looting and lawlessness which the police were unable to control, and Plymouth had been pushed beyond its limit. The bishop of Winchester reported that 'morale had collapsed' in parish after parish in Southampton (Ponting 1990: 164). In Coventry the effect was magnified by the concentrated nature of destruction; because the town was relatively small, everyone knew someone who had been directly affected by the bombing. This accelerated both the impact and the exaggeration of that impact, the Mass Observation report proffered. The city had also attracted many migrant workers to work in the aircraft industry, which expanded enormously in the late 1930s when Shadow Factories were set up by the car manufacturers, for which the city was famed, to produce arms (Hinton 1980: 93). As such, these workers had no particular allegiance to Coventry and were ready to condemn it as 'finished'. In addition, official measures to alleviate suffering were inadequate to the extent that the Mass Observation made recommendations to prevent such a failure in future, including the provision of adequate air raid shelters – something the *Daily Worker* had campaigned for – rest centres, mobile canteens and transport. Part of these recommendations included improving the public's access to information via loudspeaker vans and 'special facilities for getting newspapers delivered and sold in the streets' (Mass Observation 495: 6).

Just as the Mass Observation suggests that *the Midland Daily Telegraph's* reporting was overtly heroic, so Kelsey suggests that 'London can take it' was often far from the truth; contemporary reports of life in East End revealed a lack of staples like bread and milk, or essential services like gas and water. Crime increased by 60 per cent, juvenile crime by 41 per cent as did the systematic persecution of racial and ethnic minorities. At the same time class divides were amplified as the rich continued to enjoy a good standard of living while the working classes were sheltering underground (Kelsey 2010: 26–7). Revealing these contradictions was the *Daily Worker* which opposed the picture put forward by the *Midland Daily Telegraph* in the aftermath of the bombing by describing the city as a 'shambles'. 'The condition of the people of Coventry is indescribable. The place is crowded – with people who do not know what to do' (*Daily Worker*, 18 November 1940: 1). It described food shortages, 'no sewerage, no gas, no electricity, except in a few places, no water' (*Daily Worker*, 18 November 1940: 3). Of the population it said,

> they have neither transport facilities nor accommodation. They slept in hedges, in ditches – anywhere away from the city which had become a death trap. …
> What else were people to do but wander in this hopeless fashion and sleep in the ditches and hedges? There was no proper air raid shelter in the whole of Coventry, neither for the factory workers or the rest of the civilian population.
> (*Daily Worker*, 18 November 1940: 3)

The Daily Worker was one of the few voices to challenge the contemporary positivity of titles like the *Midland Daily Telegraph*. It condemned their treatment of the facts and dubbed them as little more than 'propaganda' sheet, produced by a process of collusion. 'No difference to them [the reader] whether it is an editor or a censor who decrees that only the "sunshine" stuff shall have the "lead"' (*Daily Worker*, 20 November 1940: 3).

But such was the strength of the myth of this sunshine perspective that it was hard for those in the thick of it to challenge. Heartfield (2005) argues that the myth also served to evoke pride for its contemporary audience; this amplified the difficulty those who felt differently faced in speaking out whatever the reality they might be facing. Those provincial voices which were prepared to speak out about their experiences were few. One civilian in beleaguered Liverpool recalled marches in favour of peace (Levine 2006: 412); another how

> Churchill was telling us how brave we all were and that we would never surrender. I tell you something – the people of Liverpool would have surrendered overnight if they could have. It's all right for people in authority, down in their steel-lined dugouts but we were there and it was just too awful. People were walking out of the town to escape the bombing. (Levine 2006: 412)

In the *Midland Daily Telegraph*, the criticism of the city's reaction to the bombing was equally muted – the odd letter of criticism, the appeal for information about a missing girl, who, it was reported two weeks later, had been dead all along, giving a hint of the chaos and grief; the suggestions of rocketing rents for those homes which remained intact, reports of homeless people who had been wandering the streets for a week in search of shelter, indicative of the lack of support for those in need. Despite this the newspaper presented a picture of unerring positivity, which was extreme to the point of being counterproductive. The Mass Observation concluded that these 'exaggerated accounts of "marvellous courage" etc. put out in the press' are 'out of key with real feeling in Coventry, the courage of which is quite enough not to require being turned into a miracle. ... Our evidence shows that the exaggerated treatment also makes people suspicious and has now been done so often that it encourages few' (Mass Observation 495: 9).

An assessment of the extent to which the provincial press was able to contribute to the morale of the civilian population is beyond the scope of this study. What can be established, however, is that the provincial press reinforced its narrative of its role of serving the good of the community by claiming to bolster morale. It is at this time that the role of newspapers in relation to communities also gained official sanction and was understood to be significant by contemporaries within and without of the industry. Therefore, concessions were made to the provincial press in terms of censorship, such as allowing them to name local targets for bombing while suppressing the same information in the national press, and by confidential briefings to local editors who could then deny unfounded rumours (Balfour 1979: 203). At the same time, though, the trading conditions created by the conflict made wartime highly profitable for provincial newspapers. Therefore, while continued publication could be justified as serving communities, it could also be seen as enabling titles to benefit from the profitable environment created by the wartime trading conditions. Even in war, then, the industry's claim to serve the good of the community has to be understood alongside its strategy to ensure the financial health of the business and maximize profitability. It is this strategy which takes centre stage in the discussion of the introduction of computer technology into the provincial newspaper industry, which is at the heart of Chapter 7.

7

The Deunionization of the Provincial Press

New technology

[The *Coventry Evening Telegraph*] has one of the most complex editorial systems to integrate its various editions. To indicate its scope, here are the titles and timings of the editions on a typical day, Friday 19 February 1988; 4 are for the Coventry area and the others are for surrounding communities. The timings are 'off-stone' times for the final page – the 'off stone' term being derived from the days of hot metal printing, now replaced by electronics. The front-page headlines are also quoted.

10.45am   *Coventry Evening Telegraph*, 'Lunch' edition.
Land Rover Deadlock: strike is on

1.00pm   *Nuneaton Evening Telegraph*
'90 More to Go sour news at Sterling' …
Bedworth Evening Telegraph
Same headlines and front page as Nuneaton.

1.10pm   *Leamington and Warwick Evening Telegraph*
'Strike Mars "Victory" at Pottertons' …
Stratford-on-Avon Evening Telegraph
Same headlines and front page as Leamington edition

1.15pm   *Rugby Evening Telegraph*
'Escape from a Takeover turns sour'

1.40pm   *Coventry Evening Telegraph*, 'Late City' edition
'Overkill on city staff is admitted' …

2.15pm   *Coventry Evening Telegraph* 'City Final' edition
'City Payroll is Over the Top' …

4.15pm   *Coventry Evening Telegraph*, 'Night Final'
The 'city centre' edition, maintained in case of major late news in the afternoon

For the 5 primary editions there are changes on up to 6 or 7 inside news pages. The Nuneaton, Leamington, Rugby, Bedworth and Stratford titles are published every day, with 2 further editions specially flagged for Kenilworth and Hinckley. The Bedworth and Stratford editions have extra slip pages 3 days a week.

(Hetherington 1989: 131–2)

Alistair Hetherington describes in detail the editorial workings of the *Coventry Evening Telegraph* in 1988. Writing about the paper as part of a survey of the local news landscape, he captures the workings of 100 journalists producing 11 editions of the established newspaper. The development of the *Coventry Evening Telegraph*, from its foundations as the *Midland Daily Telegraph*, has been charted at regular intervals in this book. Hetherington's portrait captures its operation at the zenith of its presence as a printed product, selling just shy of 100,000 copies per day in Coventry and the county of Warwickshire, via a series of editions demarcated in terms of locality and time. What made the complexity possible in practical terms was electronic technology, which facilitated 'intricate and integrated decisions' between key editorial managers. 'Stories can be stacked in word processor "baskets," and alternative versions can be prepared simultaneously. Editors, news editors, sub-editors and picture editors all have access to the texts in preparation, without interrupting whoever is working on them.'

This technologically driven operation of the *Coventry Evening Telegraph* is compared with the production of the *Huddersfield Daily Examiner*, which was owned by a small company with the editor both in charge of the paper and company chairman. With just one 1 pm edition, Hetherington described it as 'in keeping with its community. It sees itself as "solid." The office – a rabbit warren in an old building in the centre of Huddersfield – has an agreeable and friendly atmosphere. There are 42 journalists; 16 or 17 in the newsroom, 7 sub editors, 7 in sport, 7 photographers and 4 feature people.' These differential descriptions hint at the seismic changes experienced in the provincial newspaper industry in the 1970s and 1980s. This is an industry that was restructured by the introduction of computerized newspaper production, enabled by a politically motivated emasculation of the unions which had dominated the industry for the preceding eighty years. At the same time the newspaper market itself was influenced by rising production costs – which drove the will to introduce efficiency measures made possible by new technology – and an ever-increasing concentration of ownership of provincial newspapers by conglomerates for whom newspapers were just one revenue stream among many. In addition, increased competition from free newspapers and other local news providers – including television and radio – meant more people chasing what profit there was. This chapter examines the legacy of this process of technological innovation, introduced against a backdrop of the economic recession experienced by the UK during the 1970s. As such it describes at length the economic circumstances which enabled the provincial newspaper industry to harness new technology to improve profitability. The depth of this analysis acknowledges the relationship of these changes to the shape of ownership of newspapers, and also its impact on those who produced those titles in the face of more homogenized, centralized and remote working practices. The result was an increasingly commercialized provincial newspaper industry, operating in an increasingly remote relationship with the community it professed to serve, with a deunionized workforce which lacked the means to either resist or benefit from the changes.

The radical changes in production wrought by this technology are hard to understate; we think now of the newspaper industry as being part-way through a transformation wrought by digital innovation, but the impact of computerization on aspects of the newspaper industry in the 1980s was equally profound. The technology may not have shifted the business model itself, but it certainly enabled a shift in emphasis between the relevant components of it by subsuming the status of editorial to the potential profits from advertising; in turn this marked a shift in the ideology which underwrote the practices of workers in both editorial and, in particular, the production departments of the industry. The technology put production into the hands of the editorial staff and so largely wrote the place of the printer out of the history of the newspaper after their being central to its development for 300 years. Yet rather than heralding a new era of autonomy for the editorial staff, the technology can instead be seen to have facilitated an increased culture of managerialism, which reduced the status of the news worker to that of a cog in a machine designed to yield maximum advertising revenue. The apotheosis of this was the free newspaper which developed an increasingly significant role within the industry. As such, Curran has described this era as one in which the revolutionary potential of new technology – as it was then known – was a 'rainbow that came and went' (2003: 101). The fact was that computerization was harnessed by corporate businesses to lever additional profit from the advertising-based business model. This era of technological innovation has to be understood against that economic backdrop as one which facilitated the further concentration of the industry by reducing core costs and maximizing profitability to enhance the longevity of the existing business model. Additionally, the potential of the technology to reduce staffing costs meant free newspapers were able to establish themselves as competitive form, and so were used by newspaper groups to saturate markets so that they yielded as much advertising revenue from those locales as possible.

The advent of free distribution and the way in which it was employed to maximize profit also contributed to the devaluing of the regional press. In itself, the dichotomy between paid-for and free newspapers is minimal and describes a fairly minor divergence in the reality of funding for most newspapers, which have come to rely on advertising for more than 80 per cent of their total income. Initially many free newspapers were also indistinguishable from their paid-for counterparts in terms of quality and content, and indeed some editionalized titles were distributed via both free and paid-for methods. It was though the way in which free newspapers were exploited which was more problematic. The status concentrated on the newspaper as a profit centre and shifted focus away from their editorial role in relation to social contexts. This changed their status within the companies which owned them; additionally, increasingly those companies diversified their interests so that the newspaper was just one interest among many and was functionally no different as a way to make money than a wallpaper factory.

This era, therefore, had ramifications for the relationship these newspapers claimed for themselves and their communities. It subsumed the role of the newspaper in relation to the wider social good to its function as a financial instrument designed to yield shareholder benefit. Rather than emphasizing the role of the newspaper as watchdog or community supporter, editorial became just one more production process and one cost among others to be controlled (Simpson 1981: 115). This shift was facilitated by the process of rapid technological innovation which predicated the control of owners over that of employees due to the restructuring of employment relations which it enabled. Those who controlled the press abandoned claims to influence in favour of financial gain alone, embodied in Canadian media entrepreneur Roy Thomson who stated that his only interest in newspapers was profit. It is this overt pursuit which influenced the structure of the industry, and degraded the notion of the fourth estate, because it demoted the status of editorial within the organizational structure in favour of the dominance of commercial, including advertising departments. As such, news-gathering became regularized and organized along institutional lines by commercial managers who saw it as a raw material, and a cost to be controlled like any other (Simpson 1981: 116). This structure was not determined by technological developments, such as the move to direct input, but was facilitated by them in so far as it enabled owners to improve productivity and, during the 1970s and 1980s, to challenge the power of the unionized workforce in the English newspaper industry. Ideologically, the owners were assisted in this effort by the government of the day, which introduced anti-union legislation. As such, new technology failed to deliver the possibility of increased choice in newspapers – and therefore augment the fourth estate (Curran and Seaton 2003: 353). Such was the impact of the changes charted here that they are at the core of the arguments framing the relationship between provincial newspapers and their communities and the economic context which currently frames the discourse of decline surrounding the industry.

The changing motivations for newspaper ownership

Ownership of newspapers has never been straightforward; this history has already charted the interconnected motives for ownership for personal prestige and political advantage in addition to making money. This was particularly true of the national newspaper, which by the 1970s had become a dysfunctional business pulled by the twin dictators of owners, who sought social influence, and the militant unions, who capitalized on this will to prestige to hold the production process to ransom. In her analysis of the notorious Wapping dispute,[1] Suellen Littleton identifies the vanity of national newspaper owners as enabling the Fleet Street print unions to wrestle authority from managers. The unions drew on the vulnerability of the newspaper market, based as it was on a highly perishable product reaching a finite market curtailed by nationhood, to create the closed shop. In turn this led to high wages so that by 1985 the most skilled Fleet Street printers earned £40,000 a year – three times the norm for skilled manual labour. This dominance also facilitated the so-called 'Spanish practices', including overmanning and wage claims by fictitious employees; these were so numerous as to prompt an investigation by the Inland Revenue because of the tax avoidance implicit in the practice. The computerization of newspaper production offered the potential to tackle this dysfunctional relationship, and although it was first used in the provincial newspaper industry, its impact was to be greatest in the national newspaper sector.

---

[1] The Wapping dispute refers to events around the relocation of News International's newspaper production from Fleet Street to a new computerized site in London's docklands.

The circumstances described above meant the national newspaper industry had a higher proportion of production staff (58 per cent) than the provincial newspaper industry, despite the fact that generally the proportion of production staff was inversely related to circulations. The national press was able to sustain the costs incurred by overmanning because their wealthy owners would either subsidize their papers – so that they were little more than a 'rich man's hobby' (Littleton 1992: 9) – or increase the prices charged for advertising and the cover price of titles. But the provincial newspaper owners either could not, or would not, do the same because their main 'raison d'etre' was not prestige, but their ability to yield profits from advertising. This financial landscape left little room for excessive production costs. The provincial industry, though, employed more people in aggregate – 45,000 in 1974 (compared with 35,000 in the national newspaper industry) of whom 42 per cent worked in production and 22 per cent in editorial (ACAS 1974).

The book has already analysed the way in which an increasingly consolidated provincial newspaper industry enabled provincial newspaper owners to negotiate monopolistic circulation areas so they could fully exploit finite advertising markets. As this consolidation progressed, it extended integration between the ownership and publication of daily and weekly newspapers. This had, the NUJ said, provided 'economic security' for the industry (Royal Commission 1977, 2E1: 14). However, it also meant little competition at all remained in the provincial newspaper market; morning papers may still have competed somewhat with national morning titles – which also printed in regional centres in the Midlands and north – but other newspapers were co-owned inside focused, smaller circulation areas. Within these groupings, titles were expected to be profitable in their own right and not depend on cross-subsidy from other newspapers; they were also expected to contribute to the costs of shared facilities, such as London-based reporters and training and administrative facilities.

By the time of the 1977 Royal Commission on the Press,[2] there were a total of seventy-seven evening newspapers, and each one held a monopoly position in the location they served, except for in Sandwell in the West Midlands where papers in Birmingham and Wolverhampton circulated editionalized titles. It was this changing economic landscape which had been the driving force to the creation

---

[2] MPs also considered editorial standards, and a supposed anti-Labour bias (Royal Commission, vol. 1, 1977: 2–4).

of the commission – the third to be held in some thirty years. In particular, this inquiry set out to focus on whether the Monopolies and Mergers Commission, set up in 1965, had been able to regulate the ownership of newspapers. It found that the actual number of daily titles had stayed roughly the same, with nine closures and eleven launches, two of which were the editionalized papers circulating in Sandwell. There were also around 150 fewer weekly titles, leaving around 1,070 in existence. Raw numbers do not though reveal the full picture around ownership at this time, and, in particular disguise the concentration of cross-ownership and shared production within the industry. Between 1961 and 1977 the number of towns with competing weekly titles held by different companies had fallen from 226 to 146. By 1977 the number of provincial mornings had also fallen to twelve, compared with eighteen in 1948. It is worth noting that at this time the *Manchester Guardian* (considered a national title), the *Daily Telegraph* and the popular daily nationals all published a northern edition. However, with a total circulation of just one million a day, there were also gaps in the regional mornings, with the South East and East Midlands of England both without this class of newspaper because of the influence of the metropolitan mornings in this area. Additionally, those provincial newspapers held by groups were increasingly organized within 'publishing houses' – centralized units which produced and printed newspapers. A survey by ACAS (the Advisory Conciliation and Arbitration Service) in 1974 revealed 200 companies across the UK each owned between 1 and 23 titles, organized around 280 such centres. The largest group owners held multiple publishing houses so that that while seventeen morning papers were produced out of seventeen publishing houses, they were owned by just twelve different companies. The ownership of the evening press was more concentrated with seventy-five titles produced in individual houses owned by just thirty companies. These titles were often stablemates with morning and Sunday papers – all of which were published from houses that also published evening papers (ACAS 1977). The weekly newspaper market had seen the largest increase in the concentration of ownership with the top groups holding one third of all titles, as opposed to around 15 per cent in 1961. The concentration of ownership was also increasingly consolidated in geographically regional areas (Royal Commission 1977: 25), which, in effect, created monopolistic trading areas for newspaper publishers.

Those inside the industry said that the concentration was necessary because of the rising costs of newspaper production. The Guild of British Newspaper

Editors, which later became the Society of Editors, told MPs that concentration had enabled some titles to continue where otherwise they might have failed.

> Economic factors – the enormous increases that are being experienced in the cost of raw materials, plant replacement and manpower – are making it increasingly difficult for small, independent publishing companies, utilising conventional methods of production, to survive. This is regrettable. But we believe the continued publication of any newspaper as one of a large group is preferable to its going out of circulation. (Royal Commission 1977, 22E1: 5–6)

Similarly, Westminster Press argued that group ownership enabled regional variations in profitability to be evened out.

> There is decisive variation in the abilities of the different regions to sustain a newspaper. It can, perhaps, best be shown by the advertising revenue obtained by well established evening newspapers, expressed per copy of circulation on per household within each prime circulation area. In our experience, the difference is as much as 60% in terms of revenue per household. The areas consistently scoring low, in our experience, are in the North-West and the North-East. The policy we adopt is to require each newspaper company or division to achieve satisfactory financial results within its own market. This is a central feature in our policy of management autonomy. This accepts that if the fortunes of a local paper depend heavily on each particular zone, then the management have to be free to consider that this is in the longer term interests of employees because if a division or company is consistently unable to live within its means, the inducement to further investment is removed.
>
> We consider that the control of fixed costs is the vital element in maintaining financial results in less buoyant areas. Divisions or companies in this position receive useful support as part of a Group in terms of training and management services and the availability of plant transferred from other areas. (Royal Commission 1977, 17E1: 3)

At the same time, those businesses which owned provincial newspapers had also become increasingly diversified so that newspaper publishing was just one revenue stream among many, and, sometimes, a lesser stream at that. Some of these interests were allied to newspaper publishing – such as owning newsagents or paper companies – or media, such as radio and television companies. But others were completely disconnected such as North Sea oil, Scottish whisky and even laundry services. This marked a shift in the structure of companies which owned newspapers and raised the spectre of editorial bias in favour of those other interests. Among those companies which epitomized this diversification was Reed International Ltd, which described itself as a 'holding company of a group whose principal activities are pulp and lumber, paper and board, packaging and stationery; the production and marketing of decorative products, including wall covering, paint, textiles, furnishing fabrics and carpet; the printing and publishing of newspapers, consumer and business magazines, books, business directories, and general printing; and the manufacture and marketing of building products' (Royal Commission 1977: Appendix D). Among the British household names it controlled were Polycell and Sanderson, the *Whizzer and Chips* comic and the *New Scientist*; its business interests extended to Australia, Canada and South Africa. This meant its holdings of seventeen UK-based newspapers, including the *Daily Mirror* and *Sunday Mirror*, accounted for just under 20 per cent of its total profits. Even the Daily Mail and General Trust, which included Associated Newspapers, held interests as diverse as furniture and transport. Such was the impact of this change that the Royal Commission of 1977 remarked that 'the British press is now owned to an unusual extent by businesses with outside interests which have come in recent years to predominate over press interests'.

This then opened these large groups up to criticism for ignoring the special purpose of newspapers, and instead treating them as a commodity in the way the burgeoning supermarket sector treated tins of baked beans. These groups offered counterarguments that their complex structures and allied areas of interest facilitated the smooth running of the newspaper industry as a whole. For instance, in 1977 Westminster Press Ltd, as it was then known, was one of three wholly owned subsidiaries of Pearson Longman Limited, the others being the Financial Times Ltd and Longman Penguin Ltd. Clearly, while Westminster Press was the newspaper publisher of the group, publishing one morning, ten evening and an extensive range of weekly and free newspapers, this organization demonstrated business interests in the allied areas of the wider publishing industry. The advantage of this organization was that

> the mix of publishing interests coupled with the wider spread of assets normally makes it easier for Pearson Longman to borrow for expansion and re-equipment as the profitability of each form of publishing varies in relation to the other, one year with another, the cash needs of a subsidiary, which currently less profitable, can often be satisfied out of the surplus of the others within re-course to further borrowing. (Royal Commission 1977, 17E1: 2)

And, the argument continued, the nature of the provincial newspaper was that such an organization would not result in identikit titles lined up like food on a shop shelf. Drawing on the established value of the relationship between newspaper and locale, Westminster Press argued that each newspaper was individual because of the 'need for each major community to be covered specifically, under separate editors. The result of Group ownership of newspapers is quite unlike the uniformity of multiple retailing' (ibid.).

However, the newspapers which were subject to this form of ownership might have differed on this perspective. Titles were shifted between the largest newspapers groups as each jockeyed for dominance, and this often brought widespread disruption for those on the ground. Among those titles to have been bought and sold on more than one occasion was the *Stamford Mercury* in Lincolnshire, which was owned varyingly by Westminster Press, EMAP (East Midland Allied Press) and Johnston Press within the space of fifty years. The weekly title first passed into the hands of a national chain when the then Westminster Press Provincial Newspaper bought it in 1929. From then, 'its future was inextricably interwoven with numerous other newspapers and publications that were the property of the parent company', wrote the paper's biographers (Newton and Smith 1999: 225). Changes included subsuming management control to established rival the *Lincolnshire Chronicle*, which was also acquired by Westminster Press. Printing was removed from Stamford, the title was redesigned and then merged with surrounding weekly titles when they too were bought. In 1951, the title passed to the East Midland Press Group (later EMAP plc). EMAP had itself been formed by the merger of four newspaper publishers based in the east of England, at Peterborough, Kettering, Bury St Edmunds and Kings Lynn. It owned thirteen newspapers with a combined circulation of around 200,000. Westminster Press sold the *Stamford Mercury* to EMAP for £57,500 – a price justified by the title's low profit margins of just £655 in 1951. The sale to EMAP meant production was centralized and relocated; for readers this meant the paper changed size again while for production staff it meant travelling to the print centres to oversee production – then bringing the printed papers back with them, dropping them off at newsagents as they went. In short, ownership by EMAP meant 'subordination'. 'Stamford was just another regional satellite in the EMAP universe and its resources were there to be exploited or taken away' (ibid.: 251). In 1996 the title was sold for £211 million to current owners Johnston Press.

Rising costs and competition

While the cost structure of the provincial newspaper industry may not have been as dysfunctional as that of the national industry, in real terms, a newspaper page cost twice as much to produce in 1974 as it did in 1961, the Liverpool Daily Post and Liverpool Echo Ltd contended (Royal Commission 1977, 8E1: 5). This was due to a combination of rises in wage and capital costs; in particular, the cost of newsprint trebled between 1973 and 1977, which led newspapers to make the most of every column inch of space and became one driver for the modernization of production processes. At the same time, the UK also experienced a period of economic recession, which put further pressure on the profitability of those newspapers reliant on advertising revenue for profits; its effect was a fall in operating profits of between 30 and 60 per cent for provincial newspaper producers (ACAS 1977: 9). In 1975, the allocation of costs by publishers suggested that just eight of the fifteen regional morning titles were making a profit; the remainder were being kept afloat by their organization within publishing centres, which enabled cross-subsidy from the evening newspaper. However, the result of this was that the entire industry was increasingly reliant on the advertising-driven profits raised by the evening press. This meant a fragility underpinned the industry; the reliance on advertising revenues made newspapers particularly vulnerable to prevailing economic conditions which affected such income streams as classified and property advertising.

Competition from sectors like commercial radio and the free newspaper meant these titles were also selling fewer copies; revenues were preserved by increased paginations which enabled more advertising to be carried, which in turn meant a drive to incorporate technology which facilitated bigger newspapers at the smallest possible additional cost. This though did offer a defence to companies accused of damaging the industry through over concentration. Commercial television had begun in 1955, and three years later, advertising spend on ITV outstripped that of the entire press. Twenty BBC local radio stations had been established since 1962, followed by nineteen commercial radio stations enabled by legislation in 1972. Some of these included participation by the local newspaper industry, although government policy limited the extent of these holdings so that they did not have a controlling interest. Associated Newspapers had been among those to invest in the early days of commercial television, and the company formed part of Associated Rediffusion which won the franchise for

London weekly television in 1955. The company sold its interest after two years, although the franchise was to turn a profit of £5 million before the decade was out (Crisell 2002: 93). By the time of the 1977 Royal Commission, fifty-seven companies with interests in newspapers and periodicals also had investments in commercial television programme companies; around seventy also had interests in local commercial radio stations.[3] At the other end of the spectrum was competition from community newspapers; many of these were parish-magazine type publications and exact numbers are hard to quantify, although there were thought to be around twenty-two in Leicestershire alone. These titles set out to 'carry information about local events, foster a sense of community ... and provide an arena for debate on local issues' (Royal Commission, Vol 1 1977: 15). As such, they often gave a voice to people who were marginalized by the established press and earned themselves the moniker of the 'parish magazines of the dispossessed'; the most successful were often the most local (Harcup 2013: 55).

These community magazines were in addition to the political press, which had grown to around 200 periodicals by 1977. Around 150 were classified as 'alternative' – in so far as they were published by enthusiasts rather than commercial publishers. These titles also often challenged the political elite and capitalized on representing opposition, particularly to the Thatcherite offensive against the trade unions. Those writing for these titles were then accorded privileged access to communities who viewed the established press with suspicion, for instance being allowed behind the picket lines during the 1984–5 Miners' Strike when other journalists stood alongside those who were policing them. Often those working on these titles had no formal journalism training, and the titles may not have had a traditional editorial hierarchy and were instead run on a cooperative basis. Because – rather than in spite of this – they were capable of 'genuine revelation' (Harcup 2013: 56). Significantly, such was their perceived contribution to the 'diversity of voices' that the Royal Commission suggested that a method be found to support them, for instance by providing subsidized printing facilities in an argument which prefigures those rehearsed in relation to the continuance of local media in this decade (ibid.: 123–4). These two forms of publication faced problems when trying to compete with the established press. The community papers faced no problems with distribution,

---

[3] By 1977 there were nineteen independent local radio stations; this figure had grown to forty-three by 1983 (ibid.: 196–7).

because their circulation areas were small, and Tony Harcup recalls how they would often be sold by the same people who produced them via visits to pubs and clubs. However these areas were really too small to support an advertising base necessary to cover costs. Conversely, for the political periodicals, although foundation costs could be relatively low, as little as £100 the Royal Commission said (Vol 1 1977: 56), the biggest barrier to success was the cost of distribution, which was itself highly concentrated in the hands of established companies including W. H. Smith and Menzies (Whitaker 1981: 87). This meant that the political aims were often subsumed to more commercially orientated content, such as listings, in order to elicit revenue (Franklin and Murphy 1991: 127); towards the end of its twenty-year life, the *Leeds Other Paper*, for instance, became more of a what's on magazine than a newspaper and, as such, lost its original aim to 'counteract the existing establishment propaganda' of rival newspapers (Harcup 2013: 38).

One further piece in the non-traditional newspaper jigsaw were the civic newspapers, run by local authorities, of which there were around forty in 1977 (Royal Commission, Vol 1, 1977: 15) but the number of which grew rapidly in subsequent years (Franklin and Murphy 1991: 134) reaching a peak of ninety-seven. With guaranteed circulations concomitant with the number of households to which the papers were distributed for free, these titles were feared for their 'agitprop' potential, to the extent that Conservative governments introduced legislation to limit the amount of money which would be spent on them (ibid.: 132). It is noteworthy that Labour-controlled councils were more likely to publish their own newspapers than Conservative-controlled councils (ibid.: 151). These publications were largely enabled by the professional PR staff in councils, who had experience as journalists and who were able to harness new technology to produce high-quality publications to rival the commercial provincial press. While some of these were relatively simple four-page issues, others used full-colour printing and took adverts to fund up to forty-eight pages in order to offset the cost to taxpayers (ibid.: 138).

Technological innovation had also enabled new text-based broadcast platforms, including Ceefax, being developed by the BBC, the Independent Broadcast Association's version Oracle and Viewdata – a similar service which the GPO (General Post Office) was attempting to launch (NUJ, 1977: 4). All were defined as 'genuine electronic newspapers' by the Institute of Journalists, which saw itself as a champion of new technology in the newspaper industry and introduced a column, fronted by a cartoon figure called Fred the precocious caveman, who could use a computer, to keep members up-to-date with changes. The Post Office service Prestel (the trade name for Viewdata) was seen as the biggest commercial threat – possibly because of its nationwide coverage. Prestel was a text-based information service available to telephone subscribers. It enabled organizations to lease pages for information dissemination and the NUJ not only had twenty pages itself, but listed newspaper companies, including the Birmingham Post and Mail, Eastern Counties Newspapers, the Bolton Evening News and Yorkshire Post Newspapers, which had taken pages 'as an insurance policy' (NUJ 1979: 3). The technology was greeted differently by the national and provincial press and this disparity in concerns was reflected in a new structure for the NUJ, which created separate councils for each (NUJ 1976: 12). However, it was also seen to present opportunities for NUJ members and was positively championed by the Institute of Journalists (IOJ), which gave front-page coverage to British Telecom's Prestel 'Pressy' awards in their members' paper *The Journal* in June/July 1981.

Among the most successful of these products was Viewtel 202, launched by the Birmingham Post and Mail in 1978. Content included national and international news, as well as features and advertising, and by 1981 subscribers were accessing it three to four million times a year (IOJ 1981: 1). The service included 150–200 news pages a day, carrying a total of thirty stories in addition to sport and features. A total of twenty staff were employed to provide the service, which was available for eighteen hours a day, seven days a week. The aim was to update each page at least once a day with most copy coming from the Press Association or other news agencies. The service was free to those who subscribed to Prestel. Interviewed by the Institute of Journalists in the edition of *The Journal* of June/July 1981, the editor of Viewtel202, Alan Durrant, predicted that traditional newspapers would not be able to compete with Teletext and Prestel, because of the speed of the electronic versions (ibid.). Both Prestel and Oracle also had the potential to host advertising (NUJ 1977b: 14). However, as it turned out, Prestel was not the success it was forecast to be, attracting fewer than 100,000 users at its peak, while similar services, the BBC's Ceefax and ITV's Oracle, did enjoy some longevity.

This meant the biggest rival to the traditional paid-for provincial newspaper was the free newspaper, which reached a status as mature sector of the industry, after early experiments during different points in this history. Described by Franklin and Murphy as 'the single most significant development in the structure of the local press since the 1960s' (1991: 76), these free newspapers ranged from advertising-based 'shopper' newspapers to sophisticated news titles. They were born out of a variety of circumstances, ranging from entrepreneurs with no experience of journalism who wanted to benefit from advertising revenues to established publishers who would launch free titles to protect their circulation areas by deterring incursions by would-be entrants. Goodhart and Wintour (1986) chart the revival of the free newspaper in the UK back to Lionel Pickering, who brought the newspaper form from Australia, where it was well established. He established the *Derby Trader* in 1966 with just £4,800 in capital; by 1986 he had ten titles turning over £10 million a year with a 10 per cent profit margin. The success of these papers was down to a combination of factors, including a political climate which favoured the ideology of the market, and importantly the new technology which enabled them to be produced cheaply by reducing staffing levels. With minimal editorial and admin costs, they were typically run by just three or four people, yet offered blanket coverage of an area to advertisers, who 'enjoyed being courted' (ibid.: 87).

The NUJ annual reports reveal that competition from free newspapers was cause for concern. In the annual report for 1970 (which covered the year 1969–70), the union created a policy to protect journalists working for 'give-away publications'. These were defined as being 'produced by publishing enterprises usually adventitious in character outside orthodox newspaper publishing', and those 'produced by orthodox newspaper enterprises' to defend a circulation area, as market research and pilots enterprises for new publications, and as special one-off publications for readers and advertisers (NUJ 1970: 14). Often the staff producing these titles would be untrained or new entrants and, as such, deserved protection, the NUJ ruled. However, ironically perhaps, not all staff of such titles were eligible to join the union, because its own rules precluded the inclusion of staff on 'adventitious publishers of free-distribution publications'; the NUJ maintained that the biggest threat posed by free newspapers was their ability to take advertising revenue from 'orthodox' titles (NUJ 1971: 15).

In response, established newspaper companies increased their investment in this form of newspaper. Westminster Press Ltd, for instance, published twelve free titles in 1977, eleven of which had been launched since 1971. Additionally it faced direct competition from newcomers to the free newspaper market, such as the *Oxford Journal*, which had a 100,000 circulation in the same area as Westminster Press's *Oxford Times* and *Oxford Mail*. J. L. Barrons, deputy managing director of the group, claimed free newspapers enabled titles to succeed where paid-for papers had failed. A weekly paper yielded just 10 per cent of its revenue from sales, Mr Barrons explained; going 'free' therefore became a marketing exercise whereby the 10 per cent was sacrificed for a much larger advertising revenue (Royal Commission 1977, 17OE1: 13–14). Similarly, by 1991 Reed Regional Newspapers had published 100 free titles, with an aggregate circulation of 5.8 million. Reed even launched a free daily title in 1984, the Birmingham-based *Daily News*, which at its peak employed around forty journalists (ibid.: 77–8). Because of their overt dependence on advertising revenue, the number of these titles fluctuated with the state of the national economy. In 1974 there were thought to be around 150, compared with 130 two years later. While some publishers may have dismissed free newspapers as ephemeral as 'feathers in a breeze' (Franklin and Murphy 1991: 76), the impact of the proliferation of this form of publication was considerable. By 1991 Franklin and Murphy cited 1,156 free titles with a circulation of 43.5 million copies, which thrived in the monopolistic market conditions created by the established industry. Such was the opening for this newspaper form that in the new millennium the free paper has reached a new commercial pinnacle in the daily *Metro* paper, in a process explored later in this book.

Computerization. The end of an era?

While computerization of the newspaper was to be one of the most notorious industrial relations battles of the 1980s, innovation in the traditional production process was first introduced in a piecemeal fashion in the provincial newspaper industry in the 1960s. These early innovations were targeted at partial elements of production and were largely championed by group-owned titles, which had the capital to support investment. The cost benefits were also greatest for publishers of evening papers, because the high 'first-copy' cost of newspapers means high-circulation titles benefited most. This meant the technology used was far from wholesale; for instance, it was common to find visual display terminals (VDTs) being used to compose advertisements only, while the editorial pages themselves were still made up using traditional Linotype/hot metal processes. This 'phased' development then progressed through the replacement of the Linotype and hot metal with compositors instead keying words into computers which justified, stored and photoset the text which was turned out on photographic paper.

    Between 1971 and 1974, thirty-eight of the publishing houses surveyed by ACAS had introduced at least one new technology process in the composing room (where the pages were assembled) (ACAS 1977: 10). The Thomson-owned title, the *Reading Evening Post*, created from the pre-existing weekly *Reading Standard*, was widely heralded as the first 'fully-electronic' title in the country. Launched in 1965, it required an investment of £1 million to get off the ground and was seen as an experiment designed to test the potential of improved production methods – including the ability to print colour – to improve advertising yields. In the place of twenty-four Linotype machines were two photo-typesetters, each able to set a line of type a second. A £30,000 National Elliot 803 computer and a Halley-Aller web-offset press, costing £120,000, completed the equipment. Fewer than half of the Linotype operators needed for the *Reading Standard* were needed for the evening title. Similarly, greater accuracy meant fewer 'readers' were needed to spot the errors. Finally, the page make-up required fewer staff. With an increased efficiency of 30 per cent, the Thomson Computerset model epitomized by the *Reading Evening Post* was thought to enable regional titles to reach profit with a daily circulation of just 30,000 (Watts 1990). However, the savings to be had decreased with the size of the paper. For a title with a circulation of 50,000 a day, the annual cost per copy of a newspaper using photocomposition was £39,000, compared with £42,000 for hot metal, but the price was equal for a paper with a circulation of 150,000 and above.

Photocomposition, which was found in half the publishing centres by 1977, offered savings to newspapers by reducing the need for typesetters and compositors, who had produced the lines of hot metal type and then assembled them into whole page forms; instead, photocomposition meant fewer people used computers to produce type on paper, which was then 'pasted-up' into pages. However, the savings offered by the next step of shifting to wholly electronic production would replace the typesetting and composition phases altogether – and so offer substantial additional savings by eliminating an entire sector of the workforce. According to forecasts from Portsmouth and Sunderland Newspaper Ltd, which introduced photocomposition in 1969, a 'typical medium-sized' provincial newspaper, with a circulation of up to 100,000 a day and a ratio of 60–40 per cent editorial to advertising content, could expect to save £100,000 a year on labour costs by moving to direct input. The particular benefit was felt in the advertising department where adverts could be set once and kept on disc for repeat runs. In Wolverhampton the technology enabled the same staff to double the throughput of adverts (An Economic Appraisal of New Technology 1977).

This potential to 'capture the initial key stroke', which was to result in 'reporters at the keyboards of visual display unit, sending their copy direct to the computer'

(NUJ 1977b: 33), would plunge the newspaper industry into a pitched battle between those who wanted to innovate and the unionized workers who fought to retain their jobs. However, even union reaction to this process was not wholly negative, and the NUJ in particular saw aspects of technological innovation as offering increased opportunities for journalists (NUJ 1977b: 14). For the unions representing the printing and allied trades, it was a different matter. At this time, the National Graphic Association enjoyed a high level of membership, reaching 100 per cent even in places which didn't operate a closed shop; therefore, this consolidation of technological change also offered a way of undermining that unionized power by radically altering the role of labour within the newspaper industry. As such, its introduction signalled the end of wholesale union membership for this sector of the provincial newspaper industry workforce. The move was also contextualized by a widespread political offensive embodied in legislation introduced in the 1980s by the Conservative administration to limit union power across all industries.[4] Many of those involved in the newspaper industry felt that the introduction of new technology was aided and abetted by those determined to undermine the power of the unions. Such was the bitterness of the opposition of employers that industrial relations historian Gregor Gall (1993) argues that it can be characterized as an 'offensive' designed by provincial newspaper employers to undermine the unions.

Again, it was in the provincial press that these battles were initially fought between workers and modernizers. Early resistance to change had come nearly a decade before the major battles at the *Nottingham Evening Post*, which attempted to modernize the printing process in 1973. Owners of the paper, T. Bailey Forman, had successfully introduced optical character recognition (OCR) technology into accounts and advertising departments in the late 1960s. But it was the move to Letterflex printing processes – which worked in tandem with photocomposition of pages – which provoked what was called an 'all out war' by contemporaneous commentators. Opposition to change was characterized by fears that the new methods would not be as good as the old and that workers were deskilled. *The Press*, an improvised 'alternative' paper produced by striking workers in Nottingham, claimed that 'they [journalists and printers] are so

---

[4] The Thatcher-led administration introduced legislation to change the legal framework within which trade unions operated. These included the Employment Act of 1980 and 1982 and the Trade Union Act of 1984. In particular, the 1982 legislation removed immunity from legal recourse for damages from unions. This was further tightened by the 1984 act which required TUs to act in a certain way to be considered to have acted legally.

bogged down in unwieldy methods that it makes it difficult for them to maintain interest in their crafts. Good, conscientious and highly-skilled men are now treated as so many cogs or interchangeable "units"' (*The Press*, 9 July 1973: 2). In a similar vein, campaign material produced by the unions publically vilified the managing director of the paper, Christopher Pole-Carew, who, it was claimed, intended to 'drag the newspaper from its technical backwater into the computer age … by the scruff of the workers' necks'. In an undated description of the events held in the Nottinghamshire Archive, the author describes the dispute as 'all out war' (Anon: n.d. ref: DD213/1/1-2).

The unions enjoyed widespread support from the city's Trades Council and received £1,000 in funding from the miners (Anon: n.d. ref: DD213/1/1-2). They also won the support of the Labour-controlled city council which not only barred 'blackleg' staff from the *Evening Post* from its meetings, but also placed valuable adverts in *The Press*, which no doubt helped it sustain it until its final edition on 27 July, when agreement on a return to work was reached. The council justified its decision on the grounds that the circulation of the *Nottingham Evening Post* was so haphazard as to make advertising worthless (*The Press*, 11 July 1973). Following the strike, the *Evening Post*'s sister morning paper, *The Guardian Journal*, was closed and 120 editorial and production jobs were lost. This was the first step on the road to modernization. But further disputes ensued, including the exclusion of twenty-eight NUJ members for taking strike action in 1977–8 (ibid.: 34).

The dispute around Eddie Shah's *Messenger* series of newspapers in Warrington ten years later in October to November 1983 was equally – if not more – acrimonious. Shah launched his first free paper in Sale and Altrincham in 1974, and by 1982, he had expanded the company's portfolio to five *Messenger* titles (Goodhart and Wintour 1974). These titles employed a total of seventy people, just seven of whom were journalists. The dispute centred on disagreements over pay and union rights at a new typesetting plant opened in Bury in 1982; Shah employed non-NGA labour and paid workers less than the pay of the employees working for a subsidiary owned by him, Fineward Ltd. He also opened a new printing plant in Warrington in 1982 and, again, employed non-unionized labour; the NGA suggested that in fact these employees had been selected because of the vehemence of their anti-union stance. It also had a personal aspect, for instance, with Shah and his family being sent coffins as a signal of their unpopularity. John Gennard (1990), in his history of the

NGA, suggests the *Messenger* dispute was a key event because it tested the Conservative trade union law reforms. Such was the significance attached to it that at one stage the entire cohort of NGA national officers were working on the *Messenger* dispute alone. The dispute saw the use of legal action on both sides, culminating in a high court order which fined the NGA £100,000 and more than £500,000 in two separate judgements and sequestered its assets; in turn this prompted a show of support in Fleet Street so that no national newspapers were published over the weekend of 25–26 November 1983. It culminated on the nights of 29–30 November with a picket by more than 4,000 union members but ended after a series of failed negotiations in January 1984, when the NGA called a halt to action, leaving its power 'substantially curtailed'. Changes in legislation around picketing had also meant that the union was unable to halt production; while employers could move production from sites which were being picketed, the pickets were forbidden from following. The *Messenger* dispute also saw the police successfully implement tactics against mass pickets – tactics which would be seen again on a larger scale against the miners in 1984/5 and, later, during the Wapping dispute.

Gennard argues that the strength of union opposition to the *Messenger* dispute mitigated efforts by the provincial newspaper industry to force through the introduction of new technology. This approach was epitomized in the Newspaper Society's *Project Breakthrough* initiative, which was designed to introduce single keystroking, where journalists directly enter words onto a computerized system for printing without the need for 'second keystroking' by typesetters, by the end of 1984. However, the NGA was not able to win the unswerving support of fellow unionists in the NUJ and in Sogat (82). This led to independent agreements between the NGA and employers at Portsmouth and Sunderland Newspapers in 1985, which included no compulsory redundancies and the transfer of some NGA members to the editorial department where they would stay as members of the NGA. This agreement prompted a strike by the NUJ because the NGA had negotiated rights over editorial (Gennard 1990: 494). In turn this meant the NUJ did not support the NGA in a dispute over attempts to modernize the Wolverhampton *Express & Star* and in fact agreed new working practices around direct input during the NGA's dispute. Eventually the NGA abandoned its action against the title and found work for its members elsewhere; this course of action was also the result of action against the *Kent Messenger*, again because SOGAT and NUJ negotiated working agreements over the new technology. Significantly, for the future of newspaper production, the titles were able to carry on production without any NGA members being at work. As such, the power of the print unions was undermined.

Gennard suggests that the legacy of the NGA action in this respect had been to increase the cost of introducing new technology because of the costs incurred by industrial action; it was also a painful path to a joint accord between the NUJ and NGA in October 1985, which set out terms for future changes. By 1987 a total of sixty-seven such accords had been signed in the provincial newspaper industry, although these were eventually undermined by employers who negotiated agreements with the lower paid clerical workers of Sogat (82) in preference to the NGA. The NUJ was also negotiating its own New Technology agreements – 102 of which were signed between 1985 and 1991 (Gall 1993: 616). Although these agreements were negotiated at company level, and so marked the end of national bargaining between the NUJ and the Newspaper Society, Mike Noon argues that their existence is a marker of the NUJ's relative success. Many of the agreements contained verbatim tracts of the model agreement drawn up by the NUJ and, as such, were tribute to the organization and effort the union put into the move to direct input. The technology also increased the significance of the journalist to the organization. However, direct input was also being introduced without any such agreements; by 1988 fifteen companies had done this, including four subsidiaries of Westminster Press, and subsequently an increasing number of employers repudiated existing agreements (Smith and Morton 1990: 108–14). By 1988 the NGA conceded that it had failed in its fight for the provincial newspaper industry. Gall (1993) argues that from this point the spotlight fell on the NUJ and attempts by provincial newspaper employers to undermine its presence in the industry. He argues that the strategic devices employed – epitomized in Project Breakthrough – means the process of derecognition, whereby collective agreements with chapels were replaced with individual employee contracts, can be characterized as a hostile 'offensive'.

The legacy of new technology: Working practices and content

By 1976 the NUJ had begun to monitor the influence of 'technological development' and its impact on staffing levels. In the year 1975–6, 4.2 per cent of the workforce was lost to redundancy or non-replacement. In total this meant 168 people were lost from a staff of 3,869 across 115 chapels (NUJ 1976: 12).

Initially, the union had cooperated with those introducing new technology, in an attempt to gain the most benefits from it for its members.[5] But as the process developed, it expressed the view that technical innovation was in fact enabling managers to gain control of the production process, and, ultimately undermine the power of the trade unions (NUJ 1977b: 17–22). The NUJ also rightly focused on the impact of direct input on editorial staff; the immediate impact for those on the ground was often chaos – despite claims of success from management. Workers at the *Wakefield Express* complained of 'slightly fewer editions … no revision … more literals … deadlines made progressively earlier (36 hours earlier in the case of one weekly) to avoid overtime. Breakdown of computers fairly frequent, bringing everything to a halt'. The *County Express* (Stourbridge) reported: 'Printing times earlier, so late news restricted … Most early pages now 24 hours earlier … more difficult to change or revise copy once it has been set'. The *Western Mail* told of 'Copy lost in the computer, earlier deadlines, no training, no consultation', while the *Belfast Telegraph* said circulation was 'falling rapidly' because of a change to photo setting (NUJ 1977b: 24). For workers this meant earlier shift times – to account for earlier deadlines due to longer production times caused by slow outputting and correction processes. This also meant more pages had to be prepared in advance of publication – which had a greater effect on feature and inside pages, which became 'less topical' (NUJ 1977b: 27). The new processes also meant reorganized copy flow processes, including the use of more pictures, and a shift of power away from the reporter to the production subs.

In theory the move gave journalists a greater role in the production process, but direct input also brought greater responsibility, for instance demanding greater accuracy, which would 'inevitably distract attention from the more genuinely creative aspects of writing' (ibid.: 41). The journalists would become proofreaders, typesetters and stone subs (who actually shifted blocks of type) all in one, while never leaving the VDT. A survey in 1987 showed that journalists received wage increases ranging from zero to £40 as a result of these changes

---

[5] This attitude was formed against a background of substantial job losses forecast for national titles, the *Daily Mirror, Sunday Mirror* and the *Sunday People* and *Telegraph* – largely because the facsimile (fax) meant pages could be sent from London to Manchester, so regional production workers were no longer needed (NUJ 1976: 12). Such was the feared impact that the then ongoing Royal Commission issued an interim report into the national newspaper industry. The issue was debated in Parliament on 20 January 1976 – a month before the publication of the Commission's report – as signifying a de facto end to the northern editions of the national press. Speaking on the issue, the Labour MP Alan Finch said up to 700 jobs would be lost as a result of the move, which would cost the *Daily Mirror* alone £2.3 million (Hansard 1976: 1302).

(Franklin and Murphy 1991: 14). The NUJ also encountered claims that the technology was undermining once-efficient employees and production processes. The technology was also thought to be less suitable for employees aged over forty, while the health and safety concerns around eye damage, posture and radiation were also well documented. However, surveying the impact of new technology on the *Nottingham Evening Post*, Institute of Journalists' convener John Lucy said that these teething problems could be overcome. For him, the innovations meant a cleaner, slicker working environment with staff able to work more quickly to amend and edit content.

> What are the advantages for journalists? For reporters – a clean, efficient operation with no scratching about for copypaper, and a better comprehension of how the stories are developing. Easy change of text.
>
> For sub-editors – a straightforward edit function. Gone are the days of messy proofs. A to-the-millimetre read-out of the lengths of stories which enables easy and quick page make-up. The lay-out man's dream! Flexibility to change stories and design at a moment's notice.
>
> For Editors – a slicker all-round performance with information at their finger-tips. From a news system directory which gives an at-a-glance guide to the overall status of the paper. (Institute of Journalists 1982: 1)

But, critically, accompanying this innovation in production was the fact that the free newspaper had challenged the link between editorial quality and circulation. With the free paper the emphasis had shifted from the reader, who had to choose to buy a newspaper, to the advertiser for whom a circulation within a defined socio-economic group could be defined. As such the role of news was compromised; it needed to be interesting, but not so interesting as to detract from the advertising (Franklin and Murphy 1991: 78). As a direct consequence, these titles developed an amended organizational structure, including a dominant advertising department, smaller – and, critically, cheaper – editorial staffs, for instance by favouring untrained staff, who were less likely to be members of the NUJ and so were likely to be paid less and have worse working conditions (ibid.: 79–80). In a presage of complaints about the twenty-first century newsroom, the NUJ had issued warnings about the potential detrimental effect of new technology on editorial quality. The union described how 'raw untreated copy including press releases can be fed direct into the ... various editions and subsidiary publications via copy typists on a "never mind the quality, feel the width" basis. Anything can be used to fill the space between the advertisements' (1977b: 34). For the NUJ this was a result of the technology being used for 'producing private profit' (ibid.: 37) rather than for the benefit of product or employee, a process which free titles were able to exploit in the face of less resistance from unions (Franklin and Murphy 1991: 80). Significantly, this argument about the relationship between editorial quality and the reader is at the heart of concerns about the ability of the local newspaper to serve the interests of the reader today and echoes the work done by Nick Davies into the origins of editorial content for newspapers in 2008, explored in the closing section of this book.

D. H. Simpson (1981) suggests that new technology itself disrupted the relationship between editorial content and sales across the entire provincial newspaper industry because it shifted power from editorial staff and put it firmly into the hands of the commercial managers of newspapers. The innovations in production methods were used to maximize profit through cost control 'via a reduction in the labour forces and thus costs, by the introduction of greater mechanisation, providing greater managerial control inside the plant' (1981: 22). In turn this led to the 'bureaucratisation of editorial work', which conflicted with an editorial philosophy which emphasized 'artistry and flair' (1981: 86–7). Delano argues that an unforeseen consequence of the introduction of new technology was the loss of 'higher age stratum of experienced journalists who had been trained and conditioned in a way that began to disappear', choosing redundancy over the shift to computer from pencil and ruler (2000: 265). This in turn disrupted what Delano has termed the 'socialisation' of the replacement staff members into the hegemony of the newsroom. This brought the possibility that those values held dear by journalists could be open to dilution and opened the doors to a redefinition of the purpose of newspaper content. Significantly, this meant a shift in the relative emphasis put on the different justifications for editorial work, such as serving the public interest, acting as a newspaper of record, telling a good story, or simply producing copy to fill the space between adverts. Editorial workers were no longer in control and, as such, that social benefit of their work was subsumed to the purpose of profit.

> Thus news gathering, according to the commercial manager, can become ordered and even governed by strict rules. The hectic sprint for the scoop is replaced by the orderly dissemination of the news from regular and certain sources. Thus news in the main can be efficiently collected from the institutions such as the courts, council meetings, police stations etc., and from the 'wire' (news agencies), and to a large extent this is 'static news' which requires no large journalistic staff to acquire it. Indeed there is no competition to be first or

even totally up-to-date, for news that is not reported, of whatever significance, is not news because it is not reported. It may become news the next day and because there is no competition, it is seen by readers to be up-to-date. (Simpson 1981: 115)

Therefore, at a time when the space for editorial was rising through increased pagination, the work of the editorial staff was increasingly regulated and controlled. In the papers he surveyed, Simpson found a 50 per cent increase in space, with just a 10 per cent increase in staff. This changed the nature of the role of the reporter who became increasingly desk-bound and relied on easily available sources and information to provide the 'filler between the ads' in a process which Davies cites in the national press some thirty years later (2008). These staff were also low-paid, in line with their value to the organization, which led to a high turnover and subsequent lack of local knowledge. By the end of the 1980s the process of cost-cutting had become established across much of the provincial press due to the 'asset-stripping mentality of the conglomerate owners' (Franklin and Murphy 1991: 50). Citing the example of Reed International, Franklin and Murphy described an exemplar of the decline; two weekly papers each had an editor, a photographer and six reporters. First one editor oversaw both titles, then the titles were combined and half the staff lost; that paper combined with another and staffing levels were reduced by two thirds, it finally merged with a fourth title leaving 'a freesheet with one staff reporter' instead of a series of papers employing twenty-five staff. This went against the potential of new technology to offer improved plurality within the industry because in theory it reduced entry costs and introduced 'black-box' production methods which were easier to master (ibid.: 50–1). Additionally, this process took place without the resistance of journalists who were 'apparently indifferent to the opportunity for control of their professional fate offered by technology and unconcerned by drifting occupational values', due in part to the conflicting professional identity of journalism and the rupture of its tradition with the loss of experienced workers (Delano 2000: 271–2). Instead new technology had been harnessed for the benefit of the market and profit in a move defined as 'giantism, based on economies of scale', within the provincial press – a philosophy which came to characterize ownership, marketing and production of local papers. Simpson sums up the shift in purpose for these papers:

Their main aim is to make a sufficient return on capital, rather than to provide a community with information of local and national events. They still do report local and national news but this is merely a means to an end. Editorial departments are constrained in attempting to search for the 'truth' and have to report that news which is easiest to collect. (Simpson 1981: 210)

Publishers of local newspapers therefore increased their dominance in a local market by rationalizing products and establishing monopolies across increasingly large areas. The result was a provincial press which was increasingly homogenized and less local.

A new sort of commercial local press has developed: owned by conglomerates, driven by the need for advertising, employing fewer journalists who are low-paid and producing news which is geared to low-cost production in the interests of sustaining more advertising.

The localism of the local press is increasingly illusory; the market, ownership, the political system and cultural influences such as notions of style are increasingly homogenized and centralized. (Franklin and Murphy 1991: 195)

Significantly, these titles were increasingly remote from the communities they claimed to serve, and these newspapers became 'local in name only; the town or city emblazoned on the newspaper's masthead may be one of the few remaining local features of the paper' (Franklin 2006a: xxi).

8

The Digital Turn

Interpreting the crisis in local news?

The past ten years has seen the provincial press in England mired in a prevailing discourse of crisis based on tumbling revenues, which has accelerated the rate of cuts, mergers and consolidations. For the first time since it has been established as a recognized media form, the local newspaper has experienced a challenge to the trusted business model of selling readers to advertisers. It is not the case that readers have disappeared; they may have gone online, but they are still there. Instead the disruption comes in the fragmentation of the advertising market by the very nature of the internet which enables consumers and information providers to access and deliver information via hitherto unimaginable routes. This has undermined the monopolistic mastery the regional newspaper has had over those advertising markets. At the same time, total advertising revenues have been hit by the recession prompted by the 2008 banking crisis. It is this state of affairs which has underpinned predictions such as a half of all local titles closing (Culture, Media and Sport Committee 2010: 12). This reading suggests that the only reaction to the drop in income is an amplification of the strategy of concentration and rationalization which has dominated the provincial newspaper industry for nearly 100 years.

But such dire predictions have proved not to be the case. Instead of half of all 1,300 titles closing by 2014, just 100 had (*HTFP*: 16 June 2014); some of these 'closures' were also the amalgamation of geographic editions or a move to online rather than a complete withdrawal from the market place. Counter-intuitively perhaps, some legacy newspaper companies – particularly the independently owned Tindle Newspaper Group – have expanded the number of newspapers they publish. Additionally, digital platforms have facilitated new entrants to the local news market place, and increasingly those established local newspaper groups are expanding and experimenting with a range of digital platforms. All this suggests that the current range of reactions being found within the provincial newspaper industry goes beyond the 'cyclical' view of a newspaper protecting its market until an upturn in advertising revenues happens (Nel 2010). Instead, there is a structural shift in the local newspaper industry, which has been exacerbated, but not caused by, falls in advertising revenue. The drivers of change are social and technological. A more transient population means people may be bounded by, but are not tied to, localities. Local media 'increasingly faces the challenge of not only of covering local affairs, but also of identifying in ways that that resonate with their audience what is local, what makes it local, and why local is even relevant' (Nielsen 2015: 7). These structural shifts were first experienced by the highly commercialized regional daily newspaper, which, as discussed, had long been the profit power house for publishing centres. Couple these changes with the shift to digital platforms, which has changed the nature of what it means to be a news outlet – where paper may no longer be key to being a 'newspaper' – and particularly, what it means to practice as a local news worker, and the extent of the disruption looks far greater than simply facing the challenge of recouping lost revenues, however dramatic those losses might be. Understanding the future direction of travel for the local newspaper needs to account for those trends, and in this respect the narrative of crisis is too simplistic and fails to explain significant variations in response. A more useful approach frames these reactions within an evolutionary context, whereby newspapers are on the latest stage of a Darwinian journey and adapting to change (Franklin 2008: 631); such an approach frees us from the simplistic message of the imminent death of the newspaper and instead enables us to engage with the complexities of the many potential futures of local news practice.

Digital beginnings

The first newspaper in the UK credited with an online presence was The *Daily Telegraph*, which created a companion website in 1994. Although the regional newspaper industry is said by former editor Neil Fowler to have had a 'cautious' approach to the internet, local newspapers were making inroads into this area shortly afterwards. The weekly *Hereford Times* had a 'beta' website from 1995, and the online presence of local news grew exponentially as titles and groups innovated. *The Hinkley Times* created *Hnet* in February 1996, and its launch included instructions on how to use the site. Writing at the time, the then editor,

David Potter, said: 'This new development means *The Hinckley Times* becomes one of the first weekly newspapers in the country to join the growing band of forward-looking national newspapers and magazines who are publishing electronic versions.' These nascent websites were simple, based on the idea of reproducing the newspaper in an electronic form; the content largely consisted of transferring text which had already been published in the paper, online. This entailed pasting word-processed stories into boxes and individually coding them using HTML (hypertext markup language). In some cases images could be uploaded to accompany the story. Systems and support were centralized so that computer technicians could be based some miles away and so delivered assistance remotely. By 1999 the pace of innovation had quickened so that Johnston Press, which had its first site in 1997, was launching sites at the pace of two per week.

The backdrop to this period was one of prosperity for the regional newspaper industry. Hugely reliant on advertising revenue (which now accounted for around 80 per cent of total income), and heavily indebted because of continued expansion, the largest companies were reporting continued rises in profits and paying larger dividends to shareholders. Advertising revenues for the industry grew from £2.7 million in 1995 to more than £3 billion in 2004 (Franklin 2006a: 8). Profit margins of between 24 and 30 per cent were not unusual for the regional newspaper industry in 2004 and could reach as much as 40 per cent (Fowler 2011). In 1999 Johnston Press reported a 29 per cent rise in operating profit to £65.9 million; in the same year such were the prospects for the sector that Newsquest and its 180 newspapers was acquired by US news giant Gannett in what was hailed as a 'smart choice', according to its 1999 annual report. Trinity Mirror was also formed in the same year out of Trinity plc and Mirror Group plc and the new company went on to acquire a series of titles to expand its regional presence. This concentration was predicated on the sale by some companies of their regional titles – while other companies were willing to buy them because of the potential profits at stake. Those companies which withdrew from the newspaper market during this period included Thomson Corporation, which sold its English newspapers to Trinity in 1995. Reed Regional Newspapers were taken over in a management buyout to form Newsquest, which was in turn bought out by Gannett in 1999. The company went on to acquire Westminster Press (then part of Pearson). Johnston Press also expanded rapidly, incorporating newspaper groups including EMAP, which doubled its holdings, and Portsmouth and Sunderland Newspapers Ltd so that by 2006 the top four regional newspapers groups owned 65 per cent of titles. In 2005 there were 87 companies publishing local papers, down from 137 in 1998 and 200 in 1992 (Williams and Franklin 2007).

The continued significance of the advertising market to the profitability of the sector at this time was reinforced by the emergence of the free morning *Metro* commuter title as a successful product in its own right. Again, 1999 is a pivotal year with the launch of the first London Metro, which was published by Daily Mail and General Trust. It soon expanded to include editions in Sheffield, Leeds, Wales, Merseyside, the Midlands (Birmingham), Scotland and the North East, published by regional centres on a franchise basis to target an affluent audience, younger than that traditionally associated with local newspaper reading (the accepted wisdom in the industry was that you don't start reading your local paper until you have a stake on in the area signalled by home ownership and school-age children). These centres retain a share of advertising revenue and may profit by printing the title. But their adoption of the franchise was described as a 'loaded gun' (Williams and Franklin 2007: 42) where rival companies either cooperated to print and distribute the regional editions – and benefited by being paid to do so – or faced an aggressive incursion into their advertising market. The largest holder of franchises is currently Trinity Mirror, and the success of the product, which claims to be the third largest daily paper with a circulation of 1.3 million, is seen to be its ability to target young (up to 35) professionals – but the regional centres have little or no editorial input into the product, and high production values are not seen as a core part of the title.

What these companies shared was a 'mini-max' expansion strategy which sought to enjoy economies of scale over an advertising market widened by acquisition. This was designed to 'maximise revenue, especially advertising revenue, while minimising production costs' (Franklin 2006a: 7) and relied on a market organized around monopolistic titles which control a defined advertising markets. The pursuit of this strategy meant the largest decline in the number of local papers – 24 per cent –in fact took place long before the digital revolution. Between 1985 and 1995 the aggregate total of newspapers fell from 1,687 to 1,286 as companies sought to consolidate the advantages of computerization described in the previous chapter. Between 1995 and 2005 the number had been largely unchanged, and even revisiting those figures in 2014 demonstrates that the overall number of titles had declined by just 175 in nine years (see Table 8.2). Therefore, rather than closures, these high profits were predicated on a continued commitment to the rationalization of newspaper production, in an efficiency drive which drew criticism because of its impact on the perceived quality of products and the workload of editorial staff. Once the benefits of computerization had been realized at individual titles, the cost-cutting became more radical; newspapers were increasingly standardized – largely shifting to a tabloid format and with an accompanying emphasis on shorter stories and entertainment.

This process was termed 'McDonaldisation' because the way in which news was packed in homogenous newspapers serving up 'mcnuggets' of information included 'bizarre' practices, like removing subeditors with local knowledge to remote offices to work across multiple titles (Franklin 2005: 144). Critics argued that these practices undermined the ability of local reporters to exercise editorial overview of local elites and instead reduced their practice to 'McJournalism'. The *Metro* newspaper was held up as the apotheosis of this practice; it might have been the 'biggest free newspaper in the world', but it employed just six reporters in London and four in Manchester (ibid.: 148). The requirements for staff to do more to service larger papers increased. Improved print technology, which lowered production costs, meant bigger papers, capable of carrying more adverts and so bringing in more revenue. The emphasis for a successful newspaper was shifted to size so that bigger was perceived to be better. But spending restrictions meant the same number of staff were filling those pages; so regional papers were increasingly reliant on information subsidies, such as press releases from PR sources. Nick Davies interviewed a new journalist who described life on a regional newspaper as 'turning out a load of shit … in a sweatshop' (2008: 56). Similarly, research suggested that the news media had become increasingly reliant on PR sources to fill a multitude of lifestyle sections such as travel and business, which needed to be produced by the same member of staff (Lewis et al. 2008). As newspaper resources have been stretched ever thinner, the numbers of PR professionals have risen.[1] In Franklin's words, news production had been 'out sourced', reducing the journalist to a 'burger flipper'. 'The reality is McJournalism and McPapers with similar stories and even pictures, reflecting a growing reliance on agency copy. The reduced numbers of journalists, the influence of local advertisers, the increasing reliance on information subsidies from local government and other organisations with active PR staffs, means that from Land's End to John O'Groats, McJournalism delivers the same flavourless mush' (Franklin 2005: 13). Counter-intuitively, this increase in workload was not met with increases in salary but with

---

[1] Aeron Davis (2008) cites an elevenfold increase in the size of the PR sector between 1979 and 1998 as well as an increase in the sectors in which PR is found and the percentage of organizations which employ PR professionals.

low pay and what the NUJ described as a 'spiral of decline' which, to continue the burger metaphor, was driving diners out of the restaurant as readers opted not to engage with the product (Williams and Franklin 2007: 16).

Cost-cutting was, therefore, already evident when the structural changes which were to undermine the traditional advertising model were apparent. Circulations for local newspapers had been declining from their peak in 1989 when almost 48 million local newspapers were sold each week (see Table 8.1 below). By 2004 this figure had fallen to 41 million, a drop of 15 per cent. At the same time the number of free titles distributed had fallen from 42 to 29 million copies, despite the launch of the *Metro* and '*Lite*' series of titles (Franklin 2006a: 5). By the early years of the new millennium, then, the efficiency drive outlined above had translated into job cuts. In 2002 Trinity Mirror announced a two-year process to shed 800 jobs; a further 580 jobs were added onto that total in 2003, to be found overwhelmingly from among editorial and production staff.

The impact of a structural change in the advertising market began to emerge in 2004; although the UK economy grew, the advertising income for newspapers did not follow suit as might have been expected. This was because new online competitors were making incursions into the lucrative classified market, including property, cars and recruitment, which underpinned the profitability for regional newspapers. The increasing presence of national chains in the High Street also meant less demand for local advertising. This process of decline was accelerated by the development of broadband which grew from zero in 2003 to cover more than 60 per cent of the UK population in the six years to 2009

Table 8.1 Circulations of selected daily titles

Newspaper title	Circulation 1995	2005	2014
Wolverhampton Express and Star	212,739	158,130	40,119[a]
Manchester Evening News	193,063	144,201	57,104[b]
Liverpool Echo	168,748	130,145	41,489
Birmingham Mail (formerly *Evening Mail*)	201,476	93,339	82,854[c]
Leicester Mercury	118,594	82,232	36,004
Yorkshire Post (formerly *Evening Post*)	106,794	68,737	32,256
Eastern Daily Press (Norfolk)	79,596	68,599	44,957
Western Morning News	52,123	42,325	26,699

Source: Franklin 2006: 6 and Newspaper Society database.

[a]20,149 paid-for Monday to Wednesday and Friday; 19,970, Thursday.
[b]44,282 paid-for Monday, Tuesday, Wednesday, Saturday; 12,822 part-free Thursday, Friday.
[c]59,367 part-free, Friday; 23,487 paid-for Monday to Thursday, Saturday.

(Ofcom 2009). This enabled audiences to access many more forms of media – and drove innovation in those types of media – and so prompted dramatic falls in newspaper circulations, which have continued virtually unchecked.

There seems little doubt that among the dominant regional newspaper industry were those who did not recognize the nature of these shifts. William and Franklin (2007) describe the initial reaction of regional newspaper publishers to the internet as 'piecemeal'; this was the response of those who understood the downturn in revenues as cyclical – and so were focused on developing a share of the online advertising market in readiness for the upturn. A wake-up call came in the shape of the inability of DMGT to sell its regional holdings, Northcliffe Newspapers. The company had been offered for sale in 2005 but decided to reject the best offer of £1.1 billion as being undervalued. Fowler (2011) suggests the sector had perhaps started to reach the limits of concentration because of the restrictions placed on amalgamation by regulation. But it was in 2005 that the shift in patterns of advertising spend also became apparent, as exemplified by the experience of Archant Media Ltd, documented via their annual reports. Archant had grown to be the fifth largest regional newspaper publisher in the UK from its original holdings in Norwich in the east of England. In 2000 the company, then known as the Eastern Counties Newspapers Group Ltd, registered a 'record-breaking profit' from its newspapers. With a print-focused business, which also included magazines, Archant invested just £1.5 million in the internet in 2001, out of an operating profit of £26.1 million. This was focused on the Avanti project, described as a 'drive to improve efficiency' in the way adverts were produced. It also coincided with an ambitious expansion strategy to develop Archant as a 'media group of scale', according to chief executive Peter Strong, and this process of acquisitions enabled it to grow its income from regional newspaper advertising for four more years. But in 2005, Archant's operating profit fell by more than 12 per cent, largely due to the migration of recruitment and motors advertising online. Chief executive John Fry noted in the 2005 annual report for the company that 'structural change appears to be impacting the way consumers and advertisers behave. Our response … has been to accelerate developments within the business, in particular to enhance our digital solutions and to reduce costs.' Efficiency savings were made and several newspapers were turned from paid-for to free distribution in order to maximize reach. But this was accompanied by a rapid digital expansion, which meant that by 2006 all but a few of the company's newspapers had websites with a total digital audience of 945,000 per month – a growth of 68 per cent on the previous year.

In common with the major groups at this time, Archant has seen the main opportunity of the internet as being its ability to yield classified revenue. A dedicated team was created to focus on this area as print newspaper costs were cut by £15 million and the workforce reduced by 10 per cent. As early as 1999 six newspaper groups, including Newsquest, Trinity Mirror, Northcliffe and the Guardian Media Group, joined forces to launch the *Fish4* series of websites, which were designed to form a national network of regional classified advertising sites. Similarly, Northcliffe invested in *Zoopla*, the property-advertising website. Trinity Mirror had initially earmarked £150 million and created stand-alone web teams to create bespoke websites. But a revised strategy put forward in 2001 instead focused on advertising, with resulting redundancies among its web team. By 2005 the company had purchased four online advertising business, created nine local recruitment sites and ten community 'wants' sites. In 2006 it launched a series of local property sites (Williams and Franklin 2007). The issue was though, that while these strategies may have captured a section of the digital advertising market, they did not result in a proportionate rise in revenues. The industry complained that it faced competition from the free editorial content on the BBC website and from the sheer number of online competitors, which made charging substantial sums for advertising impossible. Trinity Mirror recorded a digital revenue of just £2.4 million in 2003 and it was not until 2004 that it was making more money from digital than it was investing. In 2007, total online advertising revenue for regional publishers accounted for 4.9 per cent of total advertising income. But that total (£137 million) was just one third of 1 per cent of the total amount spent on online advertising in the UK (Nel 2010). Therefore, when Archant recorded a 51.1 per cent increase in its online display advertising revenue, largely made via its jobs24 site and display advertising sales, that still only brought it to a total of £3.8 million (from £2.5 million in 2007) despite nearly 1.8 million people visiting Archant websites each month.

The decline in advertising revenues outlined above was exacerbated by the post-banking crisis recession which hit the UK in 2008. The impact of these converging trajectories was described as a 'double whammy' by the editor of a regional daily title in 2012 as advertising expenditure fell by more than £400 million – a drop of nearly 19 per cent. The speed of decline accelerated in 2009; in the first quarter the drop was nearly 30 per cent (OFT 2009) and affected both print and digital advertising revenues – and such was the concern that the government set up yet another enquiry into the future of local news in 2009.

It was here that Claire Enders said that she expected half of the 1,300 titles to close within five years. The picture painted by the report was undoubtedly bleak. Profits for GMG Regional Media fell by 85 per cent in the financial year to 2008–9; in March 2009 Johnston Press reported a loss of £429.3 million, compared with a profit of £124.7 the previous year. Trinity Mirror described the future of their newspapers as 'precarious'. In evidence to the government's enquiry into the future for local and regional media, Trinity Mirror submitted, 'the regional newspaper industry is under a three- or four-pronged attack: from an expanding choice of media outlets, from subsidized local authority newspapers, from an ever-expanding BBC and a move of traditional (mainly government) revenues on line. This is all compounded by a cyclical downturn in advertising revenues of an unprecedented nature' (House of Commons HC43-II 2009: 236).

The impact of this appeared at first sight to be straightforward – and cataclysmic. Trinity Mirror closed twenty-seven newspapers in 2008 and eight the next year (out of total of 150) and in total the NUJ documented sixty newspaper closures and the loss of more than 1,500 jobs between May 2008 and May 2009. It also recorded countless moves towards centralization in a process which has yet to end. These are typified by those experienced by the *Coventry Telegraph*;[2] in the ten years to 2015 these included the reduction in district offices from six to two; forty journalists instead of ninety (including a cut in the number of photographers from eight to four) and increased centralization for production in Trinity Mirror's Birmingham offices. The impact of this on editorial working practices was recorded. 'Our own surveys of members have shown a decline in the numbers of journalists regularly covering court or local councils,' the NUJ explained, 'with some members reporting that even in major cities a journalist only attends the local council for the most important debates. The number of specialist political correspondents has declined. There are now fewer specialist crime, court, health and education correspondents working in local newspapers' (House of Commons HC43-II 2009: 152).

Initial digital strategies required print journalists to begin to produce the same stories in a variety of formats, for instance employing the broadcast-based skills of producing video or podcasts. Subeditors were then expected to repurpose print stories for the web, upload and re-headline them. One journalist involved in Johnston's pilot project in 2006 said: 'The problem is with online you're asking the reporter to do three jobs. There's an interview where they have to write everything

---

[2]   The Coventry Telegraph dropped the word 'evening' from its title in 2006 when it moved to morning publication. This was the trend for the majority of the traditional evening newspapers which sought to extend their 'shelf-life' by being on sale in the morning.

down in shorthand for the newspaper, possibly then a sound and video interview where you have to ask different questions as it's a different format and it's gotta sound right, then if those stories then go up on the internet with no subbing or quality control you're going to have a disaster' (Williams and Franklin 2007: 55).

The NUJ reported that the demarcation between roles was becoming blurred with editorial staff expected to take, edit and upload photos; record and edit sound and video, layout and edit print pages, layout and edit websites, provide still and moving graphics, produce emails and manage multimedia workflows (NUJ 2007: 18). Often, training was perfunctory and staff forgot what they had learnt because they were given too little opportunity to practice their skills. Sometimes, investment fell short of providing the required software (Lee-Wright et al. 2012: 74). But the advent of websites – with the ability to constantly update content – has also changed shift patterns and increased working hours for editorial staff. The web was expanding the remit of editorial staff; email meant journalists were increasingly communicating directly with readers and providing 'customer relations', while staff working additional hours were unable to take time off in lieu – in part because it meant even more work for already-stretched colleagues.

> It's not just a matter of a heavier workload or even longer hours, but also different hours. As newspapers where staff have worked predictable hours go over to web-first publication, extra shifts are required at unsocial hours, notably at weekends. … The chapel at a Johnston Press daily reported that staff delivering new media 'are not paid a penny extra', despite the fact that new working practices had increased workloads. A Newsquest chapel said that increasingly integrated online/newspaper practices had led to rising workloads, but no extra money has been negotiated. (NUJ 2007: 12)

Critical appraisals of attempts by the regional news industry to innovate their traditional print practice have suggested that that the quality of work produced – particularly in relation to video where reports may simply have read out stories in front of a camera – was also so low as to be positively harmful. Staff at the *Manchester Evening News*, which moved to a multimedia newsroom in the first years of the millennium, said reporters had been asked to do too much at once; 'of course they can't handle all those things. … We thought that's what multimedia journalism was and it gave convergence a bad name' (Lee-Wright et al. 2012: 76). These strategies were also criticized for amounting to little more than a proposal to move the paper online – and integrate sound and moving image – rather than a radical approach to rethink its presentation, which required a 'paradigm shift' in the way stories are told to enable interactivity (Franklin and Williams 2007: 99). Significantly they didn't even appear to make money; when the *Manchester Evening News* was sold to Trinity Mirror, the department which produced video (Channel M) was not included in the sale.

These changes were not met without any opposition from editorial staff. At Trinity Mirror in Wales the NUJ placed a moratorium on its members handling video because no additional pay was offered. In Liverpool, members took industrial action in protest at additional workloads, which resulted in concessions around training and workloads. In Norwich, the union had negotiated a bonus system whereby staff working on Archant titles received extra payment in relation to the number of 'hits'. In 2007, staff received an additional £120 as a result (NUJ 2007: 12). But most employers justified the lack of additional pay with the response that multiskilled staff were more 'marketable' (ibid.). Editorial workers in the regional press also cited a lack of training as hampering their ability to produce good quality multimedia content. The NUJ described how at one Archant title just two of twelve editorial staff had received eighteen hours of online training at a local college. As a result, the staff said, their video was 'embarrassing'. For that reason, the NUJ report suggested that newspapers should adopt the broadcast industry's training standards of the Broadcast Journalism Training Council, in addition to the National Council for the Training of Journalists, which has traditionally set standards for newspapers, and ideally suggested the two accrediting bodies should merge (ibid.: 19). In a longitudinal study of the Newsquest-owned *Northern Echo*, MacGregor suggests that the financial context in which journalists were working between 2006 and 2011 was a significant factor in professional reactions to technology due to the 'perception of shortage of income, loss of circulation, and drastic decline in staff resources' (2013: 167). News workers described the twin demands of print and online editorial as a 'balancing act' and 'plate-spinning', which 'attest to the opacity of market logic in the day-by-day lived routines of one newsroom' (2013: 168).

Redefining the provincial press in a digital age

The disruption to editorial working practices caused by the impact of the internet has been the result of this cost-cutting. But such a disruption also goes beyond it and is reminiscent of those problems experienced by print workers with the advent of on-screen composition and described at length in this work. Indeed, the NUJ report 'Shaping the Future' drew a direct comparison to its response to new technology (NUJ 2007: 8). For journalists, therefore, these changes are profound both in respect of the skills they are expected to exercise and in terms of the relationship they have with their audience and other content producers and the nature of their professional identities. On the one hand, critics claim that the work of the local reporter has been degraded due to the additional pressures of serving a growing print and digital 'news hole'. However, at the same time, the skillset required by those same journalists has expanded. This disruption is echoed in the way the titles these journalists work for are being redefined and restructured. This process of adaptation has resulted in a change to both established workflows, but more radically the definitional categories around frequency and time of publication have been rendered irrelevant. This has in turn prompted new patterns of production and availability.

The printed versions of daily titles might now be defined as paid-for or free, a definition which has long been associated with weekly newspapers, or as distributed in a new hybrid form – that is part-paid-for and part-free in either selected areas or on selected days. Free papers are then further subdivided into papers delivered free door-to-door, or papers with an element of free pickup at selected outlets. These new definitions also extend to the weekly newspapers, and an additional frequency of publication is added via fortnightly or monthly titles. Most marked is the shift in the way that total circulations are calculated, which recognizes the significance of online editions. The Newspaper Society put total circulations for local newspapers at 40,607,310 in 2014, including all regional free dailies such as the *London Evening Standard* and *Metros*, but this total is an aggregate of paid-for, free and hybrid titles; compare this with the total cited for 1989 of 89,870,000, and the decline in printed newspaper circulations is evident. However, figures to the end of 2013 available via the Audit Bureau for Circulation suggest that individual titles enjoy a substantial online presence. The *Manchester Evening News* had 140,959 online daily browsers; the *Liverpool Echo* 124,238; the *Birmingham Mail* 68,853; *Leicester Mercury* 37,243; and *Newcastle Journal* 13,629. Of these, only the latter recorded a fall of 12.1 per cent. The others had all recorded a year-on-year rise with the *Birmingham Mail* recording a 65.9 per cent rise, the *Manchester Evening News* 34.3 per cent and the *Leicester Mercury* 32 per cent (*Press Gazette*, 27 February

Table 8.2 Local newspapers: declining number of titles 1985–2014

Newspaper type	1985	1995	2005	2014
Morning paid	18	17	19	–
Morning free	–	–	8	–
Evening	73	72	75	–
Paid dailies	–	–	–	87
Free dailies	–	–	–	12
Part-paid/part-free daily	–	–	–	2
Weekly paid	749	473	526	462
Part-paid/part-free daily	–	–	–	122
Weekly free	843	713	637	345
Sunday paid	4	9	12	11
Sunday free	–	–	9	2
Fortnightly and monthly titles	–	–	–	68
Total	**1,687**	**1,284**	**1,286**	**1,111**

Source: Franklin 2006: 4 and Newspaper Society 2014.

2014). The methodology for ascertaining circulations has also become more complex with around 100 titles opting out of the Audit Bureau of Circulation's verification process in favour of alternative independent auditors. These shifts have transformed the categorization of the provincial newspaper industry to acknowledge the irrelevance of print deadlines, as Table 8.2 demonstrates. Even the Newspaper Society has evolved and has merged with Newspaper Publishers Association to form the News Media Association. In 2014 the legacy organization had recorded a total of 1,700 'associated websites' for local newspapers which attracted 79 million unique users each week (Newspaper Society 2014b). The News Media Association instead quantifies the impact of 'news brands' including national as well as regional organizations with a total value of £6 billion a year.

Concomitant with these changes has been a shifting requirement for the physical space needed to house those who produce these products. The transformation to digital news organizations has seen the once-landmark headquarters of the *Yorkshire Post* newspaper, which physically symbolized its centrality to the city of Leeds demolished in 2014 and proposals drawn up to replace it with offices and apartments. This process largely reverses the understanding of the title as an established local institution, a position constructed in the nineteenth century, and so represents a cultural shift in the workplace; companies create 'post-industrial' newsrooms whereby the structural shift in response to digital has a physical manifestation. Nikki Usher (2014) admits that companies make money from rationalizing their property holdings, but 'ultimately the relocations make most sense because newsrooms don't need the space they historically did to create what was once an industrial product'. The nature of making newspapers is changing, and in many cases staff are leaving half-empty, run-down buildings, housing presses which no longer run, for modern work spaces which enable 'workflows that are more responsive to a digital environment' and facilitate 'a cultural shift toward a digital-first mentality'.

In tandem with this is a shift in news practice, which has created the latest iteration of what it means to be a local news worker. Just five or six years ago, the emphasis on 'web-first' and 'convergent' working dominated so that the focus was on the requirement for traditionally print-focused workers to innovate and deliver content online as well as in the newspaper. The largest newspapers groups repositioned themselves as 'webfirst' multiplatform organizations. This approach was outlined by Johnston Press plc as early as 2006 as it piloted a local newspaper, based around an 'integrated news-provision team ... the creation of digital editors to manage online content; reporters that produce video and audio as well as words on the page; sub-editors that work on paper and the web; and the introduction of a web-first news publication strategy' (Williams and Franklin 2007: 53). Simon Reynolds, editor of the *Lancashire Evening Post*, the pilot for this 'newsroom of the future' said, 'not only have we reinvented the newspaper ... but we are effectively not a newspaper any more. We have been transformed into an integrated fully converged news operation' (*Press Gazette*, 6 November 2006). However, in the era of Web 2.0, convergence has been displaced by interactivity, which is challenging the nature, as well as the skill set of news work. As a result, Trinity Mirror has restructured its editorial organization into the 'newsroom 3.1', which focuses content production on 'digital audience spikes' through the day. That same content is then 'packaged' into familiar newspaper titles (Trinity Mirror plc, 25 February 2014). Johnston Press have rationalized press centres and offices and have provided editorial staff with laptops and smartphones, which they say has 'helped to greatly improve the quality, quantity and timeliness of multi-media content available on websites, mobile sites and tablet apps' (2013: 23). Critically, mobile technology and social media mean the line between professional and amateur publishers is increasingly blurred by the ability of both to interact with each other; the technology also means established brands no longer have the monopoly on production technology. As academic Jim Hall writes,

> News is no longer a one-way process nor can news workers determine the news agenda as print and the broadcast media once allowed. Interventionist public or community journalisms, which before the web were regarded by the larger news organisations as marginal and unprofitable, and citizen journalism, have helped to show journalism how to make news a fully interactive process. If our present titles are to survive it must also be a profitable one. (2008: 222)

Research carried out into journalists' reactions to multimedia innovation revealed little resistance in principle, despite its impact on some of the basic principles of a journalists' professional identity. This may be, O'Sullivan and Heinonen suggest, because initially the technology largely complemented traditional ways of working, such as using the internet for research, emailing instead of faxing, or enjoying the speed and immediacy of social media platforms (2008: 359). However, more challenging has been those elements which blur the distinction between the audience and the professional journalist and in particular the relationship between employed journalist and 'user-generated content'. To date, research suggests that attempts to formalize the relationship between these contributing 'citizen journalists' and regional titles in England have been exploitative so that the contributors are little more than producers of free content. This is so, despite the potential to engage a wider public with the content of regional publications through what might be termed co-production. Investigations into the relationship between journalists and readers at two regional daily titles in England suggest that the systems in place limit, rather than encourage, participation – for instance by insisting on moderation of comment threads and by the lack of participation of journalists in that process. A study of a collaboration between professionals at the *Leicester Mercury* and a community reporters' network in the city suggested that 'rather than embracing citizen journalism with the civic aim of widening political engagement, it may be more realistic to suggest that local British newspapers are utilizing active readers as a form of free labour' (Canter 2013: 3).

Technology, which enables the audience to take an active role in publishing directly to the web, goes further than drawing on citizen journalists as a producer and undermines the role of the journalist as 'gatekeeper' filtering user-generated content. Individual journalists are using social media platforms to engage the audience in an increasingly participatory manner – although this may well be in spite of, rather than because of, institutional organization. This means innovation is coming from the ground up. Canter identified that 'it is individual journalists rather than their news organisations that are taking the lead in increasing interactivity with readers. … They are increasingly engaging in a two-way conversation via social media' (2013b: 492). Dickinson suggests that local reporters may be more willing to innovate 'because they are on the front line of an industry in crisis and therefore more aware of the need to cement relationships with their audiences': in this way individual editorial staff are building a name for themselves as individuals within an organization (2011: 8). The result is an opening out of the editorial process so that journalists are seen by audiences as 'ordinary, fallible individuals rather than authoritarian gatekeepers' (Canter 2013b: 493).

Even the notion of local is not what it was so that the proximity which once underwrote the relationship between local journalists and audience might be re-thought of as connectedness, facilitated by a technology which obviates the need for a physical presence. Hess and Waller (2014) suggest that 'geo-social' is a better way of defining newspapers which proclaim a link to place in their masthead in the digital age. This concept recognizes the significance of the link to place by both reader and journalist, but also recognizes that the link may be digital, the result of interest or nostalgia as well as physical location. In this instance the news provider can use place as a defining factor, but instead of location acting to delimit, it instead places the provider as 'node' within a network of information. The geo-social breaks the functionalist link between geography and community; readers are situated with a location, but are not defined by it. However, it is not certain whether digital technology is rendering the connection with place obsolete; hence why some of the latest forms of local news are capitalizing on this very aspect. Hess and Waller also suggest that the physical proximity of producer and locale remains significant within the 'geo-local' concept, because a sense of place helps to 'provide news and commentary on their audiences' place in a highly connected world' (2014: 130). For this reason, they are critical of moves to centralize newspaper production in the UK, because journalists need to preserve their connection to a geographical location in order to 'develop a specialized understanding of the land they report on' (2014: 128). This suggests that even professionals who are removed from their locale by centralization need to retain their claim to authority over a geographical area.

The local journalist now has to reach out to, and bring together, a virtual community as well as those defined by a particular geographic locality. Reader and Hatcher (2012) describe 'a community connector who has both a professional and a personal stake in that community'. Seth Lewis et al. (2014) have developed the notion of connectedness into one of 'reciprocity', where journalists actively engage with their audience – largely via social media – to build an ongoing and active relationship. Journalists are 'community builders who can forge connections with and among community members by establishing patterns of reciprocal exchange' (2014: 237). Mark Deuze describes the product of this as a form of 'open' journalism, produced by the journalist and reader-as-citizen-journalist together; the apotheosis of this is a form of 'dialogical' journalism (2003: 218) 'where the contents of a news medium … are fully maintained by journalists interacting with citizens'. The impact of this on the business of journalism is profound because the news provider no longer has a monopoly on content but is instead placed somewhere 'on a continuum between content and connectivity' (ibid.: 220), which has implications for its organization and, significantly, its role in the community.

These academic perspectives are in contrast to the dominant endorsement of digital from the regional news groups which seem to harness the technology for the promise it holds to form an 'information subsidy' to the business model. Describing who can publish to their website in 2013, Ashley Highfield, chief executive of Johnston Press, wrote, 'We now have a platform to provide greater efficiencies in our content gathering operation from our journalists, freelance contributors and readers. Using web-based editorial software the Group is now allowing trusted contributors the ability to author content direct' (Johnston Press 2013: 7–8). In 2014 Local World[3] enabled the police to upload content directly to selected news sites (*Press Gazette*, 14 March 2014). In a 2,000-word letter to staff, company Chairman David Montgomery outlined a vision of a news organization in which the reporter was largely redundant. Instead it would largely draw on user-generated content where one senior journalist would have sole charge of 'content segments', for which they would source and publish content (*Press Gazette*, 21 November 2013). This process then at best displaces the perceived role of the journalist in the information ecosystem because 'some

---

[3] The arrival of Local World in the top twenty regional newspaper groups of 2014 marked a major shift in holdings among the major players in the industry; Local World was formed in January 2013 with the acquisition of Iliffe News and Media, the publishing subsidiary of Yattendon Group, and Northcliffe Media, the regional publishing arm of Daily Mail and General Trust, which retains a 39 per cent stake in the company (DMGT 2013: 6). Trinity Mirror also has a 20 per cent stake in the company both as an investment and in order to take advantage of 'any future opportunity for industry consolidation which may emerge' (Trinity Mirror 2012: 11).

of the institutionalized communication functions of agencies and journalistic media can be performed by individual society members and organisations' (Domingo et al. 2008: 331). At worse it bypasses the editorial worker altogether, and the area in which this has had most impact is that of press photographers who have increasingly been made redundant, leaving publications wholly reliant on submitted pictures. Not unsurprisingly, this trend has been met with opposition from inside and out. As early as 2007 the NUJ stated unequivocally that this 'UGC' was 'not a replacement for quality professional journalism' (2007: 26), and journalists have articulated the growing importance of their professionalism in comparison with this 'amateur' blogosphere (O'Sullivan and Heinonen 2008: 359), perhaps in an attempt to reinforce their own significance. 'The profession has striven for its status among other professions in society since the 1800s. Even now, there seems to be an internal need to adhere to practices which ensure that status, and to maintain the particular values that both generate and legitimize those practices' (ibid.: 368).

Where now the future for local news?

The picture outlined above is simultaneously dismal, yet hopeful. This is because it suggests that the failure described is not the failure of local journalism per se, but is better understood as failure of the corporatized provincial news industry. Ofcom has suggested that 'it is local journalism, rather than local newspapers, that needs saving' (House of Commons HC43-I, 2009: 5). The NUJ argues that the corporate industry had been the architect of its own downfall because this pattern of ownership had put profit before quality.

> It is often said not much happens in Milton Keynes which is just as well because as the NUJ's workplace representative said, if it did, they would not have the staff to cover it. ... There is without doubt a crisis in local media – but the explanations of many media owners for the state they find themselves in today are too simplistic and seek to divert attention from the failure of the business model which is killing journalism at a local level. (House of Commons HC43-II, 2009: 149)

The corollary to this position is that that alternative forms of local journalism outside of the dominant corporate ownership model may not experience the same pressures.

What we have are two differing approaches underwriting the way in which the practice of provincial news can change in response to this emerging landscape. One is experimental and considers the way in which the nature of these news brands and the practice of working within them can innovate and so redefine the very nature of the relationship between news worker and community. On the other hand, we have a continued response by those large, corporate-owned, news brands to exploit these technological changes to cut costs. In 2013 Archant's strategy of rationalization resulted in the loss of fifty full-time equivalent jobs (out of a total of 1,652), including twenty-four across its East Anglian titles (*Press Gazette*, 13 March 2013). A further nineteen jobs were lost with the closure of six regional monthly lifestyle magazines. Johnston Press has shifted all of its papers to the same production template format in order to 'have a platform to provide greater efficiencies in our content gathering operation from our journalists' (Johnston Press 2013: 7). Senior staff who did not want to relocate to the Newsquest centralized subbing hub were made redundant and replaced with entry-level copy editors. The result was criticisms from industry observers for a lack of quality in subsequent products (*Holdthefrontpage*, 5 March 2014). These companies have also started to yield increasingly large proportions of profit from digital sources. The 2013 annual report for Archant reported an operating profit of £9.4 million on a turnover of £126.6 million. Significantly, 19.3 per cent of its revenue – a total of £7.2 million – was made from online with most revenue coming from display advertising, particularly jobs, mobile sites and apps (ibid.: 21). For Johnston Press, £24.6 million of its total £291.9 million revenue came from digital sources – a 19.4 per cent rise on the previous year (Johnston Press 2013: 6).

At the extreme is the move to leave print altogether, which has happened to free titles like the *St Helens News*. Trinity Mirror created one digital portal – getreading.co.uk – in the place of the former evening title, the *Reading Post*. The paper, whose history has been charted in earlier sections of this book, had moved to a weekly publication in 2009; in November 2014 it was one of a series of print publications to close in preparation for making Berkshire a 'digital-only zone'. The move followed the increasing proportion of people accessing news online via desktop and mobile devises but did not alter the core business. 'The challenge remains the same – we need to tell the stories which matter, to the people who need them but the change is the speed of delivery at which this now takes place', wrote Ed Walker, digital development editor of Trinity Mirror Regionals, of the changes (*getreading.co.uk*: The Last Post). But it also meant the closure of seven print newspapers and the loss of fifty jobs. Laura Davison, NUJ national organizer, said the impact would be detrimental to communities because 'the company has accepted they won't be able to get the breadth and depth of content in future and will be concentrating on topics that generate hits'.

Therefore, the dichotomy between public service to a community and the audience-as-profit continues to underpin perspectives on the corporatized future of the local newspaper. Ed Walker draws on an implied higher purpose when he says the stories which 'matter' will be told, while the NUJ says there will inevitably be a narrower range of content covered – a trend which is amplified by the use of web-based analytics, which demonstrate both audience volume and engagement. This has revolutionized the way in which news organizations can gauge reader reaction to their content. Previously feedback rested on sales figures or specially commissioned market research exercises; particular stories might occasionally have provoked a torrent of reaction delivered to the newsroom via letter or the telephone by readers. But analytics are now almost ubiquitous in newsrooms, particularly in the United States and United Kingdom, and have spawned an entire range of job titles, such 'audience editor' or 'audience engagement editor' in the place of the imprecise process of editorial judgement. Although systems vary in sophistication and 'bespokeness', it is now commonplace for journalists to be able to monitor how many people read their story, when and for how long. Systems can tell them where these readers are and which technology they are using to access content; additionally they can supply the route to the story taking into account both home websites but also social media and search engine sources. This information is then fed back into the editorial process including 'day-to-day tweaking of headlines, pictures, placement and promotion across social media as well as changes to workflow, like time of publication' (Cherubini and Nielsen 2016: 14). Trinity Mirror professed an aim to have analytic specialists in all of its newsrooms as part of their 'Connected Newsroom' strategy, which enables journalists to identify that content which is most engaging – and build on that information in a variety of ways which further their editorial aims, be they starkly commercial or public-interest oriented. This refined ability of analytics to segment audiences has come under fire for the way in which it conflicts with the inclusive ideal of community which has been imagined to be at the heart of the traditional local news organization. It is this ideal of the readership which I argue has underpinned the perceived social role of local news since the mid-nineteenth century. But the impact of analytics is that journalists will stop covering the type of content associated with this role if no one is reading it, particularly when the relevance of reader numbers to advertisers is considered. Whether by choice or as a result of instruction is open to question, but either way the potential is that the range of editorial content will be narrowed to what interests the public, rather than what is in the public interest, in a 'cycle which continues to gnaw away at the notion of community' (Tandoc and Thomas 2015: 247).

With technology employed to cut costs, the profit focus continues to be on advertising. Nel's work to investigate the extent to which companies were adopting an approach of structural change suggested that in 2010 the sixty-six newspapers surveyed were still relying on advertising to create a revenue stream. In July 2014, Sir Ray Tindle himself, who has retained an emphatic focus on print to the centrality of his business, forecast a return in the fortunes for the weekly newspaper industry, saying advertising revenues at a local level were beginning to make up for the loss in national revenues. Throughout the recession, though profits have fallen, his company had never made a loss, and between 2008 and 2014 he launched nineteen new titles and bought an additional twenty-one. 'We believe we have safely reached the turning of the tide and the beginning of the recovery. Forecasts of the early demise of us were certainly mistaken. The public still want their "local" and most people still want it in its present printed form' (*Press Gazette*, 9 July 2014). Even online the emphasis on the advertiser is retained, which suggests little radical shift in the basic business model. The 2013 annual report from Johnston Press described the company as a multimedia 'one stop shop' for advertisers within a 'digital first' strategy which prioritizes digital products accessed not only via computers, but also increasingly on mobile devices and via social media. The industry has also protested about ad-blocking technology, which enables users to filter out advertising material from websites to the extent that then culture secretary John Whittingdale has said it posed a real threat to the profitability of news sites (*holdthefrontpage.co.uk*, 11 March 2016).

This extreme 'mini-max' business approach facilitated by digital technology has added to the disruption to the notion of what it is to be a journalist working in the local news industry. In particular, it has enabled the principle of concentration to apply to working arrangements as well as ownership; in turn this has threatened what journalists see as their 'professional' value. At a local level the challenge to the journalists' ability to sustain the value of serving the good of the community conflicts with the requirements for remote working enforced by the business context (Russo 1998). Increasingly workers have been physically removed with the closure of local offices and printing and subediting being centralized into regional hubs. As outlined above, this has philosophical implications for the relationship between a local paper and its geography, but additionally it has a practical impact on the work routines of those staff. It might even have an impact on who those staff might be. Newsquest's centralized subbing hub means titles are no longer created by production staff aligned with them; based in South Wales, workers output titles from as far afield as Darlington and York (*holdthefrontpage.co.uk*, 5 March 2014). This means journalists are less likely to be locally based with a concomitant loss of specialist expertise often accrued over years of working in an area. The 'serious consequence here is the loss of routine contacts with the local community in which the paper circulates' (Franklin 2006a: xxi).

A useful way to envisage the provision of local news is as an ecosystem, consisting of a variety of providers of which legacy newspapers are only one. Even when just considering print alone, this work has considered 'alternative' newspapers and referenced other publications such those published by local authorities during its course. It has given less consideration to broadcast media, which largely operate at a regional level in England. Radio operates at a more localized level and is well established as a commercial and community sector, and in 2012, twenty-three local digital television licences were offered for broadcast via the Freeview service; among those, Mustard TV in Norwich is operated by Archant. At the other extreme are the parish level magazines which have often been drawn on as sources by the established local news industry. This work has also largely concentrated on the corporate-owned provincial newspaper, which has dominated the local news market for the past 100 years. Outside of this picture though are a number of alternative responses to newspaper ownership, which offer a different perspective to the 'mini-max' corporate response outlined above. These include the continued presence of family-owned, independent newspapers – predominantly weekly – which, without shareholder obligations, maintain a business structure which may still focus on the relationship with the community. In 2014 there were some five companies which owned just three newspapers in England, sixteen who owned two and twenty-nine who owned one paper. Most of these had circulations of lower than 3,000 a week. This compared with the 635 titles owned by the 'big four' companies of Trinity Mirrors, Newsquest, Local World and Johnston Press with an aggregate weekly circulation of more than 23 million.[4] There are also a

---

[4]   Source, All Regional Press Publishers, January 2014, Newspaper Society Intelligence Unit.

limited number of cooperatively owned news titles in the UK, which reinvest the money made from the product into the news organization itself. The longest standing example of this is the *West Highland Free Press* in Scotland, founded in 1972, which is unusual in its avowed left-leaning politics as well as its ownership structure. More recently the *Bristol Cable* has adopted a cooperative form of ownership based on crowdfunding and grant support to create 'an independent and accountable media source that reaches a wide audience and challenge power and received wisdom' (thebristolcable.org 2016).

The digital turn has then increased the opportunities for diversification within this ecosystem; indeed research suggests that the more precarious the business model, the greater the rate of innovation in practice and form (Powers et al. 2015). The removal of titles from their locale discussed above has been cited as a direct cause for the proliferation of 'hyperlocal' blogs and newspapers and an increased emphasis on citizen journalism which 'offers new opportunities to cover news on a town, neighbourhood or even street level' (Paulussen and D'heer 2013). In England much of this can be found at a 'grass roots level; no fewer than 550 hyperlocal websites were mapped in the country at the end of 2015 in what has been termed a "ground up renaissance"' (*Press Gazette*, 22 January 2016) for local news. These websites may also be founded along collaborative lines, with an increased emphasis on a dialogic relationship with the public. This is certainly the avowed position of the *The Bristol Cable*, which is not only cooperatively owned but which also promotes the active engagement of people in the city and holds regular workshops to facilitate that process. The form, content and motivation for these sites varies wildly; often staffed part-time or by people with no formal background in journalism, they can rely on a variety of funding sources – including grants, crowdfunding and monetizing their hyperlocal expertise – to continue. At the other extreme are independent ventures, such as the Bristol-based *Filton Voice* (as a city, Bristol has the tradition of journalistic innovation established by Sam Farley in the eighteenth century), which was launched by the former assistant editor and advertising manager of the *Bristol Post* newspaper. It distributes 90,000 print copies per quarter. Most evidence, though, suggests that the financial sustainability for these ventures is at best precarious. As such, 'it is not enough to declare hyperlocal media operations the antidote to the decline of traditional media outlets' (Kurplus et al. 2010: 372). There is also evidence that people still want professional, trusted local media outlets even within communities with thriving hyperlocal websites. Perhaps more importantly, those who work in hyperlocal news often do not position themselves as challengers to traditional providers and 'characterize themselves neither as news makers nor as journalists and are insistent that they could not and should not be seen as replacing journalists'. This is because they are often not paid for their work and so make little claim to comprehensive coverage because often the content they post is driven by personal interest and what they happen to come across in the street. This compares with the views of professional editorial staff who collaborate with citizen journalists who define themselves as trained, objective and as producing work which conforms to professional standards; as such, they have a greater 'credibility' than their community counterparts. This research by Lilly Canter suggests that both citizen and professional journalists wish to see the lines of demarcation remain (2013: 16).

In common with these community-driven newcomers, the legacy news brands, whether on paper or online, continue to lay claim to being vital conduits which provide information about public life and local affairs for communities. However, the preceding chapters have set out the contingency of this relationship. This does not detract from the traction that the notion of serving the good of the community has for news workers within the industry both past and present – exemplified for instance by the way in which it is codified in training; at the same time it has come to inform what society sees as the normative function of the local press (Conboy 2004: 272). At varying times this role has been foregrounded by the industry, particularly during the Second World War when it served the interests of profit (see Chapter 6), so that by the 1970s, the purpose had been identified as the most significant function of the local paper (1971: 273). It is a position which is still articulated by the industry, as exemplified by former London mayor and MP Boris Johnson's quote in support of Local Newspaper Week in 2013: 'The fact that local newspapers remain at the heart of communities is testimony to the energy and enthusiasm their journalists bring to the stories they tell – shining a light on what really matters to people' (Newspapersoc.org.uk 2013b). As such, serving the good of the community can be considered a 'justificatory ideology' for local news practice; for those working in the provincial press, it is actualized in the norms and routines of their working lives and is a shared norm which organizes their work.

However, while it is clear that serving the good of the community is a key concept to the local newspaper, it is far from clear whether the dominant corporate model of producing local news is focused on this purpose. Indeed, the continued process of consolidation and conglomeration which characterizes the large majority of titles has shifted the emphasis from social purpose to the bottom line so that aspects of news work aligned with that purpose – such as the coverage of local government – are increasingly absent. Most recently the economic restructuring of the provincial newspaper industry in the wake of the 2008 recession and the impact of digital competition to the traditional newspaper is also calling into question the ability of those working in the legacy industry to function in a way which aligns to this notion. Digital newcomers to the local news landscape are challenging the notions which underpin the relationship between news and community, while in equal measure using it to justify their own existence. What each of these are still able to draw on is, simultaneously, the often unquestioned assumption that local news is central to the well-being of informed, democratic communities, together with the fluidity of the notion of community itself.

This is possible because the very nature of community is itself contested; community is necessarily 'imagined' and 'limited' by a finite boundary so that while members may not actually know each other, the nature of community means they imagine that they do (Anderson 1991: 6–7). The local newspaper has been particularly successful in constituting an advertising market as a community because that very process is one way in which a local community may be 'imagined'. The operation of a local newspaper, in selecting and presenting a certain body of content aligned with a locale, both employs and creates a form of 'parish pump patriotism' (Franklin and Murphy 1991: 56). Anderson suggests that the newspaper is a powerful instrument in this imagining; not only is content significant, but in a process appropriate for the mass-circulation printed newspaper of the pre-digital era, the very act of reading it also becomes a 'ceremony' which simultaneously links members of the community. This may be a visible process in which the reader observes 'exact replicas of his own newspaper being consumed' and so it becomes 'visibly rooted in everyday life' (ibid.: 35–6). This notion is particularly compelling for the traditional pattern of sale for provincial newspapers, produced for instance on market days in their earliest forms when readers would gather together in a regular event, or as a mass-market evening title sold at times to coincide with the end of the working day. Anderson argues that this regular pattern of publication also creates a sense of 'temporal coincidence' (ibid.: 24) that reinforces the construction of community. Increasingly, though, this notion is disrupted by the fact that 'newspapers' are available in an atemporal, digital format, those titles which are printed are produced as early as possible – to make their 'shelf-life' as long as possible – so that the coincidence of purchase is also disrupted.

Despite this, the narrative of the local community by a local newspaper may continue to normalize its ideological construction. Hall suggests that the media order events in terms of 'maps of meaning' to enable the audience to 'make sense' of events according to an assumed shared knowledge in a 'social process – constituted by a number of specific journalistic practices, which embody (often only implicitly) crucial assumptions about what society is and how it works' (1978: 55). The notion of community is constructed and reinforced by that mapping, which itself refers to a system of shared values and beliefs, which, it is assumed, the audience shares. The process creates a 'consensus' that community exists and is reflected in journalists' concept of the role of the paper.[5] Martin Conboy (2002 and 2006) has demonstrated this process in the British popular press – and in particular the tabloid press – to show how it constructs a particular notion of community. These titles exploit language to communicate a 'shared idealization' (2006: 10) while at the same time the newspaper's use of language to articulate a form of British national community is also a highly successful commercial strategy which enables it to retain a large share of the national newspaper market (2006: 13). In a similar way local newspapers exploit place to create a community centred on a geography concomitant with this circulation area and foreground localness with such strategies as signalling its name in its title and by including stories which have a connection to its circulation area. Simultaneously they create an advertising market, which claims confluence with that geographical area, although in reality it is aligned with only those people the advertisers want to target. This strategy is an organizing principle for the type of content included and prioritized by the newspaper. Chief among these is an overwhelming emphasis on local content; a title gives prominence to and campaigns for causes and issues within the geographical area with which it is aligned. As described in the course of this history, the title becomes part of 'the establishment', even moving into landmark buildings to rival those of key institutions and so assumes a mandate for its watchdog role. The corollary to this is the need for accuracy, because expert local readers would notice mistakes. Additionally, Franklin and Murphy argue that the embodiment of the community is its

---

[5]   This process is explored in my paper 'The ideological challenge for the regional press; re-appraising the community value of local newspapers'.

institutional representation so that council, MP, court, emergency services are all given prominence as sources (1991: 58).

However, this notion of community is not absolute or inclusive, and, because of its alignment with the business structure of the newspaper, it is open to change and exploitation. Analysts have been arguing that the cracks in the relationship between community and newspaper were beginning to show half-a-century ago because of 'consensus-seeking market journalism' (Jackson 1971: 286). Therefore, while the notion of the local press serving the good of the community may remain 'an essential part of its public legitimacy' (Conboy 2004: 127), the extent to which that role is fulfilled has long been open to question. Cox and Morgan (1973) and Franklin and Murphy (1991) criticize the proposition that communal life depends on this form of news production; instead, they suggest it creates an ideology of news production which serves the economic interest of the localized provincial newspaper industry. This question of the social role of local news has gathered renewed urgency with the challenge to a highly commercialized provincial press by digital media. As such, the idea that the journalist serves the good of the community may go beyond degradation and simply be abandoned by a newsroom for whom the pursuit of profit has been accelerated by recession and structural shifts.

Despite this lies the significance of these traditional media brands which might go beyond the stark figures of analytics. Nielsen suggests that in the disrupted media landscape, independent information, produced by professional journalists, about local affairs can accord an organization the status of 'key stone' media, which have an impact on the wider news ecosystem disproportionate to their perceived size. They might be perceived to have a diminished reach, for instance because of falling circulations, but in fact their impact goes beyond the stark figures provided by sales or analytics. This has implications for the range of content papers might like to include – whatever the analytics might say. In this reading, even if readers do not engage with reports of local government, those reports still resonate across the wider political landscape. And if those reports are dropped – for instance because the analytics demonstrates a lack of audience – then that environment is all the poorer for it. 'Many citizens would not feel this directly … but they would live with the ecological consequences as the media that they do rely on for information would have to make do without the steady stream of local news coverage produced by the local newspaper' (Nielsen 2015: 69). Perhaps acknowledging this potential impact, in March 2016 the UK government announced business rate relief for those newspaper companies which continue to operate offices in local areas. Its consultation articulated the normative role of newspapers and their perceived importance to the actual and imagined local landscape explored here; 'local newspapers ... are an important source of information for local communities and a vital part of a healthy democracy' (DCMS 2015: 4).

However, whether, what is in effect, a public subsidy is justifiable for news organizations which seek only to maximize profits remains to be seen, and so we must first return to the reframed question about the role provincial newspapers play in relation to their communities. If we believe the local press should be a vital part of democratic accountability, then what sort of business model can support a local press which would be able to take on that mantle? This work has established that there is nothing absolute about the relationship between the corporate-owned news brand which dominates the English provincial newspaper market and this role. Indeed, the typology of historical development set out here demonstrates that the emphasis on social benefit has been neither consistent nor continually evidenced, during that history. Just as the earliest entrepreneurial printers in the eighteenth century made no claim to community benefit, but prioritized their utility to the business customer, so the evidence presented here demonstrates that the dominant news brands are no longer operating within a business structure which supports that function. Indeed, this history demonstrates that, rather than being an ideological pillar for the corporate-owned provincial news industry, the good of the community is little more than a mythological value, which may have coincided with a way of working which served the interest of the business, but never went so far as to underwrite its organization. To reiterate, this retrospective look at the workings of the newspaper industry suggests that profit has always been at the heart of this business. For this reason, those who would seek to establish the 'golden age' for the corporate local newspaper which put public service before profit will find that, like the crock of gold at the end of the rainbow, this era is little more than an idealized chimera. Times of disruption such as now prompt varying responses from alternative news providers who, for instance, institute themselves as not-for-profit businesses which invest in ways of working which centralize that value. In doing so, they contribute to the undermining of the mythology of community benefit which the corporate business has successfully defended since the nineteenth century by drawing on its failure in this respect. In light of this, it is appropriate to question the way in which that corporate industry continues to draw on this value as a claim to legitimacy or as a claim to public support. The challenge for this legacy newspaper industry as it seeks to carve out a future as a re-imagined digital offering may not, therefore, be to master the technology in a way which revives its ability to make money from advertising. Instead it might be the way in which it can revalue its place as part of the public landscape and recapture the idea that it can serve the good of the community.

Bibliography

ACAS (1977), *Industrial Relations in the Provincial Newspaper and Periodical Industries*. Cmnd 6810-2, HMSO, London.

Anderson, B. (1991), *Imagined Communities*. Verso, London.

Aspinall, A. (1946), 'The Circulation of Newspapers in the Early Nineteenth Century'. *Review of English Studies*, 1946, pp. 29–43.

Aspinall, A. (1973), *Politics and the Press, 1780-1850*. The Harvester Press, Brighton.

Asquith, I. (1978), 'The Structure, Ownership and Control of the Press', in, Boyce, G., Curran, J. and Wingate, P. (eds), *Newspaper History from the Seventeenth Century to the Present Day*. Constable, London, pp. 98–116.

Bainbridge, C. (1984), *One Hundred Years of Journalism: Social Aspects of the Press*. The MacMillan Press Ltd., Basingstoke.

Balfour, M. (1979), *Propaganda in War 1939-1945*. Routledge and Keegan Paul, London.

Barker, H. (1998), *Newspapers, Politics and Public Opinion in Late Eighteenth-Century England*. Oxford Scholarship Online, Oxford University Press, Oxford.

Baylen, J. (1972), 'The New Journalism in Late Victorian Britain'. *Australian Journal of Politics and History*, 18, pp. 367–85.

Belsey, J. (1992), *Hold the Front Page: 60 Years of Great Stories from the Evening Post*. Bristol Evening Post, Bristol.

Bennett, E. A. (1898), *Journalism for Women: A Practical Guide*. John Lane and The Bodley Head, London.

Benson, J. (2009), 'Calculation, Celebrity and Scandal'. *Journalism Studies*, 10:6, pp. 837–50.

Bigmore, E. C. and Wyman, W. H. (2014), *A Bibliography of Printing*. Cambridge University Press, Cambridge.

Bingham, A. (2012), 'Ignoring the First Draft of History?' *Media History*, 18:3–4, pp. 311–26.

Bingham, A. and Conboy, M. (2013), 'Introduction Journalism and History: Dialogues'. *Media History*, 19:1, pp. 1–2.

Black, J. (1987), *The English Press in the Eighteenth Century*, Croom Helm. Reprinted in 1991 by Greggs Revivals, Aldershot.

Black, J. (2001), *The English Press 1621-1821*. Sutton Publishing, Stroud.

Briggs, A. S. A. (1949), 'Press and Public in Early Nineteenth-century Birmingham'. *Dugdale Society Occasional Papers*, No. 8.

Briggs, A. and Burke, P. (2002), *A Social History of the Media: From Gutenberg to the Internet*. Polity, Oxford.

Bromley, M. and Hayes, N. (2002), 'Campaigner, Watchdog or Municipal Lackey? Reflection in the Inter-war Provincial Press, Local Identity and Civic Welfarism'. *Media History*, 8:2, pp. 197–212.

Burke, R. (1970), *The Murky Cloak: Local Authority Press Relations*. C. Knight, London.

Burnby, J. (1988), 'Pharmaceutical Advertisement in the 17th and 18th Century'. *European Journal of Marketing*, 22:4, pp. 24–40.

Calder, A. (1991), *The Myth of the Blitz*. Pimlico, London.

Camrose, Viscount. (1947), *British Newspapers and their Controllers*. Cassell and Company Ltd, London.

Canter, L. (2013a), 'The Source, the Resource and the Collaborator: The Role of Citizen Journalism in Local UK Newspapers'. *Journalism*, 0:0, pp. 1–19 (published online 19 February 2013).

Canter, L. (2013b), 'The Interactive Spectrum: The Use of Social Media in UK Regional Newspapers'. *Convergence: The International Journal of Research into New Media Technologies*, 19, pp. 472–95.

Chalaby, J. K. (1996), 'Journalism as an Anglo-American Invention: A Comparison of the Development of French and Anglo-American Journalism, 1830s-1920s'. *European Journal of Communication*, 11, pp. 303–26.

Chalaby, J. (2000), ' " Smiling Pictures Make People Smile": Northcliffe's Journalism'. *Media History*, 6:1, pp. 33–44.

Chambers, D., Steiner, L. and Fleming, C. (2004), *Women and Journalism*. Routledge, London and New York.

Cherubini, F. and Neilsen, R. K. (2016), *Editorial Analytics: How News Media are Developing and Using Audience Data and Metrics*. Reuters Institute for the Study of Journalism. University of Oxford, New York.

Clampin, D. (2014), *Advertising and Propaganda in World War II*. IB Tauris and Co Ltd, London.

Conboy, M. (2004), *Journalism: A Critical History*. Sage, London.

Conboy, M. (2011), *Journalism in Britain: A Historical Introduction*. Sage, London.

Cook, E. (1920), *The Press in War-time*. Macmillan and Co Ltd, London.

Cox, H. and Morgan, D. (1973), *City Politics and the Press: Journalists and the Governing of Merseyside*. Cambridge University Press, Cambridge.

Cranfield, G. A. (1952), 'The First Cambridge Newspaper'. *Proceedings of the Cambridge Antiquarian Society*, XLV, pp. 5–16.

Cranfield, G. A. (1962), *The Development of the Provincial Newspaper 1700-1760*. Clarendon Press, Oxford.

Cranfield, G. A. (1978), *The Press and Society from Caxton to Northcliffe*. Longman, London.

Curran, J. (1978), 'The Press as an Agency of Social Control', in Boyce, G., Curran, J. and Wingate, P. (eds), *Newspaper History from the Seventeenth Century to the Present Day*. Constable, London, pp. 51–75.

Curran, J. (2002), 'Media and the Making of British Society c1700-2000'. *Media History*, 8:2, pp. 135–54.

Curran, J. and Seaton, J. (2003), *Power without Responsibility* (6th edn). Routledge, London.

DMGT (2013), Annual Report. Available at http://www.dmgt.com. Accessed 24 June 2014.

Davies, N. (2008), *Flat Earth News: An Award-winning Reporter Exposes Falsehood, Distortion and Propaganda in the Global Media*. Chatto and Windus, London.

Davies, Robert (1868), *A Memoir of the York Press, with Notices of Authors, Printers and Stationers in the Sixteenth, Seventeenth and Eighteenth Centuries*. Nichols and Son, Westminster.

Dawson, M. (1998), 'Party Politics and the Provincial Press in Early Twentieth Century England: The Case of the South West'. *Twentieth Century British History*, 9:2, pp. 201–18.

Delano, A. (2000), 'No Sign of a Better Job: 100 Years of British Journalism'. *Journalism Studies*, 1:2, pp. 261–72.

Department for Culture Media and Sport (2015), *The Case for a Business Rate Relief for Local Newspapers. Consultation*. https://www.gov.uk/government/consultations/the-case-for-a-business-rates-relief-for-local-newspapers. Accessed 10 August 2016.

Deuze, M. (2003), 'The Web and its Journalisms: Considering the Consequences of Different Types of Newsmedia Online'. *New Media and Society*, 5, pp. 203–30.

Deuze, M. (2005), 'What is Journalism? Professional Identity and Ideology of Journalists Reconsidered'. *Journalism Theory, Practice and Criticism*, 6:4, pp. 442–64.

Dickinson, R. (2011), *The Use of Social Media in the Work of Local Newspaper Journalists*. Paper presented at Future of Journalism Conference, Cardiff, 8–9 September 2011. Available at https://lra.le.ac.uk/handle/2381/10155. Accessed 4 July 2014.

Domingo, D., Quandt, T., Heinonen, A., Paulussen, S., Singer, J. B. and Vujnovic, M. (2008), 'Participatory Journalism Practices in the Media and Beyond'. *Journalism Practice*, 2:3, pp. 326–42.

Duncum, A. P. (1952), *The Westminster Press Provincial Newspapers*. Westminster Press Provincial Newspapers Ltd, Fleet Street, London.

Elliott, P. (1978), 'Professional Ideology and Organization Change: The Journalist since 1800', in Boyce, G., Curran, J. and Wingate, P. (eds), *Newspaper History: From the 17th Century to the Present Day*. Constable, London, pp. 172–91.

Feather, J. (1985), *The Provincial Book Trade in Eighteenth Century England*. Cambridge University Press, Cambridge.

Ferdinand, C. Y. (1997), *Benjamin Collins and the Provincial Newspaper Trade in the Eighteenth Century*. Clarendon Press, Oxford.

Finn, M. (2002), 'The Realities of War'. *History Today*, August: 26–31.

Fletcher, L. (1946), *They Never Failed: The Story of the Provincial Press in Wartime*. Newspaper Society, London.

Foucault, M. (1972), *The Archaeology of Knowledge*. Routledge, London.

Foucault, M. (1984), 'Nietzsche, Genealogy, History', in Rabinow, P. (eds), *The Foucault Reader*. Penguin, London.

Fowler, N. (2011), *Have They Got News For You? The Rise, the Fall and the Future of Regional and Local Newspapers in the United Kingdom*. 17th Guardian Lecture, Nuffield College, Oxford.

Franklin, B. (2006a), 'Attacking the Devil? Local Journalists and Local Newspapers in the UK', in Franklin, B. (eds), *Local Journalism and the Local Media, Making the Local News*. Routledge, London.

Franklin, B. (2006b), 'A Right Free for All! Competition, Soundbite Journalism and Developments in the Free Press', in Franklin, B. (eds), *Local Journalism and the Local Media, Making the Local News*. Routledge, London.

Franklin, B. (2008), 'The Future of Newspapers'. *Journalism Studies*, 9:5, pp. 630–41.

Franklin, B. (2013), 'Editorial'. *Digital Journalism*, 1:1, pp. 1–5.

Franklin, B. and Murphy, D. (1991), *What News? The Market, Politics and the Local Press*. Routledge, London.

Gall, G. (1993), 'The Employer's Offensive in the Provincial Newspaper Industry'. *British Journal of Industrial Relations*, 31:4, pp. 615–24.

Gall, G. (1998), 'Resisting the Rise of Non-unionism: The Case of the Press Workers in the Newspaper Industry'. *Capital & Class*, Spring, 22, pp. 43–61.

Gardner, V. (2008), 'John White and the Development of Print Culture in the North East of England, 1711-1769', in Hinks, J. and Armstrong, C. (eds), *Book Trade Connections from the Seventeenth to the Twentieth Centuries*. Oak Knoll Press and the British Library, New Castle, DE, pp. 71–92.

Gennard, J. (1990), *A History of the National Graphical Association*. Unwin Hyman, London.

Gent, T. (1832), *The Life of Mr Thomas Gent, Printer of York, Written by Himself*. Thomas Thorpe, Covent Garden.

getreading.co.uk: *The last Post. The Future of News Reporting in the Digital Age*. http://www.getreading.co.uk/news/reading-berkshire-news/last-post-future-news-reporting-8300764. Accessed 14 March 2016.

Gibb, M. A. and Beckwith, F. (1954), *The Yorkshire Post Two Centuries*. The Yorkshire Conservative Newspaper Company, Leeds.

Gliddon, P. (2003), 'The Political Importance of Provincial Newspapers, 1903-1945: The Rowntrees and the Liberal Press'. *Twentieth Century British History*, 14:1, pp. 24–42.

Goodhart, D. and Wintour, P. (1986), *Eddie Shah and the Newspaper Revolution*. Coronet, Sevenoaks.

Gopsill, T. and Neale, G. (2007), *Journalists: 100 Years of the NUJ*. Profile Books, London.

Grant, J. (1871), *This History of the Newspaper Press: The Metropolitan Weekly and Provincial Press*. Routledge, London.

Gregory, A. (2004), 'A Clash of Cultures: The British Press and the Opening of the Great War', in Paddock, T. (eds), *A Call to Arms, Propaganda, Public Opinion and Newspapers in the Great War*. Praeger, Westport, CT and London, pp. 15–50.

Hadwin, S. (2006), 'Real Readers, Real News', in Franklin, B. (ed.), *Local Journalism and the Local Media*. Routledge, London, pp. 140–9.

Hall, J. (2008), 'Online Editions: Newspapers and the "New' News"', in Franklin, B. (ed.), *Pulling Newspapers Apart: Analysing Print Journalism*. Routledge, London and New York, pp. 215–23.

Hampton, M. (2004), *Visions of the Press in Britain, 1850-1950*. University of Illinois Press, Urbana and Chicago.

Hampton, M. (2005), 'Defining Journalists in Late-Nineteenth Century Britain', *Critical Studies in Media Communication*, 22:2, pp. 138–55.

Hampton, M. (2008), 'The Objectivity Ideal and its Limitations in 20th-century British Journalism', *Journalism Studies*, 9:4, pp. 477–93.

Hampton, M. and Conboy, M. (2014), 'Journalism History – A Debate. Journalism History and Media History'. *Journalism Studies*, 15:2, pp. 154–71.

Hansard (1946), *Press (Control and Ownership)*. HC Deb 29 October 1946, vol. 428, cc452–577. http://hansard.millbanksystems.com/commons/1946/oct/29/press-control-and-ownership. Accessed 14 August 2014.

Harcup, T. (2002), 'Journalists and Ethics: The Quest for a Collective Voice'. *Journalism Studies*, 3:1, pp. 101–14.

Harcup, T. (2013), *Alternative Journalism, Alternative Voices*. Routledge, Abingdon.

Holdthefrontpage.co.uk (5 March 2014), 'Dyson at Large. Newsquest's little hub of horrors'. http://www.holdthefrontpage.co.uk/2014/news/dyson-at-large-newsquest's-little-hub-of-subbing-horrors/. Accessed 18 March 2014.

Holdthefrontpage.co.uk (16 June 2014), 'Editor's Blog: Why Claire Enders was Wrong about Newspaper Closures'. http://www.holdthefrontpage.co.uk/2014/news/editors-blog-why-claire-enders-was-wrong-about-newspaper-closures/. Accessed 18 March 2014.

Holdthefrontpage.co.uk (11 March 2016), 'Trinity Mirror boss declares "war" on ad-blocking industry'. http://www.holdthefrontpage.co.uk/2016/news/regional-publisher-declares-war-on-ad-blocking-industry/. Accessed 14 March 2016.

Harris, M. (1975), 'Newspaper Distribution during Queen Anne's Reign', in Hunt, R. W., Philip, I. G. and Roberts, R. J. (eds), *Studies in the Book Trade In Honour of Graham Pollard*. The Oxford Bibliographical Society, Oxford, pp. 139–51.

Harris, M. (1978), 'The Structure, Ownership and Control of the Press, 1620-1780', in Boyce, G., Curran, J. and Wingate, P. (eds), *Newspaper History from the Seventeenth Century to the Present Day*. Constable, London, pp. 82–97.

Harris, M. (1981), 'Periodicals and the Book Trade', in Myers, R. and Harris, M. (eds), *Development of the English Book Trade, 1700-1899*. Oxford Polytechnic Press, Oxford, pp. 66–94.

Hartley, N., Gudgeon, P. and Crafts, R. (1977), *Concentration of Ownership in the Provincial Press*. Royal Commission on the Press. Research Series 5. Cmnd. 6810-5. Her Majesty's Stationery Office.

Haste, C. (1977), *Keep the Home Fires Burning: Propaganda in the First World War*. Allen Lane, London.

Heartfield, J. (2005), *Revisiting the Blitz Spirit: Myths about the Second World War won't Help us Understand What is Happening Today*. http://www.spiked-online.com/ newsite/article/869. Accessed 14 August 2014.

Herd, H. (1927), *The Making of Modern Journalism*. George Allen and Unwin Ltd, London.

Hetherington, A. (1989), *News in the Regions: Plymouth Sound to Moray Firth*. MacMillan, Basingstoke.

Hinton, J. (1980), 'Coventry Communism: A Study of Factory Politics in the Second World War'. *History Workshop Journal*, 10:1, pp. 90–118.

Hobbs, A. (2009), 'When the Provincial Press was the National Press (c 1836-1900)'. *International Journal of Regional and Local Studies*, Spring 2009, 5:1, pp. 16–43.

Hobsbawm, E. J. (1967), *Industry and Empire: An Economic History of Britain since 1750*. Weidenfeld & Nicolson, London.

Hodgson, G. (2015), *War Torn: Manchester, its Newspapers the Luftwaffe's Blitz of 1940*. University of Chester Press, Chester.

Hollis, P. (1970), *The Pauper Press: A Study in Working-class Radicalism of the 1830s*. Oxford University Press, Oxford.

House of Commons (2010), HC43-I. *Future for Local and Regional Media. Vol I*. The Stationary Office, London.

House of Commons (2010), HC43-II. *Future for Local and Regional Media. Vol II*. The Stationary Office, London.

Hoyer, S. and Pottker, H. (eds) (2005), *Diffusion of the News Paradigm 1850-2000*. Nordicom, Goteborg, Sweden.

Institute of Journalists (1978), *The Journal: The Magazine for the Profession of Journalism*. May.

Institute of Journalists (1981a), *The Journal: The Magazine for the Profession of Journalism*. June/July.

Institute of Journalists (1981b), *The Journal: The Magazine for the Profession of Journalism*. December.

Institute of Journalists (1982), *The Journal: The Magazine for the Profession of Journalism*. June/July.

Jackson, A. (2009), 'Football Coverage in the Papers of the Sheffield Telegraph c1890-1915'. *International Journal of Regional & Local Studies*, 5:1, pp. 63–84.

Jackson, I. (1971), *The Provincial Press and the Community*. The University Press, Manchester.

Jarvis, J. (2007), 'News Organisations will be Built on Large Advertising Networks in 2020', in *Envisioning the Newspaper 2020*. World Association of Newspapers. http://www.wan-ifra.org/microsites/research-reports-shaping-the-future-of-news-publishing

Johnston Press plc (2013), *Annual Report and Accounts 2013*. Available from http://www.johnstonpress.co.uk/investors/reports-results-presentations. Accessed 23 June 2014.

Kelsey, D. (2010), *Mentioning the War: The Myth of the 'Blitz Spirit' in British Newspaper Responses to the July 7th Bombings*. PhD, Cardiff School of Journalism, Media and Cultural Studies.

Koss, S. (1984), *The Rise and Fall of the Political Press in Britain. Vol. 2 The Twentieth Century*. Hamish Hamilton, London.

Kurplus, D., Metzgar, E. and Rowley, K. (2010), 'Sustaining Hyperlocal Media'. *Journalism Studies*, 11:3, pp. 359–76.

Labour Research Department (1946), *The Millionaire Press*. LRD, London.

Larson, C. (1941), 'The British Ministry of Information'. *Public Opinion Quarterly*, 5:3, p. 412.

Layton, W. (1946), *Newsprint: A Problem for Democracy*. P O'Donoghue, London.

Lee, A. J. (1976), *The Origins of the Popular Press in England*. Croom Helm Ltd, London.

Lee, A. J. (1978), 'The Structure, Ownership and Control of the Press', in Boyce, G., Curran, J. and Wingate, P. (eds), *Newspaper History from the Seventeenth Century to the Present Day 1855-1914*. Constable, London, pp. 117–29.

Lee-Wright, P., Phillips, A. and Witschge, T. (2012), *Changing Journalism*. Routledge, Abingdon.

Levine, J. (2006), *Forgotten Voices of the Blitz and the Battle of Britain*. Ebury Publishing, London.

Lewis, J., Williams, A. and Franklin, B. (2008), 'A Compromised Fourth Estate'. *Journalism Studies*, 9:1, pp. 1–20.

Lewis, S., Holton, A. and Coddington, M. (2014), 'Reciprocal Journalism'. *Journalism Practice*, 8:2, pp. 229–41.

Littleton, S. M. (1992), *The Wapping Dispute: An examination of the Conflict and its Impact on the National Newspaper Industry*. Avebury, Aldershot.

Liverpooldailypost.co.uk (10 December 2013), 'The Liverpool Post to cease publishing'. http://www.liverpooldailypost.co.uk/news/liverpool-news/liverpool-post- cease-publishing-6391108. Accessed 18 December 2013.

Liverpooldailypost.co.uk (18 December 2013), 'Live updates: Final edition of the Liverpool Post is put together'. http://www.liverpooldailypost.co.uk/news/liverpool-news/live-updates- final-edition-liverpool-6416365. Accessed 18 December 2013.

Loftus, D. (2002), 'Capital and Community'. *Victorian Studies*, 45:1, pp. 93–120.

Lovelace, C. (1982), *Control and Censorship of the Press During the First World War.* Unpublished PhD, Kings College, London.

MacGregor, P. (2013), 'Siren Song or Path to Salvation? Interpreting the Vision of Web Technology at a UK Regional Newspaper in Crisis, 2006-11'. *Convergence*, 20, pp. 157–75.

MacInnes, J., Rosie, M., Petersoo, P., Condor, S. and Kennedy, J. (2007), 'Where is the British National Press?' *The British Journal of Sociology*, 58:2, pp. 187–206.

Mackie, J. B. (1894), *Modern Journalism, A Handbook of Instruction and Counsel for the Young Journalist.* Crosby Lockwood and Son, London.

Marr, A. (2004), *My Trade: A Short History of British Journalism.* Macmillan, London.

Marzolf, M. T. (1984), 'American "New Journalism" Takes Root in Europe at End of 19th Century'. *Journalism Quarterly*, 61:3, pp. 529–691.

Mass Observation File Report 495 (18 November 1940), *The Tom Harrisson Mass-Observation Archive, Part One: File Reports, 1937-1941.* Harvester Press, Brighton, 1983 (accessed via Warwick University Library call number (microfiche) 296).

Matheson, D. (2000), 'The Birth of News Discourse; Changes in News Language in British Newspapers, 1880-1930'. *Media Culture Society*, 22, pp. 557–73.

Matthews, R. (forthcoming), 'The Ideological Challenge for the Regional Press: Reappraising the Community Value of Local Newspapers'. *Journal of Media Business Studies.*

McClaine, I. (1979), *Ministry of Morale: Home Front Morale and the Ministry of Information in World War II.* George Allen and Unwin, London.

McNair, B. (2006), 'News from a Small Country; the Media in Scotland', in Franklin, B. (ed.), *Local Journalism and the Local Media, Making the Local News.* Routledge, London.

Milne, M. (n.d.), *The Newspapers of Northumberland and Durham: A Study of their Progress during the 'Golden Age' of the Provincial Press.* Frank Graham, Newcastle upon Tyne.

Milton, F. (2009), 'Uncle Toby's Legacy: Children's Columns in the Provincial Newspaper Press'. *International Journal of Regional and Local Studies*, 5:1, pp. 104–20.

Money, J. (1971), 'Birmingham and the West Midlands, 1760-1793: Politics and Regional Identity in the English Provinces in the Later Eighteenth Century'. *Midland History*, 1:1, pp. 1–19.

Morris, C. (1963), *I Bought a Newspaper.* Arthur Baker Ltd, London.

Murdock, G. and Golding, P. (1978), 'The Structure, Ownership and Control of the Press, 1914-76', in Boyce, G., Curran, J. and Wingate, P. (eds), *Newspaper History from the Seventeenth Century to the Present Day.* Constable, London.

National Council for the Training of Journalists (2011), *NCTJ 60th Anniversary Video.* http://www.nctj.com/resources/nctj-60th-anniversary-video. Accessed 17 September 2012.

National Council for the Training of Journalists (2014), http://www.nctj.com/ journalism-qualifications. Accessed 12 March 2014.

National Union of Journalists (1946), *National Executive Council's. Minutes XII.* March 1945–April 1946. Modern Records Centre, Warwick University.

National Union of Journalists (1947), *National Executive Council's. Minutes XIII.* April 1946–April 1947. Modern Records Centre, Warwick University.

National Union of Journalists (1970), *Annual Report 1969-70.* National Union of Journalists, London. Modern Records Centre, Warwick University.

National Union of Journalists (1971), *Annual Report 1970-71.* National Union of Journalists, London. Modern Records Centre, Warwick University.

National Union of Journalists (1972), *Annual Report 1971-72.* National Union of Journalists, London. Modern Records Centre, Warwick University.

National Union of Journalists (1976), *Annual Report 1975-76.* National Union of Journalists, London. Modern Records Centre, Warwick University.

National Union of Journalists (1977a), *Annual Report 1976-77.* National Union of Journalists, London. Modern Records Centre, Warwick University.

National Union of Journalists (1977b), *Journalists and New Technology.* National Union of Journalists. London. Modern Records Centre, Warwick University.

National Union of Journalists (1979), *Annual Report 1978-1979.* National Union of Journalists, London. Modern Records Centre, Warwick University.

National Union of Journalists (2007), *Shaping the Future. Commission on Multi-media Working.* www.nuj.org.uk/documents/shaping-the-future/. Accessed 3 July 2014.

Neilsen, R. K. (2015), *Local Journalism: The Decline of Newspapers and the Rise of Digital Media.* IB Tauris, London and New York.

Nel, F. (2010), 'Where Else is the Money?' *Journalism Practice*, 4:3, pp. 360–72.

Nerone, J. and Barnhurst, K. G. (2003), 'US Newspaper Types, the Newsroom, and the Division of Labor, 1750-2000'. *Journalism Studies*, 4:4, pp. 435–49.

Nerone, J. and Barnhurst, K. G. (2012), 'Stead in America', in Laurel Brake et al. (eds), *William T Stead: Newspaper Revolutionary.* British Library Publishing, London, pp. 98–114.

Newton, D. and Smith, M. (1999), *The Stamford Mercury: Three Centuries of Newspaper Publishing*, Shaun Tyas, Stamford.

Newspaper Society (2009), 'Local Newspaper Week'. http://www.newspapersoc.org.uk/ Default.aspx?page=4400. Accessed 23 October 2009.

Newspaper Society (2014), 'Top 10 facts about local media'. http://www.newspapersoc. org.uk/top-ten-facts-about-local-media. Accessed 16 August 2014.

Noon, M. (1991), 'Strategy and Circumstance: The Success of the NUJ's New Technology Policy'. *British Journal of Industrial Relations*, 29:2, pp. 259–76.

Norfolk News Company (1951), *The Norwich Post: Its Contemporaries and Successors.* Norfolk News Co, Norwich.

Norris, H. E. (1910), *Notes and Queries*, Ser. 11. II, 17 December, pp. 481–2.

Northampton Mercury (1901), *1720-1901. History of the Northampton Mercury. Illustrated.* Northampton Mercury Offices, Market Square, Northampton.

Ofcom (2009), Local and Regional Media in the UK. *Discussion Document.* Available at http://stakeholders.ofcom.org.uk/market-data-research/other/tv-research/lrmuk/. Accessed 16 March 2016.

OFT (Office of Fair Trading) (2009), *Review of the Local and Regional Media Merger Regime.* Final Report.

Ogilvy-Webb, M. (1965), *The Government Explains: A Study of the Information Services.* A Report of the Royal Institute of Public Administration. Allen and Unwin Ltd, London.

O'Malley, T. (2014), *Was there a National Press in World War II?* Symposium presentation.

Onslow, B. (2000), *Women of the Press in Nineteenth-Century Britain.* Macmillan Press Ltd, Basingstoke.

Ornebring, H. (2006), 'The Maiden Tribute and the Naming of Monsters'. *Journalism Studies*, 7:6, pp. 851–68.

O'Reilly, C. (2014), '"Dirt, Death and Disease": Newspaper Discourses on Public Health in the Construction of the Modern British City'. *Journal of Historical Pragmatics*, 15:2, pp. 207–27.

O'Sullivan, J. and Heinonen, A. (2008), 'Old Values, New Media'. *Journalism Practice*, 2:3, pp. 357–71.

Packer, I. (2006), 'A Curious Exception? The Lincolnshire Chronicle and the "Starmer Group"'. *Journalism Studies*, 7:3, pp. 415–26.

Paulussen, S. and D'heer, E. (2013), 'Using Citizens for Community Journalism: Findings from a Hyperlocal Media Project'. *Journalism Practice*, 7:5, pp. 588–603.

Peacocke, E. (1930), 'Openings for Women', in Cranfield, W. T. (ed.), *Journalism as a Career.* Sir Isaac Pitman and Sons Ltd, London.

Penny, J. (2001), *All the News that's Fit to Print: A Short History of Bristol's Newspapers since 1702.* Bristol Branch of the Historical Association.

Political and Economic Planning (1938), *Report on the British Press.* PEP, London.

Ponsford, D. (31 July 2016), 'Heartbroken' reporter Gareth Davies says Croydon Advertiser print edition now thrown together collection of 'clickbait'. *PressGazette. co.uk*, http://www.pressgazette.co.uk/heartbroken-reporter-gareth-davies-says-croydon-advertser-print-edition-now-thrown-together-collection-of-clickbait/. Accessed 10 August 2016.

Ponting, C. (1990), *1940; Myth and Reality.* Cardinal, London.

Porter, R. (1986), 'Before the Fringe: Quack Medicines in Georgian England'. *History Today*, 36:11, pp. 16–22.

Pottker, H. (2005), 'The News Pyramid and its Origin form the American Journalism in the 19th Century', in Hoyer, S. and Pottker, H. (eds), *Diffusion of the News Paradigm 1850-2000.* Nordicom, Goteborg, Sweden, pp. 51–64.

Powers, M., Zambrano, S. V. and Baisnee, O. (2015), 'The News Crisis Compared: The Impact of the Journalism Crisis on the Local News Ecosystems in Toulouse (France) and Seattle (US)', in Neilsen, R. K. (ed.), *Local Journalism: The Decline of Newspapers and the Rise of Digital Media.* IB Tauris, London and New York, pp. 31–50.

Pratt Boorman, H. R. (1961), *Newspaper Society, 125 Years of Progress.* Kent Messenger, Maidstone.

Press Gazette (6 November 2006), 'Johnston Evening's Multimedia Newsroom Adds Readers and Online Traffic'. http://www.pressgazette.co.uk/node/36207. Accessed 3 July 2014.

Press Gazette (13 March 2013), '24 Editorial Jobs to Go as Archant Look to Share Content across East Anglia'. http://www.pressgazette.co.uk/24-journalism-jobs-face-axe-archant-looks-share-content-across-suffolk-and-norfolk-titles. Accessed 23 June 2014.

Press Gazette (28 August 2013a), 'Sales Fall by Average of 10.5 Per cent for UK's Regional Dailies'. http://www.pressgazette.co.uk/sales-fall-average-105-cent-uks-regional-dailies. Accessed 1 January 2014.

Press Gazette (28 August 2013b), 'ABC Figures Show only One Local Weekly Growing Print Sales in First Half of 2013'. http://www.pressgazette.co.uk/abc-figures- show-only-one-local-weekly-growing-print-sales-first-half-2013. Accessed 1 January 2014.

Press Gazette (21 November 2013), 'Who Needs sub Editors? Read David Montgomery's 2,200-word Missive on the Future of Local World in full'. http://www.pressgazette.co.uk/print/content/who-needs-sub-editors-read-david-montgomerys-latest-unsubbed-2200-word-missive-future-local. Accessed 23 June 2014.

Press Gazette (27 February 2014), 'How Digital Growth is Countering Print Decline. Title by Title ABC Breakdown'. http://www.pressgazette.co.uk/how-digital-growth-countering-print-decline-regional-press-title-title-abc-breakdown. Accessed 3 July 2014.

Press Gazette (14 March 2014), 'Story Uploaded by Torquay Police to Herald Express Highlights Shortcomings of Monty's "Content Harvesting" plan'. http://www.pressgazette.co.uk/content/story-uploaded-torquay-police-herald-express-highlights-shortcomings-montys-content. Accessed 23 June 2014.

Press Gazette (9 July 2014), 'Sir Ray Tindle "totally Convinced" of Almost Complete Return to "Full Viability" for Local Press'. http://www.pressgazette.co.uk/sir-ray-tindle-totally-convinced-almost-complete-return-full-viability-local-press. Accessed 10 July 2013.

Press Gazette (22 January 2016), 'Signs that We are on the Cusp of a Ground-up Renaissance for Local Journalism'. http://www.pressgazette.co.uk/content/signs-we-are-cusp-ground-renaissance-local-journalism. Accessed 14 March 2016.

Raven, J. (2014), *Publishing Business in Eighteenth-Century England.* Boydell Press, Woodbridge.

Raymond, J. (1996), *The Invention of the Newspaper; English Newsbooks, 1641-49.* Clarendon Press, Oxford.

Reader, B. and Hatcher, J. (2012), *Foundations of Community Journalism*. Sage, London.

Rhodes, P. (1981), *Coventry Evening Telegraph: Birthday Telegraph*, supplement published 9 February 1981.

Rhodes, P. (1992), *The Loaded Hour: A History of the Express and Star*. SPA Ltd and The Express and Star, Wolverhampton.

Riley, E. (2006), *Life is Local: The History of Johnston Press plc*. Edinburgh, Johnston Press Plc.

Rosie, M., Petersoo, P., MacInnes, J., Condor, S. and Kennedy, J. (2006), 'Mediating which Nation? Citizenship and National Identities in the British Press'. *Social Semiotics*, 16:2, pp. 327–44.

Royal Commission on the Press (1947–9), Cmnd. 7700. Report. HMSO, London.

Royal Commission on the Press (1947–9), *Minutes of Evidence Taken before the Royal Commission on the Press*. HMSO, London.

Royal Commission on the Press (1962), *Cmnd. 1811. Report*. HMSO, London.

Royal Commission on the Press (1977), *Cmnd. 6810. Vol 1. Final Report*. HMSO, London.

Royal Commission on the Press (1977), *Cmnd. 6810-1. Vol 2. Final Report*. HMSO, London.

Royal Commission on the Press (1977), *Evidence Submitted to the Commission: With Miscellaneous Papers*. National Union of Journalists 2E1, London.

Royal Commission on the Press (1977), *Evidence Submitted to the Commission: With Miscellaneous Papers*. Liverpool Daily Post and Liverpool Daily Echo Ltd 8E1, London.

Royal Commission on the Press (1977), *Evidence Submitted to the Commission: With Miscellaneous Papers*. Westminster Press 17E1, London.

Royal Commission on the Press (1977), *Evidence Submitted to the Commission: With Miscellaneous Papers*. Guild of British Newspaper Editors, 22E1, London.

Royal Commission on the Press (1977), *Evidence Submitted to the Commission: With Miscellaneous Papers*. An Economic Appraisal of New Technology, London.

Schudson, M. (2008), *Why Democracies Need an Unlovable Press*. Polity Press, Cambridge.

Seymour-Ure, C. (1996), *The British Press and Broadcasting since 1945*, 2nd edn. Blackwell Publishers, Oxford.

Simpson, D. H. (1981), *Commercialisation of the Regional Press, The Development of Monopoly, Profit and Control*. Gower Publishing Company Ltd, Aldershot.

Smith, P. and Morton, G. (1990), 'A Change of Heart: Union Exclusion in the Provincial newspaper Sector'. *Work, Employment and Society*, 4:1, pp. 105–24.

Sommerville, C. J. (1996), *The News Revolution in England, Cultural Dynamics of Daily Information*. Oxford University Press, Oxford.

Spender, J. A. (1927), *Life, Journalism and Politics*. Frederick A. Stokes Company, New York.

Stoker, D. (2014), 'Another Look at the Dicey-Marshall Publications'. *The Library*, 7th series, 15:2, pp. 111–56.

Stott, R. (2002), *Dogs and Lamposts*, Metro Publishing Ltd, London.

Tandoc, E. C. and Thomas, R. J. (2015), 'The Ethics of Web Analytics'. *Digital Journalism*, 3:2, pp. 243–58.

Taylor, J. (2006), '"Town" versus "Gown" The Establishment of the Cambridge Daily News as a Modern Newspaper at the End of the 19th century'. *Journalism Studies*, 7:3, pp. 403–14.

Trinity Mirror plc (2012), *Annual Report 2012*. Available at http://www.trinitymirror.com/investors/financial-information. Accessed 23 June 2014.

Trinity Mirror plc (25 February 2014), 'Trinity Mirror North East Unveils Plans for Digitally-Led Operation'. http://www.trinitymirror.com/pressrelease/trinity-mirror-north-east-unveils-plans-for-digitally-led-news-operation/2044. Accessed 24 June 2014.

Tunstall, J. (1996), *Newspaper Power: The New National Press in Britain*. Oxford University Press, Oxford.

Turner, M. (1991), *The Making of a Middle Class Liberalism in Manchester c 1815-32: A Study in the Politics of the Press*. Unpublished PhD thesis, Oxford University.

Usher, N. (2014), *Moving the Newsroom; Post-industrial News Spaces and Places*. Tow Center for Digital Journalism, New York.

Walker, A. (2006a), 'The Development of the Provincial Press in England c. 1780-1914: An Overview'. *Journalism Studies*, 7:3, pp. 373–86.

Walker, A. (2006b), 'Reporting Play'. *Journalism Studies*, 7:3, pp. 452–62.

Watts, A. T. (1990), *The Newspaper Press in the Town of Reading 1855-1980*. Unpublished PhD, University of Stirling.

Whitaker, B. (1981), *News Limited: Why You Can't Read All About It*. Minority Press, London.

Whorlow, H. (1886), *The Provincial Newspaper Society 1836-1886: A Jubilee Retrospect*. Page, Pratt and Turner, London.

Wiener, J. H. (1969), *The War of the Unstamped: The Movement to Repeal the British Newspaper Tax, 1830-1836*. Cornell University Press, New York.

Wiener, J. H. (1994), 'The Americanization of the British Press, 1830-1914'. *Studies in Newspaper and Periodical History* (Now *Media History*), 2:1/2, pp. 61–74.

Wiles, R. M. (1965), *Freshest Advices, Early Provincial Newspapers in England*. Ohio State University Press, Columbus.

Williams, J. B. (1916), 'The First English Provincial Newspaper'. *Notes and Queries*, Ser. 12. II, 29 July, pp. 81–2.

Williams, K. (2010), *Read All About It! A History of the British Newspaper*. Routledge, Abingdon.

Index

ACAS (Advisory Conciliation and Arbitration Service)   169, 178
Advertisement Duty   28
advertising
  commercial logic of   15
  free newspapers   7, 54, 118, 165–6, 176–8
  newspapers and   49–54
  and profit   49–54
  proportion of paper dedicated to   103
  revenue   6–7, 29, 50, 69, 104, 114, 118, 129, 135, 154, 165–6, 178, 190–2
Allied Newspapers Ltd   89, 113, 123, 126–7
American Civil War   87
Anglo-Newfoundland Development Co Ltd 129
Aris's Gazette   51, 70
Arnold, Matthew   95
Aspinall, Arthur   32, 62–3
Asquith, Ivon   64, 82
Associated Newspapers   120, 127, 129–30, 136, 150, 171, 173
Associated Rediffusion   173
Association for Promoting the Repeal of the Taxes on Knowledge   69
Audit Bureau for Circulation   200–1
Auto Trader   194

Bailey, Sir William   140, 145–6
Baines, Sir Edward   73
Baker, Thomas   42
Barker, Hannah   33, 39–40, 56, 57, 60
Barnhurst, Kevin   27–8, 37, 77
Barnsley Chronicle   142
Barrons, J. L.   177–8
Bath Chronicle   44
Bath Journal   44, 64
Battle of Sargossa   37
Baxter, W E   73
Baylen, Joseph   93

BBC. *See* British Broadcasting Corporation (BBC)
BBC Radio 4   17
Beaverbrook Newspapers   120
Beckwith, Frank   50
Belfast Telegraph   184
Bennett, E. A.   79
Benson, John   95
Bernstein, Carl   16
Berrow's Newspapers Ltd   112
Berrows Worcester Journal   32
Berry, John   33
Berry, Sir William   124
Bicycling News   99
Bingham, Adrian   27
Birmingham Chronicle   39
Birmingham Daily Post   149
Birmingham Gazette   39, 89, 156
Birmingham Gazette Ltd   158
Birmingham Mail   22, 200
Birmingham Post   12, 120, 126, 150
Birmingham Post and Mail   176
Bishop, Philip   56
Black, Jeremy   14, 24, 34, 35–6, 39, 45, 58, 74, 79
Blade Runner   1
blogs/blogging   20, 211
Bolton Evening News   176
Boyce, George   60
Bradford Weekly Telegraph   97
Brice, Andrew   53
Brice's Weekly Journal   53
Brighton Gazette   70
Brighton Guardian   70
Bristol Cable   211
Bristol Evening News   126
Bristol Evening Post   128, 150
Bristol Evening World   123–4, 127
Bristol Mercury   64
Bristol Observer   72
Bristol Post   211

Bristol Post Boy 36
Bristol Post Man 36
Bristol Times and Mirror 126
Bristol United Press 126
Bristol Weekly Mercury 36
British Broadcasting Corporation
      (BBC) 140, 175–6, 197
British Expeditionary Force 143
British Navy 37
British Press 146
Broadcast Journalism Training
      Council 199
Bromley, Michael 24, 135
Browne, Phillis 78
Bucks Herald 3, 136
'Bulgarian Horrors' 93
Burbage, George 53
Burges, Elizabeth 45–6, 50
Burges, Francis 45
business models/business strategy 10–11,
      27, 46, 59–61, 66–9, 80–3

Cambria Daily Leader 124
Cambridge Chronicle 57
Cambridge Daily News 109
Cambridge Evening News 24
Cambridge Independent Press 81
Cambridge Intelligencer 57
Cambridge Journal and Weekly
      Flying Post 47
Camrose, Viscount 112–13, 123, 129,
      131, 146
Canter, Lilly 204, 212
Capitalism 36
Carlisle Conservative Newspaper
      Company 71, 82, 126
Carlisle Patriot 62, 65, 71
Carnegie, Andrew 96, 115
Ceefax 175–6
Chalaby, Jean 91, 92
Chelmsford Chronicle 40, 56
Churchill, Winston 155
circulation 2–5, 20–3, 42–6, 117–22,
      129, 194
City Politics and the Press (Cox and
      Morgan) 20
Civil War 35
Clachar, William 56

Clampin, David 145, 152
Cluer, John 48–9
Cobbett, William 66
Collins, Benjamin 44, 47, 50
'commerce of information' 36
community
      commercial practice and the
            good of 135–7
      newspapers and 79–83
computerization
      deunionization of the provincial
            press and 178–83
      newspapers and 178–83
Conboy, Martin 11, 27, 55, 56, 58, 92, 214
conflict, as good news for
      newspapers 139–41
Conservative Party 71
conservatives 60, 62, 71–2, 175
consolidation of ownership 115–22, 130–5
Contagious Diseases Act 93
Control of Paper (No 48) Order of March
      1942 152–3
Copleston, Jonathan 93
Corn Laws 69
The Cornishman 2
corporatization of the provincial press
      commercial practice and the good of
            the community 135–7
      consolidation of ownership 115–22,
            130–5
      growth of chain control 111–14
      newspaper costs as a driver for
            consolidation 128–30
      Rothermere and 122–7
      Royal Commissions 130–5
County Express 184
Coventry Evening Telegraph 146, 164
Coventry Telegraph 98, 197
Coventry Times 99
Cowdray, Viscount 89
Cowen, Joseph 73–4
Cox, Harvey 10, 20, 110, 215
Craighton, William 52
Cranfield, Geoffrey 32, 39, 41, 51
Crimean War 75
Cross-grove, Henry 33
Croydon Advertiser 7
Cumberland Evening News 126

Curran, James   11, 23, 81–2, 147, 165
The Cyclist   99

Daily Express   21, 97
Daily Herald   130
Daily Mail   21, 86, 92, 113, 128
Daily Mail and General Trust
    (DMGT)   127, 171, 192, 195
Daily Mirror   113, 147, 150, 171
Daily Mirror Group   120. *See also* Reed
    International
Daily News   89, 178
The Daily News Ltd   150
The Daily Telegraph   17, 169, 190
Daily War Telegraph   75
Daily Worker   147, 156, 158–60
Darlington Evening Despatch   9
Davies, Gareth   7
Davies, Haydn   134, 136
Davies, Nick   186–7, 193
Davison, Laura   208
Dawson, Michael   89
Defence of the Realm Regulations
    (DORA)   143
democracy   4, 23, 59, 216
Denman, Trudie   146
Derby Daily Telegraph   123–4, 127
Derby Telegraph   2
Derby Trader   177
Derbyshire Journal   47
deunionization of the provincial press
    changing motivations for newspaper
        ownership   167–72
    computerization and   178–83
    new technology   163–7
    rising costs and competition   173–8
    working practices and content   183–8
Deuze, Mark   19, 205
Dicey, Cluer   48
Dicey, William   42–4, 47–8, 53
Dicky Bird Society   97
digital age, redefining the provincial
    press in   199–206
digital technology   2
Disraeli, Benjamin   69
Dixon, Steve Anderson   20
DMGT. *See* Daily Mail and General Trust
    (DMGT)

DORA. *See* Defence of the Realm
    Regulations (DORA)
Dorset Daily Echo   149
Dr Bateman's Pectoral Drops   48, 53
Dr Williams' Pink Pills   102
Durrant, Alan   176
Dyson, Steve   20

East Cumberland News   82
East Midland Press Group
    (EMAP plc)   172
Eastern Counties Newspapers Group
    Ltd   176, 195
Eastern Morning News   85, 88
eBay   194
editorial workers, in provincial
    press   16–20
education   18, 79–80, 106–7
Elliott, Philip   18, 75
Empire News   22
Empire Paper Mills   129
Enders, Claire   197
English Civil War   35
Evans, Harold   17
Evening Post   149, 157, 181
Evening Star   96
Evening World   119, 140, 149, 157
Evershed, Sir Patrick   126

Farley, Felix   36
Farley, Sam   36, 211
Feather, John   39
Ferdinand, C. Y.   35, 47, 52
Filton Voice   211
Financial Times Ltd   171
First World War   89, 115, 141, 144,
    145–6, 155
    community in   141–5
    provincial press in   141–5
Fish4 series of websites   196
F. Johnston and Company   120. *See also*
    Johnston Press
Fletcher, Leonard   152
Flower, Benjamin   57
Foucault, Michel   11
Fountain, Phil   3
fourth estate   22–4, 59, 109–12, 133, 166–7
Fowler, Neil   190, 195

Franklin, Bob   10, 25, 176, 178, 187, 195,
      214–15
free press   61–9
Fry, John   195
FTI Consulting   21

Gainford, Thomas   35
Gall, Gregor   180, 183
Gannett   191
Gardner, Victoria   41
Gazette   40–1, 46
A General History of Executions   53
Gennard, John   181
Gent, T.   45
The Gentlewoman   107
George, Lloyd   123
George I, King of Great Britain and
      Ireland   56
Gibb, Mildred A   50
Gladstone, William Ewart   93
Glasgow Evening News   128
Gliddon, Paul   24, 89
Gloucester Citizen   123, 127
Gloucester Journal   31, 42, 44–5, 48, 53,
      55, 80
Gloucestershire Echo   123, 127
GMG Regional Media   197
golden age   12, 135, 216
Golding, Peter   113, 119, 120
good of the community   5–11, 79–83
Goodhart, David   177
Gopsill, Tim   17
GPO (General Post Office)   175
Graham, Malcolm   96
Graham, Thomas   96–7
Granada TV   20
Grant, James   69, 71–2
Grantham Times   3
Great Exhibition of Victorian
      Times   123. *See also* North East
      Coast Exhibition
Great Thunderstorm   91
Great Train Robbery   17
Green, Wilfred   126
Green 'Un   98
Griffiths, Ivor   112
Grimsby Daily Telegraph   127
Grimsby Evening Telegraph   123

The Guardian Journal   181
Guardian Media Group   196
Guild of British Newspaper Editors   146,
      169–70

Hadwin, Sara   9
Hall, Jim   203, 214
Hampshire Chronicle   40, 42, 47, 52, 56, 57
Hampshire Independent   64
Hampton, Mark   23–4, 26, 81, 92, 106
*Handbook of Instruction and Counsel
      for the Young Journalist*
      (Mackie)   92
Harcup, Tony   175
Harmsworth, Alfred   92, 94, 119
Harris, Michael   35, 46
Hasbert, Samuel   33, 45–6
Hatcher, John   205
Hayes, Nick   24, 135
Heartfield, James   155, 160
Heinonen, Ari   203
Hereford Journal   56
Hereford Times   190
Herne Bay Gazette   3
Hetherington, Alistair   67, 164
Highfield, Ashley   205
Hinkley Times   190–1
History of the Old and New Testaments   47
Hobbs, Andrew   63
Hodgson, Guy   139
Hollis, Patricia   66, 68
Howgrave, Francis   33, 49
Howgrave's Stamford Mercury   33
Hoyer, Svennik   87
HTML (hypertext markup language)   191
Huddersfield Daily Examiner   164
Hull Daily Mail   123, 127, 143
Hulton Readership Survey   21
Humphrys, John   17

I Bought a Newspaper (Morris)   3
Iliffe, William   99, 112, 123
Independent Broadcast Association   175
Independent Press Standards Organisation
      (IPSO)   18
industrialization, newspapers and   74–9
Institute of Journalists (IOJ)   17, 75,
      106–7, 112, 131, 175, 176

inverted pyramid   19, 87, 90–1, 92 n.5,
        102, 104–5, 108
IOJ. *See* Institute of Journalists (IOJ)
IPSO. *See* Independent Press Standards
        Organisation (IPSO)
Ipswich Journal   52
Ives, Chester   97

Jackson, Ian   6–8, 24–5, 110, 136
Jarvis, Jeff   13
Johnson, Amy   123
Johnson, Boris   212
Johnson, Samuel   36
Johnston Press plc   21, 23, 120, 172,
        191, 197, 202, 207, 210. *See also*
        F. Johnston and Company
Joint Industrial Council   132
Jones, L   64
Joseph Rowntree Social Service Trust   89
journalism
    local   54–8
    photographers   96, 131, 206
    specialist journalism   78–9, 97–9
    watchdogs   5–10, 24–5, 166, 214
    women as journalists   78
Journalism; A Critical History
        (Conboy)   11
journalists
    editors   57, 70–1, 106–7, 146, 164
    as a professional   8, 19, 39, 75, 105, 108
    professional ideology   7
    reporters   28, 61, 78, 105, 156
    subeditors   105, 197
    training   9
    wages   7, 132–3
    women   78, 107
Joyce, Clive   3

Kelsey, Darren   155
Kemplay, Christopher   80
Kemsley   112, 123
Kemsley Federated Group Chapel   133
Kemsley Newspapers   115, 120
Kent Messenger   182
Kidderminster Shuttle   3
Koss, Stephen   23

Lancashire Journal   33, 47

Lawrence, Edward   95
Layton, Sir Walter   145
Lee, Alan   74, 76–7, 81, 94
Leeds Intelligencer   50, 57
Leeds Mercury   48, 65, 70, 71, 73, 80, 106
Leeds Other Paper   175
Leeds Times   97
Leicester Mail   108, 124
Leicester Mercury   200, 203
Letterflex printing processes   180
Lewis, Seth   205
Liberal Party   70 n. 5, 123
*Lincoln, Rutland and Stamford
        Mercury*   65
Lincolnshire Chronicle   119, 172
Lincolnshire Echo   127
Linotype   61
Lionel Pickering   177
Littleton, Suellen   167
Liverpool Daily Post   20, 87, 173
Liverpool Echo   20, 200
Liverpool Echo Ltd   173
Liverpool Post   20, 25
Liverpool Weekly Mercury   78
local government   8–9, 25, 65, 135,
        213, 215
local journalism, emergence of   54–8
local news, future for   206–17
Local Newspaper Week   3
Local World   127, 205, 210
London and Country Journal   47
London Can Take it   155
London Evening Standard   200
London Express Newspapers Ltd   150
London Metro   192
London Society of Compositors   131
Longman Penguin Ltd   171
Lovett, William   72
Lucy, Henry   78
Lucy, John   185
Ludlow, J. M.   64
Ludlow Post-Man   37

Mcdonaldisation   193
MacGregor, P.   199
MacInnes, John   22
Mackie, A   73
Mackie, John   92, 105–6

Macliver, Peter Stewart 72, 80
Maiden Tribute campaign 94
Manchester Daily Despatch 22
Manchester Daily Times 75
Manchester Evening News 3, 126,
    198–9, 200
Manchester Guardian 21, 63, 69, 72, 73,
    107, 109, 120, 126, 150, 169
Marr, Andrew 16
Marshall, John 108
Marzolf, Marion 109
Matheson, Donald 90
McWhirter, William 127, 135–6
Mencken, L. 16
Menzies 175
Metro newspaper 193–4
Metros 200
Middlesex County Chronicle 70
Midland Counties Herald 70
Midland Daily Telegraph 98–105, 108,
    140, 150, 153, 156–60
Midland Daily Tribune 147
Midland News Association 96
Mill, John Stuart 60
The Millionaire Press 133
Milne, Maurice 64, 94
mini-max expansion strategy 192, 209–10
The Mirror 3
Mirror Group plc 191
Mitchell, Charles 115, 119
Moll Flanders (Defoe) 55
Money, J. 62
Monopolies and Mergers
    Commission 135, 169
Montgomery, David 205
Morgan, David 10, 20, 110, 215
Morris, Claud 3
Murdoch, Rupert 119
Murdock, Graham 113, 119, 120
Murphy, David 10, 176, 178, 187, 214–15

National Association of Journalists 75
National Council for the Training of
    Journalists 9, 136, 199
National Graphical Association
    (NGA) 180–3
National Savings Committee 148
National Society of Operative Printers and
    Assistants (Natsopa) 131
national titles 2
National Union of Journalists 17, 22, 75,
    106–7, 112, 131
Neale, Greg 17
Nero 56
Nerone, John 27–8, 37, 77
Newbury, John 49
Newcastle Chronicle 2, 73, 74, 106
Newcastle Courant 45
The Newcastle Courant 40–1
Newcastle Daily Chronicle 61
Newcastle Evening World 123–4, 127
The Newcastle Gazette 37
Newcastle Journal 22, 70, 149, 200
Newcastle United 96
Newcastle Weekly Chronicle 97
New Journalism 24, 28–9, 85–7, 88
    commercial success as an organizing
        factor 105–10
    emergence of 'news' 85–8
    influence on content and
        production 92–8
    and the *Midland Daily
        Telegraph* 98–105
    news presentation as a sales
        technique 89–92
New Scientist 171
news
    emergence of 85–8
    local 189–90
    presentation as a sales technique 89–92
news agencies 78, 176
News International 120. *See also* News of
    the World
News Media Association 201
News of the World Organisation
    Ltd 120, 136, 150. *See also* News
    International
newspaper content
    childrens content 97
    sport 55, 73, 96–103, 147, 153
newspaper industry, early ventures
    in 36–41
newspaper ownership
    changing motivations for 167–72
    consolidation of 115–22, 130–5
Newspaper Press Directory 115, 119

Newspaper Proprietors' Association   112, 132, 144, 153. *See also* Newspaper Publishers Association
Newspaper Publishers Association   132, 201. *See also* Newspaper Proprietors' Association
newspaper publishing in wartime   149–54
Newspaper Society   2, 21, 112, 132–3, 143, 147, 156, 182–3, 200, 201
Newspaper Supply Company   153
newspapers
    advertising and profit   49–54
    alternative   174, 210
    communities of interest and profit   69–74
    computerization and   178–83
    conflict as good news for   139–41
    costs as a driver for consolidation   128–30
    daily   115, 118, 129
    demarcation and news work   74–9
    digital beginnings   190–9
    emergence of local journalism   54–8
    establishing market   42–6
    evening   115–22
    free   7, 54, 118, 165–6, 176–8
    freshest advices and circulation wars   42–6
    future for local news   206–17
    good of the community and representation   79–83
    industrial action   183, 199
    industrialization and   74–9
    online   190–9
    pamphlets   34, 81
    place in commercial landscape   33–6
    political bent   59–61
    reader, cure-alls and books   46–9
    stamped   61–6
    unstamped   45, 66–7
    technology and   163–7
news presentation, as a sales technique   89–92
Newsprint Supply Company   145, 150
Newsquest   191, 196, 210
NGA. *See* National Graphical Association (NGA)
Norfolk News Company   46

Norris, H. E.   43
North East Coast Exhibition   123. *See also* Great Exhibition of Victorian Times
North Eastern Daily Gazette   87
North of England Newspaper Company   89
North Mail   149
Northampton Journal   45
Northampton Mercury   20, 42–5, 52
Northcliffe Newspapers Ltd.   115, 122–4, 127–8, 135, 195–6
The Northern Courant   37
Northern Daily Times   75
Northern Echo   82, 89, 93, 108, 119, 126, 199
Northern Star   57, 128
Northern Weekly Leader   97
Norwich Gazette   33, 46
Norwich Post   32, 33, 45, 55
Norwich Post-man   46
Nottingham Evening Post   180, 185
Nottingham Journal   81, 89
Nottinghamshire Journal   53
NUJ   132–4, 177, 180, 182–5, 194, 197–200, 206
Nuneaton Newspapers Ltd   158

objectivity   11, 19, 87, 92, 92 n.5
Odhams Press   120
Okell, Benjamin   48
O'Malley, Tom   21, 26
optical character recognition (OCR) technology   180
Oracle   175
Oracle   36
O'Reilly, Carole   82
Ornebring, Henrik   94
O'Sullivan, John   203
Ottoman Empire   93
Oxford Flying Weekly Journal   47
Oxford Journal   177
Oxford Mail   177
Oxford Times   177

Packer, Ian   119
Pall Mall Gazette   85, 94–5, 106, 107
Palmerston   64
Parks, William   37

Pasham, James   45
Peacocke, Emilie   17, 108
Pearson Longman Limited   171
Penarth Times   17
People's Journal   97
photocomposition   179
Plymouth Herald   2
Plymouth Weekly Journal   51
Pole-Carew, Christopher   181
Political and Economic Planning   26
political economy   15, 27
Political Register   66
politics, and the battle for a free
    press   61–9
Poor Man's Guardian   66–7
Porter, Roy   48–9
Portsmouth and Sunderland Newspapers
    Ltd   191
Portsmouth Evening News   152
The Post   20
Post-man   46
Post Office Clerks of the Road   51
Post Office service Prestel   176. *See also*
    Viewdata
Potter, David   191
Pottker, Horst   87, 90, 105
Power Without Responsibility (Curran and
    Seaton)   23
Prentice, Archibald   72
The Press   180–1
Press Amalgamation Court   135
Press Association   76–7
Press Bureau   143
Press Complaints Commission   18
Press Council   17–18
Press Gazette   21
Preston Herald   78
printers   28, 32–50
Printing Act of 1662   35
Printing and Kindred Trades
    Federation   131
profits, and newspapers   49–54
Progress of the Working Class, 1832-1867
    (Ludlow and Jones)   64
Project Breakthrough initiative   182–3
Provincial Newspaper Society   67, 68–9,
    75, 76, 80, 148
Provincial Newspapers   115

provincial press
    communities of interest and
        profit   69–74
    and the community in the First World
        War   141–5
    contemporary conundrum   1–16
    corporatization of   111–37
    editorial workers in   16–20
    and morale   155–61
    national *vs.*   20–7
    and political patronage   59–83
    politics and the battle for a free
        press   61–9
    reappraising   27–30
    redefining, in a digital age   199–206
publishing, and Second World War
    145–9
Pugh, Charles   56

Raikes, Mary   53
Raikes, Robert   31, 42–4, 47–8, 53,
    54, 56
Raikes, Robert, Jr.   53, 57, 80, 82
Raven, James   39, 46, 54
Reader, Bill   204
The Reading Evening Post   179
Reading Mercury   37, 49, 77
Reading Observer   77
Reading Post   207
Reading Standard   179
Reed International Ltd   120, 171, 187.
    See also Daily Mirror Group
Reed Regional Newspapers   178, 191
Reform Act   81
Reid, Sir Thomas Wemyss   106
Report of *Royal Commission*
    of 1977   129
representation, newspapers and   79–83
Reynolds, Simon   202
Reynolds, Vaughan   12
Rochdale Observer   143
Rothermere, Lord   112, 119, 122–7
Royal Commission of 1947   21, 127,
    134–5
Royal Commission of 1947-9   130, 136–7
Royal Commission of 1974-7   129
Royal Commission of 1977   118, 171, 168
Royal Commission on the Press   25, 118

Royal Commissions   6, 112, 121, 130–5
Rutland Times   2

Salisbury Herald   71
Salisbury Journal   39, 42, 44, 47, 50, 52
Salopian Journal   40
Saunders, William   78, 85
Schudson, Michael   23
Scott, Ridley   1
Seaton, Jean   23
Second World War   7, 15, 24, 26, 29, 99,
    112–33, 116, 118, 134, 139–41,
    144–6, 148, 155, 158, 212
  publishing in the face of the adversity
    of   145–9
Shah, Eddie   181
Sheffield Evening Telegraph   142
Sheffield Independent Company   89
Sheffield Weekly Telegraph   97–8
Shields Daily News   77
Shrewsbury Chronicle   78
Shropshire Journal   47
Simmons, James   53
Simpson, D. H.   10, 186, 187
Six Acts   66
Smart, Anna Maria   37
Smith, Adam   54
Smith, Henry   81
Society for Promoting Public
    Improvements   80
Society for Women Journalists   75
Society of Editors   146, 170
Society of Graphical and Allied Trades
    (SOGAT)   182
Society of Women Journalists   107
SOGAT. *See* Society of Graphical and
    Allied Trades (SOGAT)
Sommerville, C. J.   1, 34, 35
Southern Daily Echo   149
Southern Newspapers Ltd   149, 150
South Wales Daily Post   124, 127
South Wales Weekly   78
Spender, John Alfred   85, 88
Staffordshire Evening Sentinel   127
Stamford Mercury   172
Stamp Act of 1712   35, 49–50, 57
Stamp Act of 1725   49, 51
Stamp Duty   28, 50, 54, 59–60

abolition of   61, 75–6
politicians and   62
preservation of   68
Temperance Society and   63
Starmer, Charles   82, 126
Starmer Group   119
Stationer's Company   40
Stead, William Thomas   78, 93–4,
    106, 109
St Helens News   207
The St Ives Mercury   42–3
St Ives Post   43
St Ives Post-Boy   43
Storey, Samuel   96
Stott, Mary   108
Stott, Richard   3, 17
Strong, Peter   195
Sturmey, Henry   99
Sunbeam Society   97
Sunday Mirror   171
Sunday Pictorial Ltd   150
Sunday School movement   57, 80
Sunday Times newspaper   17
Sunderland Echo   96
Sunderland Newspaper Ltd   179

Taylor, Jane   24
T. Bailey Forman   180
technology
  deunionization of the provincial
    press and   163–7
  newspapers and   163–7
telegraph   18, 61, 74–7
Temperance Society   63
Thirty Days War   34
Thomas, Mark   25
Thompson Organisation   136
Thomson, Roy   131, 166
Thomson Corporation   191
The Times   22, 67, 73, 76, 107, 120
Tindle, Sir Ray   209
Tindle Newspaper Group   189
Today   17
Trinity Mirror   196–9, 202, 207–8, 210
Trinity plc   191
Tyne Mercury   70

United Newspapers   136

Usher, Nikki 202

VDTs. *See* visual display terminals (VDTs)
Victoria, Queen of England 103, 105
Viewdata 175. *See also* Post Office service
  Prestel
Viewtel 176
visual display terminals (VDTs)
  178, 184

Wakefield Express 184
Walker, Andrew 24, 50, 55, 57, 95
Walker, Ed 207–8
Walker, Robert 47
War Aims committee 144
wartime, provincial press in
  business of newspaper publishing in
    wartime 149–54
  conflict as good news for
    newspapers 139–41
  newspaper publishing in 149–54
  provincial press and the community in
    the First World War 141–5
  provincial press and morale 155–61
  publishing, and Second World
    War 145–9
Ward, Anne 56
War of Spanish Succession 37, 54
Warwick and Staffordshire Journal 47
Weekly Herald 67
Wellsman, Walter 87
West Highland Free Press 211
West Sussex Gazette 70
Western Daily Press 72, 126
Western Evening Herald 149
Western Mail 184
Western Morning News 85, 149
Westminster Gazette 85, 89
Westminster Press 89, 115–16, 118, 123,
  126, 150, 170, 183, 191
Westminster Press Group 136
Westminster Press Ltd 171–2, 177

Westminster Press Provincial
  Newspaper 172
Westmorland Gazette 65
Whig party 64
White, Grace 45
White, John 40–1, 45
Whittingdale, John 209
Whizzer and Chips comic 171
Whorlow, H. 65, 68, 77
W. H. Smith 76, 175
Wiener, Joel 66, 88
Wiles, Roy 36, 45, 49, 51, 55–6
Wilkes, John 56
William II, King 40
Williams, K. 147
Wintour, Patrick 177
Withy Grove (Thomson)
  Chapel 133
Wolverhampton *Express & Star* 95–7,
  115, 182
Wolverhampton Wanderers 96
Woman 79
Wood, Joseph Snell 107
Woodward, Bob 16

Yarmouth Gazette 46, 50
York Chronicle 39
York Courant 39, 56
York Mercury 45, 51
Yorkshire Conservative Newspaper
  Company 71
Yorkshire Daily Observer 108
Yorkshire Evening News 113
Yorkshire Evening Post 22, 113
Yorkshire Evening Press 157
Yorkshire Herald 157
Yorkshire Observer 89
Yorkshire Post 3, 50, 57, 71, 91, 120,
  150, 201
Yorkshire Post Newspapers 176

Zoopla 196